DOWN BY THE
LOS ANGELES RIVER

Friends of the Los Angeles River's
Official Guide

WRITTEN AND ILLUSTRATED BY
Joe Linton

🦫 **WILDERNESS PRESS** *... on the trail since 1967*

BERKELEY, CA

Down by the Los Angeles River

1st EDITION 2005
Copyright © 2005 by Joe Linton

Front cover illustration copyright © 2005 by Joe Linton
Interior illustrations, photos, and maps, except where noted, by Joe Linton
Cover design: Joe Linton, Larry Van Dyke
Book design: Lisa Pletka
Book editor: Eva Dienel

ISBN 0-89997-391-4

Manufactured in the United States of America
Distributed by Publishers Group West

Published by: **Wilderness Press**
1345 8th Street
Berkeley, CA 94710
(800) 443-7227; FAX (510) 558-1696
info@wildernesspress.com
www.wildernesspress.com
Visit our website for a complete listing of our books and for ordering information

Cover illustration: Fletcher Drive Bridge on the LA River
Frontispiece: Good Stuff Park in Elysian Valley;
   Butterfly Bench in Studio City

SAFETY NOTICE: Although Wilderness Press and the author have made every
attempt to ensure that the information in this book is accurate at press time, they
are not responsible for any loss, damage, injury, or inconvenience that may occur
to anyone while using this book. You are responsible for your own safety and
health while following the walking and biking trips described in this book.
Always check local conditions, know your own limitations, and consult a map.

Note from Friends of the LA River: From FoLAR's founding almost 20 years ago,
there has been confusion and disagreement over ownership, maintenance, and
access to the Los Angeles River and its tributaries. Some of the walks in this book
take place in areas where access is in dispute and which may officially be closed,
though in reality are widely used by both riverfront communities and visitors.
Except in cases of rainy weather, FoLAR has always stood for total access to the
river. For specific access questions or issues, contact FoLAR at 323-223-0585 or
mail@folar.org.

To Merrill Butler—

May we all craft lasting, useful, beautiful, and inspiring legacies for our communities.

MERRILL BUTLER
LA Engineer of Design, 1923-1961
Photo courtesy of LA City Bureau of Engineering

ACKNOWLEDGMENTS

This book would not have come to fruition without the efforts of the following essential individuals. I stand on their shoulders: Marge Linton, my mother, for instilling me with caring, creativity, culture, and persistence; Lewis MacAdams, for inspiring me, encouraging me, and for demonstrating to me his unique and vital mix of creativity, style, care, and mischief; Chuck Arnold, for being a sharp, thoughtful, caring, persistent, diplomatic advocate for rivers and bikes; Honorable City Councilmember Ed Reyes, for having integrity, savvy, respect, and a real passion for the LA River; Maria Lopez, Los Angeles County's LA River level-headed go-to person, for expertise, diplomacy, and wisdom; Blake Gumprecht, for writing the book where I learned LA River history; Patt Morrison, for writing a wonderful introduction and a clever and insightful book on the LA River book; and Roslyn Bullas, Eva Dienel, Lisa Pletka, Laura Keresty, Larry Van Dyke, and the rest of the staff at Wilderness Press, whose expertise brought my work to completion, and made it much clearer and stronger.

Thanks to all who were vitally important to my river advocacy and in the creation this book: Alex Baum, Rebecca Belletto, Paul Bournhonesque, Dore Burry, Shelly Backlar, Jennifer Carno, Dan Cooper, Lynne Dwyer, Belinda Faustinos, Arthur Golding, Brett Goldstone, Jessica Hall, Michael Oppenheim, Angel Orozco, Jennifer Petersen, Jill Sourial, Aaron Thomas, Martin Schlageter, Rick Schoonover, Joy Spain, Dave Stonerod, Melanie Winter, and Thiago Winterstein.

The book would not have been possible without the able assistance of courteous and helpful staff at the Los Angeles Downtown Public Library and the Los Angeles City Archives.

Thanks to the folks who were instrumental in creating the parks, bikeways, bridges, art, landscaping, and other features that you'll tour on the river. Without their efforts and accomplishments, this would have been a very short book: Peter Aeschbacher, Michael Amescua, Arroyo Arts Collective, Andrea Azuma, Vik Bapna, Lane Barden, Lahni Baruck, Honorable Xavier Becerra, Matt Benjamin, Jon Bishop, Honorable Barbara Boxer, Tim Brick, Kathleen Bullard, Honorable Yvonne Burke, Paul Burton, Netty Carr, Jeff Chapman, Jan Chatten-Brown, Wenn Chyn, Jeff Carr, Arturo Chavez, Honorable Laura Chick, Maria Chong-Castillo, Ruth Coleman,

Glen Dake, Jim and Nina Danza, Gray Davis, Honorable Hector De La Torre, Nishith Dhandha, David Diaz, Ray and Cecilia Dominguez, Michael Drennan, Lisa Duardo, Tom Dwyer, Pete Echeverria, Joe Edmiston, Cecilia Estolano, Joe Evelyn, Jay Field, Mike Feuer, Phil Franco, Tim Fremaux, Annette Fuller, Honorable Eric Garcetti, Astrid Garcia, Irma Garcia, Nidia Garcia, Robert Garcia, Jose Gardea, Alan Gee, Honorable Jackie Goldberg, Dario Gomez, Bob Gottlieb, Dorothy Green, Joan Greenwood, Adel Hagekhalil, Holly Harper, Rick Harter, Tom Hayden, Jill Hill, Suzi Hoffman-Kipp, Ted Jackson, Wendell Johnson, Wendy Johnson, Noa Jones, Diane Kane, Lynnette Kampe, Larry Kaplan, Shahram Kharaghani, Katie Klapper, Honorable Don Knabe, Gideon Kracov, Chris Kroll, Honorable Tom LaBonge, Stephanie Landegran, Mia Lehrer, Honorable Lloyd Levine, Leo Limon, Andy Lipkis, Honorable Alan Lowenthal, Kastle Lund, Raul Macias, George Magallanes, Stephanie Mancillas, Ted Masigat, Mike May, Ejike Mbaruguru, Ron Milam, Honorable Gloria Molina, Michelle Mowery, Chi Mui, Mike Mullin, Ana Munsell, Jessica Murray, Mary Nichols, Jared Orsi, John Pearson, Tony Perez, Nicole Possert, Jenny Price, Rick Reid, Guillermo Reyes, Joel Reynolds, Clark Robins, James Rojas, Mario Romo, Sarah Rose, Honorable Lucille Roybal-Allard, Bruce Saito, Denis Schure, Dan Sharpe, Jose Sigala, Larry Smith, Heather Speight, Nancy Spiller, Sara Starr, David Sundstrom, Carrie Sutkin, Eileen Takata, Terry Taminen, Heather Trim, Lupe Vela, Honorable Antonio Villaraigosa, Teresa Villegas, Thea Wang, Bob Warnock, Deborah Weintraub, Bill Wenk, Rosemarie White, Scott Wilson, Gaby Winqvist, Sean Woods, Honorable Zev Yaroslavsky, and Jody Yoxsimer.

Thanks to the following for inspiring my art and writing: The Beehive Collective, Robert Crumb, Barbara Kingsolver, Alphonse Muchá, Arundhati Roy, Mehmet Sander, Ben Shahn, and Alice Walker.

Thanks to friends and family who I depended on for information, support, and inspiration. Now that the book is done, I look forward to spending time with you again: Esfandiar and Homeyra Abbassi; Sarah Acevedo; I'ila Ali'i; Lois Arkin; Stefan Cajina; Kara Carlisle; Camille Cimino; Andrea Clemons; Mike Eberts; Liz, Tom, Garrett, Miles, and Paige Gastil; Dedan Gills; Hana Hammer; Kreigh Hampel; Jen Hofer; Yuki Kidokoro; Dale Kreutzer; Joe Krovoza; Mark Lakeman; Fletcher, Laura, Rachel, and Owen Linton; Matt and Liz Linton; Jimmy Lizama; Mara and Ixchel Mark; Rex and Brian McDaniel; Randy Metz; Lara Morrison; Brad Mowers; George Patton; Emily Ramsey; Ted Russell; Aaron Salinger; Julio Santizo; Julio R. Santizo; Marcelino Sepulveda; Andrea Solk; Somerset Waters; and Michelle Wong.

Willow trees and powerlines reflected in the waters of the LA River in Elysian Valley (Walk 12)

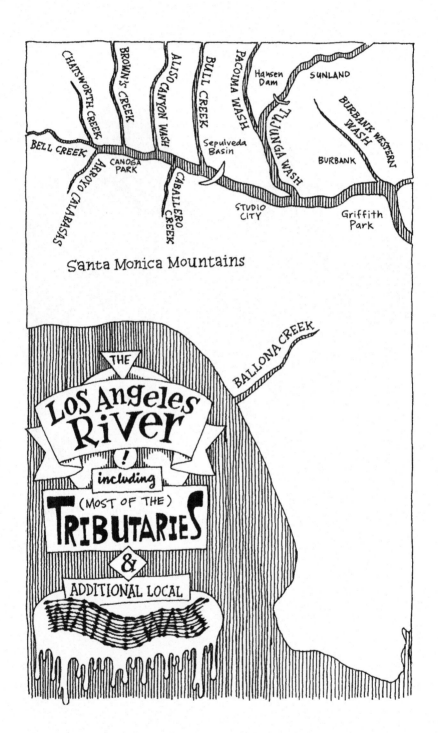

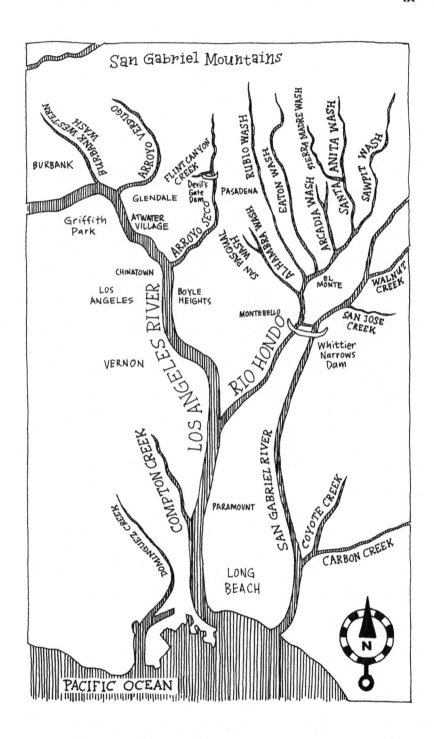

Egret Park in Elysian Valley (Walk 12)

TABLE OF CONTENTS

Walks

Historic Bridges

FOREWORD

This book you've got your mitts on right now is not fiction. There really is a Los Angeles River.

This book is, in fact, an owner's manual. Every Angeleno owns a piece of this much-mocked waterway, every Angeleno should take the time to appreciate it, and every Angeleno has a stake in the care and maintenance of the river, for what becomes of the river will be—like that sacrificial coal-mine canary—a signal for what becomes of Los Angeles itself.

Some Sierra Club newsletter past made the argument that the river should be transformed "from a bad joke for Johnny Carson back into a real river." I thought we'd turned that corner—turned that bend, to use a riverine word—and that the LA River was in its post-punchline epoch.

But there, in the June 2005 issue of *Los Angeles* magazine, was comedian Ellen DeGeneres, interviewing herself. Ellen asked Ellen to "describe your perfect weekend or weekday."

"On weekends, I like to swim in the LA River," Ellen told herself. "It's kind of exclusive. You won't see a lot of touristy people there."

I wouldn't be surprised if there were more tourists than locals down by the riverside. Tourists pay attention to maps and signs. We locals just zip across the bridges that span the vast chasm of riverbed.

So whoa, people. Slow down and get down—to ground level, to water level—and check out your river. Joe Linton's book is a user-friendly guide whose amusing maps and drawings make the river accessible, and even inviting.

That's a switch, because for decades the powers that be, one, didn't want you to know that it's really a river, and has been since, oh, about the late Pleistocene epoch, and, two, didn't want you to go anywhere near it.

Now there's a little money and a lot of interest in re-greening stretches of this survivor-river that is the reason the city of Los Angeles even managed to sprout and flourish in the first place.

Don't settle for a virtual river experience. You've seen it on TV. I've seen it on TV. Heck, I've even been at the river being filmed for TV. Now lay your peepers on the real thing.

Linton's book is the closest thing to hiring a personal tour guide: all the practical and vital particulars about parking, bike paths, wheelchair access, gates, and toilets that lyrical travel books don't condescend to give you, and some sprightly writing that the routine how-to guides don't bother with.

What will surprise newcomers to the river and charm its "creek freak" regulars are details about riverside walks and parklets, like the traditional Japanese garden—"Suiho-En Garden of Water and Fragrance" in Van Nuys—fed for more than 20 years on reclaimed water, and Ernie's Walk. Ernie's Walk is a riverside garden that reminds me of the Watts Towers: the singular and quirky undertaking of one man. Retiree Ernie La Mere cultivated plants his neighbors tossed out, built seats, set out fruit for passers-by, and ultimately had his ashes scattered there so that, as he told a *Los Angeles Times* reporter, "I'll always be with the walk and no one will ever be alone."

My personal fave is the Bette Davis Picnic Area. As the actress herself wasn't the most gorgeous of Hollywood stars, so is this not the prettiest part of the river. But pairing "Bette Davis" and "picnic"—what is with *that*? Maybe if she spread out a mink stole instead of a red-checked tablecloth ... but Warner Brothers' studios were along the river, and Bette was a Warner's supernova. How close did we come, I wonder, to a Humphrey Bogart Picnic Area?

The movies are like LA, and LA is like its river. It reinvents. It loses and makes comebacks. This book delivers you the entire river, the star stretches and the bit-player sections, less lovely but no less loved, and no less vital to the life of a waterway, which, like Mark Twain, found that reports of its demise were greatly exaggerated. Long live the riv!

—*Patt Morrison is a* Los Angeles Times *columnist whose own credits include being host and commentator on PBS and NPR programs, and author of the best-selling* Río LA: Tales from the Los Angeles River.

FROM THE FRIENDS
OF THE LOS ANGELES RIVER

When Pat Patterson, Roger Wong, and I began Friends of the Los Angeles River in 1985, our first official act was to borrow a pair of wire cutters, slice a 5-foot-wide hole in a fence bearing a sign that read NO TRESPASSING: $500 FINE OR 6 MONTHS IN JAIL—one of the fences that had kept people away from the river for decades—and declare the river open. Friends of the Los Angeles River has been inviting people down to the river ever since.

Very early on we realized that the river needed a constituency, and the only way to reach that constituency was to create it. So we sponsored kayak trips for politicians and journalists. We created La Gran Limpieza, the Great Los Angeles River Cleanup. More recently, we began a series of River Education Days for elementary, middle, and high school students. In collaboration with the Los Angeles Conservation Corps' Clean & Green program, we conducted a yearlong water-quality monitoring effort every month at 22 sites up and down the river. Every one of these events was aimed at cleaning up trash, doing good science, advancing education, and bringing people down to the river—often one at a time—to see for themselves what was worth preserving, what was worth fighting to change.

One of our most successful programs has been our ongoing series of river walks. For these we have been supremely fortunate in inspiring the talent and commitment of Joe Linton, an artist who has led walks—strolls, really—along the Los Angeles River from the San Gabriel Mountains to the Pacific Ocean one Sunday a month for more than five years. In the process, he has come to know more about the Los Angeles River than almost anyone else alive today. That he is an artist who is able to capture, with pen and ink, the spirit of this mysterious ad hoc collaboration between man and nature is an incredible bonus for us all.

A few years ago, FoLAR did a yearlong "Re-Envisioning the Los Angeles River" series of collaborations with Occidental College. One of them was a commission for Dana Plays, then an Occidental film professor, to create a 15-minute montage of movie scenes shot along the LA River. It was limited to films we could rent at local video stores, and most of the scenes turned out to be unremitting catalogues of urban isolation and despair.

After screening the piece, there was a panel discussion featuring Ella Taylor, the *LA Weekly* film critic, the writer/director Robert Towne, and the filmmaker Wim Wenders. Wenders told the audience that he had often scouted the river for shooting possibilities, but concluded that he just didn't make that kind of movie. FoLAR doesn't either.

This book will change the way we see the Los Angeles River. With Joe as your guide, I believe you will see the Los Angeles River through fresh eyes. You will experience sublime beauty, high irony, weird juxtapositions, total ugliness, the power of nature, anger at short-sighted human stupidity, humor, inspiration, and hope. Take it with you as you explore the Los Angeles River, and let Joe's spirit guide you along its path. And don't forget to bring along a few friends.

—Lewis MacAdams, Chairman of the Board
of Friends of the Los Angeles River

La Gran Limpieza is an annual FoLAR event to clean up the LA River.

Trees along the soft-bottom Rio Hondo behind the Whittier Narrows Dam

Introduction

"To the extent that it is possible... you must live in the world today as you wish everyone to live in the world to come. That can be your contribution. Otherwise, the world you want will never be formed. Why? Because you are waiting for others to do what you are not doing; and they are waiting for you, and so on. The planet goes from bad to worse."

—Alice Walker, *The Temple of My Familiar*

I first encountered Friends of the Los Angeles River (FoLAR) in 1993 when I was living in Long Beach. I was at a meeting of the Long Beach Area Citizens Involved (LBACI), a progressive coalition group that worked on various issues, including environment, education, and human rights.

Founder Lewis MacAdams, executive director Martin Schlageter, and technical advisory board chair Jim Danza were there representing FoLAR. They were urging local groups to oppose a proposal by the county's Flood Control District and the Army Corps of Engineers to spend hundreds of millions of dollars to raise the Los Angeles River's concrete walls even higher. The proposal, called the Los Angeles County Drainage Area project (LACDA), would further separate communities from the river in their midst.

I was impressed with these environmentalists. They weren't campaigning for a distant rainforest or desert. The concepts they were talking about weren't vague ones, like global warming or sprawl. Don't get me wrong, forests, deserts, warming, and sprawl are very important causes; they just weren't as present and immediate to me as the water and the land where I lived.

The FoLAR folks were idealistic, creative, contrarian, and even visionary. They were calling for radical change—including "de-paving LA"—but they were also grounded with
strong technical expertise.
Their enthusiasm was palpable. They were even dressed sharply (complete with very cool vintage ties) for a presentation before an informally dressed LBACI crowd.

I knew the river a bit, and it really appealed to me. The river was only a couple of blocks from the downtown Long Beach studio where I lived, and I frequently biked to work along it. Along the way, I'd see pelicans, egrets, and ducks—as well as a lot of concrete and trash.

Like many people, I had some sense of what the river looked like now, but I hadn't thought about what it could be. When I was growing up in Tustin, I would bicycle to the beach along the channelized Santa Ana River. I hadn't given a lot of thought to what these rivers might be.

The FoLAR folks had a vision for the future of the Los Angeles River: a lot less concrete, and a lot more nature—a greenway for the surrounding communities. I was hooked. I decided to volunteer for the group. I made a flier for a very small fundraiser to collect money for a campaign against the concrete walls. I went to cleanups. I even started to hang out with the local "creek freaks."

Later, I moved to Los Angeles and got more involved. I continued to contribute my artistic skills for fliers and outreach materials. In 1998, I was invited to join FoLAR's board of directors.

Michael Amescua's welcoming Guardians of the River Gate at Los Feliz

Our early efforts tended to focus on basic awareness. Our message frequently was, "Yes, there is a river in LA," and, "Yes, it was a river before they poured all the concrete." Many Angelenos drive over the river every day and don't even know it's there. Those who have seen it assume it's just a place the engineers picked to put in a big storm drain.

When people asked how they could get involved, Lewis replied that they should go down to the river to see it, listen to it, and begin a relationship with it. He often said that if only he could bring all of the decision-makers to the river, they would truly see it and would get involved in its restoration.

On his advice, I began a program of monthly Down by the River walks that continues to this day. Initially, I did a lot of preparation, biking out to scout the sites well in advance of the walks, and lining up experts to speak to participants. Gradually, through preparing for and leading these walks, I developed a fair amount of on-the-ground expertise about the river. I began to know where to find the holes in the fences, where the red-tailed hawks roosted in the powerline towers, and the locations of the vacant lots and right-of-ways that could become parks and trails. I learned a great deal more working as a council deputy for two years for Los Angeles City Councilmember Ed P. Reyes. During that time, I assisted in coordinating the city's river revitalization efforts.

Through the hard work of FoLAR and many other groups and individuals, there are dozens of new parks, miles of bikeways, a variety of public art installations, frequent tree-plantings, and much more planned. The momentum has shifted. What was a neglected, hidden, and degraded waterway is emerging as a welcoming greenway.

The river is by no means a paradise. It's obviously not a "wild and scenic" river. Some wildlife purists look down on it, but to me it's something special. It tells a story of nature's persistence. As much as we have bulldozed, concreted, and generally trashed the Los Angeles River, it's still around, and it's still full of life.

It has willow trees growing three stories tall, graceful herons and egrets hunting, mother ducks with a dozen ducklings in tow, fish, turtles, and much more. Yes, it's degraded. Yes, there's a lot of trash hanging in those trees (and we need to do more about that). But it is a real river. It was a real river a thousand years ago, and it will still be one a thousand years from now.

Wild, scenic rivers are great. If you hike up into the Los Angeles River's headwater tributaries, such as the Arroyo Seco above Jet Propulsion Laboratory in Pasadena, it's lush and beautiful. But most of us in the city won't get out and explore these wild areas, so restoring our river is a way of bringing that nature, that wildness, into our everyday lives.

Working on the restoration of the Los Angeles River initially appealed to me as a local cause: a way of being rooted in the community where I live. Gradually, though, I became aware that river restoration is not just a Los Angeles thing. Restoring the LA River is a local manifestation of a global effort. Communities all over the world are working to protect and restore their rivers.

When I go to other cities, such as San Jose, Berkeley, and Toronto, I visit river and creek projects and bring back ideas. I read Arundhati Roy and others who make me aware of misguided projects to dam and concrete rivers all over the world. The issues differ from place to place, but there are similar currents of deep connections with place and nature.

A couple years ago, I led a group of freshman English students from Cal Poly Pomona on a walking tour of the river. We began at Steelhead Park and covered one of my favorite sections in Elysian Valley (Walk 12), where the streambed meanders along the earthen bottom. The area has tall willow trees and ducks and, in quiet moments, you can hear the river gently trickling around smooth stones.

I've led a lot of walks for the public, schools, pre-schools, Girl Scouts, girlfriends, journalists, and others. Sometimes folks express their enjoyment, but a lot of times I'm unsure whether they're really interested in the river. So after this walk, I asked the English professor if I could read the essays that the students were writing about the experience. He agreed to let me.

I enjoyed many of the essays, but one brought tears to my eyes. In ever so slightly broken English, the student wrote that she had never known of the Los Angeles River. When she first came to the walk, she didn't realize it was a river. (This makes sense; it's difficult to see the water behind the trees and brush across from Steelhead Park.) She wrote that before she saw the water, she spotted an insect that she associated with rivers in her home country. (I suspect it was a dragonfly.) When she saw that insect, she knew that it really was a river. She said that this was confirmed when she walked farther and saw the water flowing.

"I come from a culture where rivers are important," she wrote, and she went on to emphasize the value of respecting and honoring the river by bringing it back to life.

I think that we all come from cultures, all over the world, where rivers are important. In Los Angeles and in many places across the county and around the world, we've literally turned our back on the rivers that have given birth to great cities.

I hope that this book will inspire you to go down to the river. Listen to the river. Begin to fall in love with it. Protect it. Restore it.

A Brief History of the River

The Los Angeles River is the reason the city of Los Angeles was founded where it was, but that's certainly not the beginning of our river's story. Long before Europeans arrived here and about 12,000 years before the opening of the first LA River bike path, the region's river waters sustained indigenous peoples.

Local Native Americans, known as the Tongva (or Gabrielinos), had various dialects, hence a few different names for the LA River, including *Pieme Pahite*, *Otcho'o*, and *Wenoot*. Most Tongva place names ended in "-ngna," and these names still grace our landscape: Tujunga, Cahuenga, Topanga, Cucamonga, Azusa (shortened from Azusungna), and others. Tongva people, too, are still around today, and many are working to protect their sacred spaces.

Indigenous people's villages were located in many places along the river and its tributaries, from Long Beach to the San Fernando Valley. These included Yangna, which was located in what is today downtown Los Angeles.

The earliest written account of the Los Angeles area, in 1769, describes the confluence of the Los Angeles River and the Arroyo Seco (Walk 13) as a lush and pleasant spot with tall trees, abundant water, and plentiful game. It was because of this pleasant spot that the Spanish established a pueblo outpost. The river and subsequent pueblo were named after "Nuestra Senora de Los Angeles de la Porciúncula." The name has less to do with the river and the land than the day that the Spaniards arrived here. August 1 was a day of rest celebrating the jubilee of Our Lady of the Angels of the Small Portion. The name commemorates St. Francis of Assisi's church in Italy. The long, elaborate name was quickly shortened to plain old Los Angeles, though early accounts refer to the Rio Porciúncula.

Leaning willow tree in the Glendale Narrows section of the LA River

For years after the region was settled, water from the Los Angeles River sustained bounteous local agriculture. Los Angeles was among the most agriculturally productive counties in the entire nation from the mid-1800s to the mid-1900s, sustained entirely on river water until the construction of the Los Angeles–Owens River Aqueduct in 1913.

Throughout the history of Los Angeles, the river flooded every 10 to 20 years. Large floods in 1914, 1934, and 1938 were especially devastating. From early in Los Angeles history, locals built up levees and other reinforcements to attempt to contain the river. After the 1938 floods, the city fathers brought in the federal Army Corps of Engineers to "improve" the river and prevent future flooding. As a result, the river was straightened, deepened, and armored. Its entire length was reinforced with concrete. Only three areas retained their earthen bottom: the Sepulveda Basin (walks 1 through 3), the Glendale Narrows (walks 7 through 13), and the estuary in Long Beach (walks 18 and 19).

The concrete reinforcement has prevented flooding and property damage, and it has made development possible throughout the floodplain. These benefits were achieved at great cost. In today's dollars, the armoring of the river cost more than $5 billion. The price was much greater for the environment: The river could no longer support wildlife and wetlands; anadromous steelhead trout could no longer migrate up its concrete bed.

From time to time in the ensuing years, a few individuals proposed greening and other improvements on the LA River, but, other than a few bike paths, these proposals were not actualized.

In the mid-1980s, a small group of river advocates formed the Friends of the Los Angeles River (FoLAR). The people of FoLAR had a vision that one day the Los Angeles River would be restored as a greenway from the mountains to the sea. To this end, FoLAR has engaged in educational efforts, events, campaigns, and lawsuits. FoLAR is certainly not alone in its work. The group joined forces with many other organizations—national, regional, and local—including other nonprofits, neighborhood associations, businesses, and governmental agencies.

In the beginning, FoLAR had a tough time just getting people to take the river seriously. To change this, the group began offering educational events aimed at teaching young and old about the history of the river and the nature one encounters there today. FoLAR also hosted the annual "La Gran Limpieza," the Great Los Angeles River Cleanup, where thousands of volunteers hauled several tons of trash out of the river each year. FoLAR even sponsored cultural events, from poetry readings to film screenings to opera performances. And the organization brought people to tour the river on foot, on bicycle, and by kayak.

In the late 1990s, the tide seemed to turn. Many more people began to learn about the Los Angeles River, and, as a result, many became interested in its future. Today, there is a political and public consensus that the river is worth investing in, and that it's an important avenue to making our city a more livable place. In some circles, the river is even hip.

Because of this, dozens of new pocket parks—also called mini-parks—have been created, thousands of native trees have been planted, and more than a dozen additional miles of bikeways have been opened. The California Department of State Parks has purchased two large former rail-yards, and new parks at these sites are under construction.

This is just a brief historical overview. The history of the river is still being written. New projects are being planned and built each year, and the face of the river is changing. While it may never again be the pristine, beautiful, natural river that the Spaniards encountered, it is re-emerging as natural resource in our midst.

Additional river history can be found peppered throughout this book, and much more thorough and detailed histories of the river are available in other books. For an extensive listing, see the Resources section on page 300. Among many useful books, I highly recommend two: *The Los Angeles River: Its Life, Death, and Possible Rebirth,* by Blake Gumprecht, and *Río LA: Tales from the Los Angeles River,* by Patt Morrison.

The soft-bottom river upstream of Los Feliz Blvd.

Accessing the River

When the US Army Corps of Engineers embarked on its project to encase the Los Angeles River in concrete in the 1940s, '50s, and '60s, engineers never imagined that the river would be used for anything more than flood control. As such, they built countless fences, but very few trails, and hardly any public access or parking.

But this didn't keep people away from the river. Even before it was channelized, people had been walking along the river, and they continued to access the river after the channel was armored. Sometimes they found gaps in the fencing; sometimes they made their own holes. At nearly every street end and every bridge along the river, you will find a spot in the fence where people have climbed through.

As residents of a city with the lowest percentage of public open space and parkland of any major urban center in the nation, Angelenos used the river as a natural refuge. By the late 1980s, residents of Los Angeles and surrounding communities began to demand increased access to the river. When FoLAR was founded in 1986, the group helped focus this movement on a cause—the creation of a greenway from the mountains to the sea.

By the 1990s, the county of LA, which administers much of the land surrounding the river, responded to public pressure by developing the LA River Master Plan, which incorporated a new goal—to provide a safe environment and a variety of recreational opportunities along the river. This has translated into the development of new facilities, including bike paths and mini-parks, and the opening of previously restricted areas of the river.

While access to the river has gradually expanded, much remains officially closed today. Nonetheless, people are out there every day, walking, biking, jogging, or just sitting and enjoying the solitude. Because access is changing and many of these areas are not signed to the contrary, people assume that the river is open to the public.

Today, many agencies from all levels—federal, state, county, and local—regulate access to the river, and they are justifiably concerned about the danger the river presents during wet weather. While many of these agencies don't look favorably on unrestricted access to the river, they haven't enforced access restrictions.

Because of the ever-changing access restrictions around the LA River,

this book covers only those walks that are in areas commonly used by the public. While most of these are fully and officially open the public, a few of these walks are not yet officially open, and, in some cases, parts of these walks are not officially open. Nonetheless, they are frequented daily by walkers, birders, and bicyclists, and they likely will be opened officially in the future. I have included an Access Note for the walks in this book that may include sections that are not yet officially open. All of these are safe places I and many other people visit and enjoy regularly.

I've deliberately omitted parts of the river where you have to scramble over railings, fences, and/or railroad tracks. While I've done my share of that and it can be fun, I can't recommend these areas for the general public. There are some great stretches, like Taylor Yard, that I didn't include here because access is an issue.

FoLAR and other nonprofit organizations are actively working to increase access to the LA River. If you have questions about the status of access in a certain area or would like to learn how you can help support the effort to increase public access to the river, please contact FoLAR at 323-223-0585. The county of LA does issue permits for group events planned in areas that are not currently open to the public. To obtain a permit, call the Los Angeles County Department of Public Works at 800-675-4357.

To Park or Not to Park

Each walk includes information about where to park. With the notable exception of the LA River Center, there aren't too many public parking lots on the river. This causes some concern among local residents who don't want to see their streets inundated with people driving in from all over the southland to see the LA River. If you are parking in someone else's neighborhood, please be considerate.

Whenever possible, leave you car at home and ride your bike or take public transit to the river (directions for public transit are also provided). All of these walks are in the developed areas of the city, so transit is usually convenient. If you've got a large group and you're meeting up for a walk where the only parking is on a neighborhood street (this includes much of the Glendale Narrows), I suggest that you gather somewhere else and carpool to the river.

Parking becomes a big issue in the parks along the river. Every space allotted to a car means less natural space for recreation and generally less permeability and more storm-water runoff.

If you park your car, please use common sense security measures: Lock your car and don't leave valuables out in the open. Throughout most of Los Angeles, parked cars in isolated areas are vulnerable to break-ins.

Safety

Wet Weather Safety

When it comes to weather, there is good news and bad news. The good news is that, for more than 300 days each year, it doesn't rain in this region. All of these are great days to enjoy the LA River. The bad news is that on rainy days, the river runs at a higher flow, which puts visitors at greater risk. Please avoid trips to the river when it's raining. Gates are locked, surfaces are slippery, and the high-water flows are very dangerous.

Many years, the river will claim the life of a child or two. These are generally kids who see the raging water and try to do something stupid like riding it on a boogie board. The current is very strong, and the water carries a lot of debris. People who enter the high-flowing water generally don't escape.

Mike Mullin, a city of Los Angeles' storm-water expert, told me the following story about the power of the river's flow: In the late 1990s, a crew of workers with a cement truck was in the LA River channel downtown. It wasn't raining where they were working, but it was raining in the upper watershed—in the north end of the San Fernando Valley. Soon, the water began to rise. When the water reached only 2 or 3 feet, it began to carry the cement truck away. The workers had to be rescued by a county sheriff's helicopter.

Natural rivers have their dangers, but channelized rivers are, in many ways, designed to be about as deadly as possible. A natural river has pools or shallows along the edges of the river where the current isn't very strong. Given the geometry of concrete channel walls, however, the entire LA River flows with deadly force when the water rises.

In most places, the river has been straightened. This straightening acts in two ways to make the water flow faster: It has fewer curves to slow it down, and it is steeper, causing the water to flow even faster. In addition, the impermeability of our paved watershed means that water drains to the river very quickly, which also results in sudden increases in flow.

I frequently get questions about where to watch the river during rainstorms. I have occasionally seen the river in high flow, and while it can be a dramatic sight, I don't recommend going to the river in the rain. It's not worth the risk. Curling up with a good book safe at home is a much better way to spend a rainy day.

*Morning glory flowers growing on the barbed-wire fence
at the Village Gardens of the LA River in Sherman Oaks*

Dry Weather Safety

The walks in this book take you along the top of the channel. (In fact, all of FoLAR's monthly walks are on the access roads or bike trails along the top.) This is an excellent way to experience the river, with safe, wide, flat, and even surfaces to walk on. These are generally wheelchair accessible. You also get excellent views of the flora and fauna in the channel below, and you don't need to get your feet wet or scramble through thick vegetation.

Although county officials frown on this, many intrepid river explorers walk into the channel every day. Every year, during FoLAR's La Gran Limpieza Cleanup, thousands of people walk down into the channel without serious incident. The cleanup and any other events in the channel are permitted through the Los Angeles County Department of Public Works.

While the walks in this book don't include specific instructions for going into the river channel, if you decide to enter it, you are doing so at your own risk and should observe the following important precautions:

Visit only in dry weather. The river can rise rapidly, and when this happens, the surrounding area becomes impassable, slippery, and very dangerous. If it has been raining in the last few days, the sandbars can be very muddy. Do not enter the channel if it's been raining that week, or if it's raining elsewhere in the watershed.

Be careful of slippery slopes. Concrete becomes slippery when it is wet—especially around storm-drain outlet flows on sloped concrete. Over the years, I have seen a couple of people lose their footing and slide precariously into the bridge piers below the storm drain by Fletcher Drive. I

still shudder recalling this, and I'm grateful that the injuries weren't more serious. Don't walk where it's wet, especially if the ground is sloped. Dry slopes can be precarious, too, especially if they are covered with gravel, mud, uprooted vegetation, or other debris. Walk, don't run, and watch your step. Rocks in the water, just like in any river, are very slippery. If you're unsure, please stay on the path at the top of the levee.

Avoid the water. While most adults won't touch it, a lot of kids want to enter the water. Please don't let them. I generally recommend avoiding all contact with the water. The water quality can be unhealthy at any time of the year, but it is generally worse during the dry summer months. Don't drink the water and avoid contact with your eyes, mouth, nose, or any open sores. Having said this, I want to dispel the myth that the water is deadly, poisonous, or corrosive. It's not. It's actually cleaner than most people would expect it to be. I've stepped into it a few times and lived to tell the tale.

Watch out for sharp trash. There is plenty of trash in the river and some of it, like broken bottles, is sharp. Keep an eye out for sharp objects and avoid them.

Be nice to animals. Be careful not to harm the wildlife that lives in the riverbed. If you encounter bird nests on the ground or in the branches, please do not disturb the nests or eggs.

Red Car River Park in Atwater Village

How to Use This Book

This book is broken down into three sections: Walks, Bikeways, and Historic Bridges. The format for each section is somewhat different, so please read this section to orient yourself before plunging into the rest of the book.

All walks, bikeways, and bridges are listed in order from upstream to downstream. These begin with the main stem of the Los Angeles River and are followed by the tributaries, also in upstream-to-downstream order. The following is a list of waterways featured in this book (this is not a comprehensive list of tributaries):

Los Angeles River	Flint Canyon Creek
Arroyo Calabasas	Rio Hondo
Bell Creek	Sawpit Wash
Brown's Creek	Santa Anita Wash
Bull Creek	Sierra Madre Wash
Haskell Creek	Arcadia Wash
Tujunga Wash (Big Tujunga Wash)	Eaton Wash
Pacoima Wash	Rubio Wash
Burbank Western Wash	Alhambra Wash
Arroyo Verdugo (Verdugo Wash)	San Pasqual Wash
Picken's Canyon Creek	Compton Creek
Arroyo Seco	

Walks

For the most part, the walks are accessible for all ages and people of all abilities. Nearly all walks are along the flat access roads at the top of the levees. These are not hikes and are not meant to be strenuous. They are relatively short distances, generally 1 to 2 miles, doable at a casual pace in an hour and a half to two hours.

Because they parallel the waterway, most of the walks are linear. If they are too long for you, you can easily turn back early. If a walk is too short, multiple walks can be combined for longer excursions.

Anything you are comfortable walking in—sneakers, sandals, running shoes, etc.—is appropriate footwear for these trips. Hiking boots are not required. Follow common sense and bring water if you are doing a longer walk during the summer. Drinking fountains are few and far between.

Many of these trails are shared by pedestrians, joggers, dog-walkers, and sometimes by skaters, bicyclists, and equestrians. Please share the road and be courteous of others. When you're walking on a bikeway, don't spread out over the entire area. Bicyclists should yield to pedestrians and equestrians.

Walks on the Los Angeles River are divided into four sections: San Fernando Valley, Glendale Narrows (Griffith Park to Elysian Park), Downtown Los Angeles, and Downstream (Vernon to Long Beach). These four sections are identified on the overall walks map on pages 26 and 27. Each section includes an introduction characterizing the area, as well as a section map that shows the location of each walk in that area.

The river walks are followed by walks on four of the main tributaries: Tujunga Wash, Arroyo Seco, Rio Hondo, and Compton Creek. Each tributary includes an introduction and a map showing the location of the walks along it.

Each walk includes two illustrated maps showing how to get to the starting location and the walk route. Starting locations are marked with a star. The first map shows the freeways, transportation systems, or bikeways that are useful in getting to the start. The walk route map shows which way to go from the starting point and the features you'll encounter along the walk. The maps aren't necessarily drawn to scale; features are enlarged or condensed for readability. The actual walk mileage is listed on the facing page.

Each walk also includes distance, other attractions, a summary of the trip highlights, directions to the starting point (including bike, public transit, and car directions), and a description of the walk itself.

OTHER ATTRACTIONS

The following symbols represent other attractions that can be found on the walk. These include:

Good place for bird-watching.

Features one or more historic bridges.

Features off-street parking.

Adjacent to a large park.

Features one or more new natural "pocket parks."

Features public art, including gates, murals, and more.

Features interpretive signage.

Wheelchair accessible.

Recommended for kids.

Restroom available at the starting point.

HIGHLIGHTS AND OTHER INFORMATION

Each trip also includes brief highlights describing features of the walk, the starting point and directions to the start, and the walk directions. Some walks also include sidebars with additional information on current and planned projects or features. Others feature side trips to nearby nature centers and gardens, generally near (but not on) the river. The side trips are within walking or biking distance of the main walk. Side trips also include descriptions, directions, and other attractions.

Bikeways

Bicycling is a great way to experience the LA River. I first experienced the river biking to work along it from my home in Long Beach. I remember seeing what I now know is an egret and wondering, "What's that big bird doing out there?"

The bikeways chapter features a comprehensive listing of the existing bike paths along the Los Angeles River and its tributaries. There are 11 bike paths, covering a total of 126 miles. These are concrete and/or asphalt surfaces and are best for road bikes. In the upper watershed, there are mountain biking trails, but these are not included in this book. Rides range in length from less than 1 mile to 23 miles; some are more suitable for experienced cyclists, and others are appropriate for families or newer riders.

Each bike trip describes one specific bike path facility. In many cases, multiple bike paths can be combined for longer rides. The final trip includes directions for bicycling from the river's headwaters (Canoga Park) to its mouth (Long Beach). This 55-mile ride (approximately half on city streets) can be enjoyable as a long ride, or it can be useful in making connections between multiple bikeways.

Most of the LA River and its tributaries still lack bikeways. For the most part, there is plenty of right-of-way, so future bikeway construction shouldn't be too difficult. The most costly part of the project is completing all of the needed grade crossings. Some areas, especially in downtown Los Angeles and the city of Vernon, are difficult because there are no existing access roads. FoLAR and others are pushing for a continuous bikeway from the mountains to the ocean along the LA River and its tributaries.

SAFETY

Please be aware that all of these bike paths are closed and locked when rain is predicted. Unfortunately, agency staff who lock the gates don't work on weekends, so gates may be locked on perfectly gorgeous Sundays after Saturday storms.

Never ride on the bikeways when it's rainy. The pathways become slick and the river can rise rapidly when it's raining—a dangerous combination for riders. Please enjoy these bikeways during the 300-plus days of dry weather we have in Southern California.

Bike Events on the River

For those interested in group rides on the LA River, two big rides take place each spring. Each features various distances for all types of bicyclists, from the beginner to the more experienced rider. Routes and distances can vary a bit from year to year, so check with the appropriate organization for the latest information on the rides listed below:

The River Ride: Hosted by the Los Angeles County Bicycle Coalition, this event takes place in May. The event begins in Griffith Park on the LA River and features rides measuring 15, 35, and 70 miles. For information, visit www.labikecoalition.org.

The Tour De Sewer: Hosted by the Bell Gardens Lions Club, this event is in March. It begins at John Anson Ford Park on the Rio Hondo and features rides measuring 15, 30, and 62 miles. For information, visit www.bellgardenslions.com.

BIKES AND PUBLIC TRANSIT

Metro, Los Angeles County's transit system, welcomes bikes on buses and trains. Permits are not required to bring bikes aboard Metro trains, however, bikes are not allowed on trains during peak hours in peak commute directions. There are no restrictions during weekends and holidays. When riding, allow other passengers to exit and enter before you board with your bike, avoid crowded trains, don't block the doorway of the train operator, and hold onto your bike on the train. Bikes are not allowed on escalators; use the elevator or stairs. All MetroLink trains are equipped with easy-to-use bike storage areas; look for the bike decal on the train door. Amtrak trains vary; generally, the only local trains that have consistently easy bike access are the Surfliner trains.

Metro, Foothill Transit, Long Beach Transit, and Montebello buses have front racks that hold two or more bikes. Follow easy step-by-step loading directions on the rack itself. If the rack is full, wait for the next bus. You are responsible for loading and unloading your bike.

Regulations may change and other rules may apply, so be sure to check the appropriate website or call for more information:

Amtrak: www.amtrak.com or 800-872-7245.

Foothill Transit: www.foothilltransit.org or 626-967-3147.

Long Beach Transit: www.lbtransit.com or 800-266-6883.

Metro: www.mta.net or 800-266-6883.

MetroLink: www.metrolinktrains.com or 800-371-5465.

Montebello Bus Lines: www.cityofmontebello.com or 323-887-4600.

TERMINOLOGY

I use a variety of terms to explain the type of bikeway I'm describing. These include:

Bike Paths: Called "Class I," these are facilities designed for bikes only (though generally shared with skaters and pedestrians), completely separate from car traffic.

Bike Lanes: Called "Class II," these are on-street lanes specially striped and designated for bicyclists, adjacent to car lanes.

Bike Routes: Called "Class III," these are streets recommended for bicycling, without any special lane striping for bikes. There are a number of signs alerting riders to the "Los Angeles River Bicycle Route," which should more appropriately say bike path.

Bike Trails: Today, this generally refers to mountain biking areas. In the 1970s and '80s, this term was commonly used for what we now call bike paths. The older county bike paths are generally labeled bike trails, such as the Lario Bike Trail.

Bikeways: This inclusive term can be used to describe any of the facilities listed in this section.

BIKE TRIP FEATURES

The bikeway section begins with an overall map showing the location of all the bikeways (pages 198 and 199). Each trip includes a map illustrating that path, as well as text describing the distance, route highlights, and recommended starting points (including how to get there and where to park). Some trips feature route notes that describe connecting bikeways and other useful route information. The route cues tell you where to go at key points in the ride. They are listed upstream to downstream. Depending on where you start and which direction you ride, you may need to start in the middle of the cues and follow them in forward or reverse order.

Each trip also includes a comprehensive listing of access points, in case you want to start the trip from somewhere other than the recommended starting point. Many of these bikeways are easily accessible from upstream and downstream at all cross streets, but in some cases, access is unavailable or difficult to find. Access points are also listed upstream to downstream, with mileage corresponding to route cues.

Within the bikeways section are two additional side trips describing spur bike paths off of the main facility. The side trips also feature maps and similar trip information.

Historic Bridges

The Los Angeles River has some great bridges. The Historic American Engineering Record, a government program that documents important architectural, engineering, and industrial sites throughout the US, describes them as a "group of the finest examples of City Beautiful bridges and viaducts in the United States." Though heralded when they were built, these historic bridges are often overlooked today. They generally do not appear in local architectural or historical guidebooks. When they are acknowledged, documentation generally focuses on a dozen or so of the most celebrated bridges, leaving out many other great historic structures throughout the watershed.

The best, longest, and most well-known local bridges are in downtown Los Angeles and date from 1910 to the 1932. Also fairly renowned are bridges over the Arroyo Seco in Pasadena and northeast Los Angeles. There are many more excellent historic bridges in locations from Tujunga to Glendale to Long Beach. Some are modest, but others rival the downtown and Arroyo bridges in beauty and grace.

This chapter includes an almost comprehensive listing of historic

KEY TO WALKS

WALK	Birding	Bridges	Parking	Large Park	Pocket Park	Public Art	Interp. Signs	Wheelchair	Kids	Restroom
SAN FERNANDO VALLEY										
W1 Sepulveda Basin Balboa Upstream	X		X	X						X
W2 Sepulveda Basin Balboa Downstream	X		X	X						X
W3 Sepulveda Basin Wildlife Reserve	X		X	X			X	X	X	X
W3-S Side Trip: Japanese Garden	X		X	X				X	X	X
W4 Ernie's Walk						X		X		
W5 LAR Village Gardens						X	X	X		
W6 Studio City						X	X	X		
GLENDALE NARROWS										
W7 Bette Davis Picnic Area	X	X		X						
W8 Los Feliz	X				X	X	X	X		X
W9 Atwater River Walk	X	X				X	X			
W10 South Atwater Village	X	X				X	X			
W11 Rattlesnake Park	X	X				X	X	X		
W12 Egret Park	X					X	X	X	X	
W13 River Center		X	X			X		X	X	X
DOWNTOWN LA										
W14 Cornfields and Chinatown		X			X					
W14-S Side Trip: Elysian Park		X	X				X			
W15 Downtown Bridges		X								
DOWNSTREAM										
W16 Maywood Riverfront Park		X			X			X		
W16-S Side Trip: Augustus Hawkins Nature Park		X	X			X	X	X	X	X
W17 Dominguez Gap	X							X		
W18 Estuary at Willow Street	X					X		X		
W19 River's Mouth	X		X	X		X				X
TRIBUTARIES										
W20 Tujunga Wash–Hansen Dam		X			X			X		X
W21 Tujunga Wash–The Great Wall of Los Angeles						X	X	X		
W22 Lower Arroyo Seco Nature Park–Pasadena	X	X	X	X					X	X
W22-S La Casita del Arroyo		X	X	X						
W23 Lower Arroyo Seco–Highland Park, S. Pasadena		X	X	X			X			
W23-S Audubon Center at Debs	X		X	X		X	X	X	X	X
W24 Rio Hondo—Bosque Del Rio Hondo	X		X	X				X	X	X
W24-S Whittier Narrows Nature Center	X		X	X		X	X		X	X
W25 Rio Hondo—Whittier Narrows Dam	X		X	X				X		X
W26 Compton Creek Regional Garden Park		X						X		
W27 Lower Compton Creek	X		X					X		

bridges on the Los Angeles River, its tributaries, and in surrounding areas. Bridge listings include where to find the bridge, which walk or walks it is featured in, when it was built, who designed it, whether it has an historic designation, and a brief description.

The chapter includes a section called "Cruising Merrill Butler's Los Angeles" (page 289), a 15-mile bicycling/driving tour that features 14 historic bridges in the downtown Los Angeles area. Historic bridges are also featured on various walks and bike rides.

KEY TO BIKEWAYS

	BIKEWAY	DISTANCE (miles)
B1	Sepulveda Basin Bike Path Loop	9.1
B2	Glendale Narrows LA River Bike Path	8.3
B3	South County LA River Bike Trail	4.8
B4	Lario Bike Trail	23.5
B4-S	Rio Hondo Coastal Basin Spreading Grounds Bikeway	1.8
B4-S	Long Beach Shoreline Bikeways	7.1
B5	Brown's Creek Bike Path	1.5
B6	Hansen Dam Bike Path	2.5
B7	Arroyo Seco Bike Path	2.1
B8	Upper Rio Hondo Bike Trail	5.2
B9	Santa Anita Wash Bike Path	0.9
B10	Compton Creek Bike Path	2.9
B11	Lower Compton Creek Bike Path	1.9
B12	Headwaters to River's Mouth	55.0

Best Trips

BEST FIRST WALK

For your inaugural walk, I recommend the portions of the soft-bottom areas that have been most improved for access. These include:

Glendale Narrows: Walks 8, 10, and 11.

Sepulveda Basin Wildlife Reserve: Walk 3.

Estuary at Willow Street—Long Beach: Walk 18.

Lower Arroyo Seco Nature Park—Pasadena: Walk 22.

Rio Hondo: Walks 24 and 25.

BEST OF THE SEASON

Most of these sites have subtle changes throughout the year, including migratory birds, trees turning color and dropping leaves, and more. It's good to check out various places at various times and see what appeals to you. Here are a few seasonal highlights:

Spring: I enjoy the flowers blooming at many sites, including Ernie's Walk (Walk 4), Village Gardens (Walk 5), Studio City (Walk 6), and South Pasadena's Arroyo Seco (Walk 23).

Summer: Enjoy the ocean breezes on walks 18 and 19 or rest in the shade of tall cottonwoods at Atwater River Walk (Walk 9).

Fall: Some concrete-lined downstream areas, walks 16 and 18, develop a coat of sediment by the fall. The sediment grows plants, attracting insects, ducks, and other natural life to otherwise desolate areas like Vernon. While these aren't the most natural areas on the river, the fall is the best time to visit them.

Winter: Large flocks of migrating Canada geese convene at the Sepulveda Basin Wildlife Reserve (Walk 3). Other visiting migratory fowl can be seen at various soft-bottom sites, including migratory shorebirds at the estuary (Walk 18) and Lower Compton Creek (Walk 27).

BEST BIRD-WATCHING

Almost all the soft-bottom areas have very good birding. Recommended bird-watching sites include: Sepulveda Basin Wildlife Reserve (Walk 3), Whittier Narrows (walks 24 and 25), Lower Compton Creek (Walk 27), Long Beach Estuary (walks 18 and 19), and all the walks along the Glendale Narrows (walks 7 through 13).

BEST ART

My favorite art pieces on the river are the beautiful artistic gates. Check out both of Brett Goldstone's gates at Fletcher Drive (walks 10 and 11) and Whittier Narrows Nature Center (Walk 24's side trip), Michael Amescua's gate at Los Feliz (Walk 8), and Lahni Baruck's gate at Studio City (Walk 6). *The Great Wall of Los Angeles* (Walk 21) is an excellent and long mural.

BEST HISTORIC BRIDGES

My favorite bridges are downtown, with Macy Street (now Cesar Chavez Ave.), Fourth Street, and North Broadway topping the list. Walk 15 features four great bridges. Walks 10, 14, 22, and 23 feature multiple excellent historic bridges, and walks 7, 9, 11, 13, and 16 each showcase a single outstanding bridge.

BEST GRAFFITI

I see graffiti, or "graf-art," as a mixed blessing. Some of it is intricate and beautiful, though a lot of it is just disrespectful tagging. It's disheartening to see it marring beautiful sculptures, structures, and vistas. In a way, the vast concrete scars of the channels and the freeways call out for aesthetic improvement, but I wish that graf-artists would show more respect for things of beauty, including historic bridges, sculptures, and murals. Some graffiti scares people away, and some attracts visitors.

People ask me where to go to see the best graffiti, so here are some recommendations. These, of course, change throughout the year. There are often elaborate murals under the 2 Freeway (Walk 11). The most elaborate graf-art I've seen is in downtown Los Angeles, some of which is visible on Walk 15 (some best viewed by entering the channel under the Sixth Street Bridge).

BEST BIKEWAYS

For families and beginners, I highly recommend the Glendale Narrows (Bikeway 2), Sepulveda Basin (Bikeway 1), or Hansen Dam (Bikeway 6). For more experienced riders looking for an excellent long ride, I recommend starting at Peck Road Park and combining the Upper Rio Hondo (Bikeway 8), Lario Bike Trail (Bikeway 4), and the Long Beach Shoreline to beach to Queensway (Bikeway 4's side trip) for a 60-mile out-and-back trip.

Entryway to Ernie's Walk, Sherman Oaks

South Pasadena's Arroyo Seco Woodland and Wildlife Park (Walk 23)

Walks

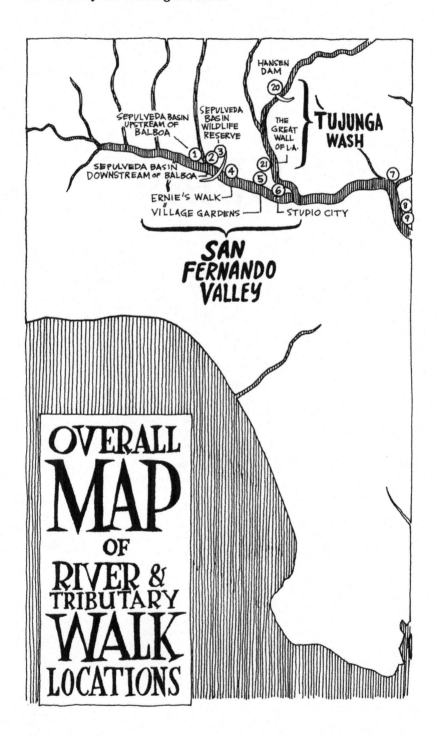

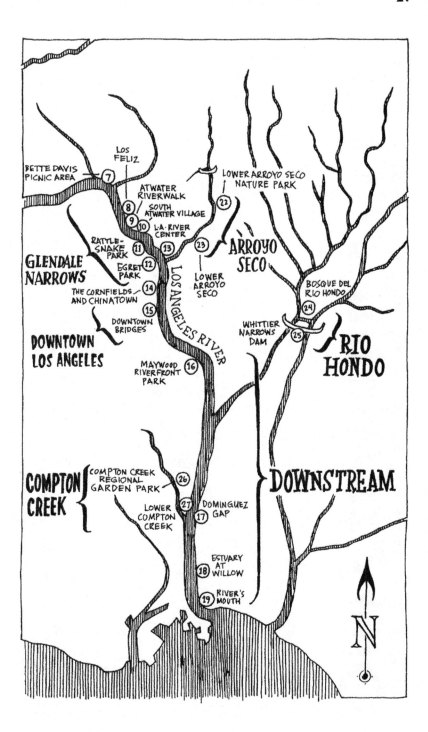

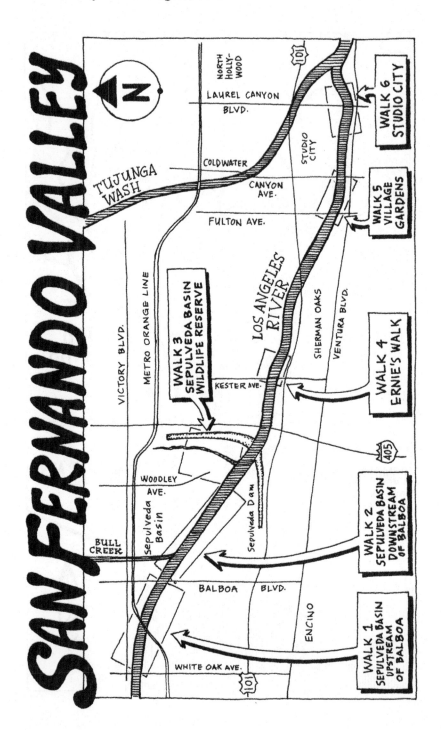

There are nearly 20 miles of the Los Angeles River in the San Fernando Valley. Although the river is what makes the Valley a valley, much of it is relatively unassuming and nearly anonymous. Many locals are unaware of the name or the significance of the channel they cross daily.

The river begins in the west Valley. The headwaters are behind the stadium of Canoga Park High School, where Arroyo Calabasas and Bell Creek converge. In the east Valley, the river flows through the communities of Canoga Park, Winnetka, and Reseda before entering the soft-bottomed Sepulveda Basin. The basin serves as a popular central park for the Valley, and the river is central to the basin. Below the basin, the river wends its way through Sherman Oaks, Studio City, and Toluca Lake, and then runs along the edge of the cities of Burbank and Glendale.

In addition to the river itself, the Valley is home to numerous tributaries. Their names are varied and colorful: Limekiln Canyon Wash, Tujunga Wash (see page 149), Caballero Creek, Santa Susana Wash, Dayton Creek, Mormon Canyon Creek, Pacoima Wash, and many more. These undervalued waterways can become greenways: a system of linear parkways that connect neighborhoods together.

The Sepulveda Basin is an important confluence for the Los Angeles River. Historically, the site of the basin was a confluence of a half dozen creeks, including Bull Creek and Haskell Creek. Today, the site is a major transportation confluence, with the intersection of the 405 and 101 freeways. It is where diverse residents of the Valley come together for many different kinds of recreation. The basin also contains some of the best wildlife areas along the river.

Interestingly enough, the San Fernando Valley is the birthplace of do-it-yourself river reclamation. Valley residents don't wait for the county, FoLAR, or anyone else to beautify their stretch of riverbank. They've taken it upon themselves to create beautiful and unique projects at Ernie's Walk (page 51) and the Village Gardens (page 57). It's probably happening out there somewhere else right now, and I just haven't noticed it yet.

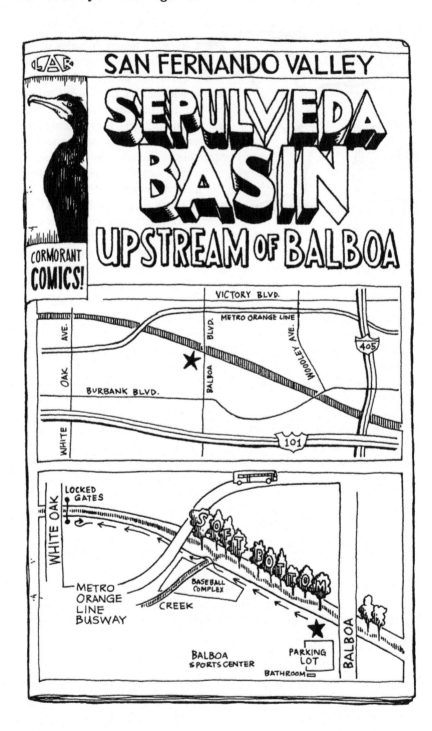

Walk 1

SEPULVEDA BASIN
Upstream of Balboa

HIGHLIGHTS   **2.2 MILES**

The Sepulveda Basin, a lush, green oasis in the middle of
the San Fernando Valley, is the Valley's Central Park. This
walk showcases the tall trees and plentiful birds of the soft-
bottom channel in the west end of the basin.

Access Note: Although many people visit this area every
day, this trip may include places that are not yet officially
open to the public.

STARTING POINT
Parking lot on Balboa Blvd., directly south of the LA River
(*Thomas Guide* p. 561, D1).

WALK DIRECTIONS
From the parking lot on Balboa, go north toward the river. I
suggest starting the walk by going out on the Balboa Blvd.
Bridge and looking upstream. From this vantage point, you
can often spot ducks, coots, cormorants, and other birds.

Walk back and then upstream on the concrete bike path.
A few feet before the path U-turns, go to the left of the bikeway fence and continue walking upstream on the flat grassy
area (used as an access road) along the top the channel.

The path goes along the fences of the sports complex on
your left. Walk to the right around the large tree that blocks
the access road. Carefully, stepping on the dry horizontal
surfaces, cross the outlet of a small tributary, which is slippery when wet. At the Metro Orange Line Bridge, the channel narrows and becomes concrete-bottomed. There is a
walkable asphalt access road continuing to White Oak
Ave., but the gate is locked at White Oak.

Turn back and retrace your steps back to Balboa Blvd.

DIRECTIONS TO THE START

BIKE

The walk's starting point is located just off the parking lot on Balboa Blvd., on the Sepulveda Basin Bike Path. Getting there is an easy 7-mile ride from the Metro Red Line North Hollywood Station. From the station, bike west on Chandler Blvd., which is located directly across Lankershim Blvd. from the Metro station (Chandler is split into two one-way streets; take North Chandler to go west). Chandler, with an intermittent bike lane/route, is a pleasant ride. Continue directly west 4.2 miles until Chandler veers right and puts you on Van Nuys Blvd. Turn left onto Burbank Blvd. Cross over the 405 Freeway and Sepulveda Dam. Enter the Sepulveda Basin Bike Path on your right at the corner of Burbank Blvd. and Woodley Ave. Continue biking west, parallel to Burbank Blvd., and follow the path as it turns right at Balboa Blvd. At the LA River, take the right fork to go left under the Balboa Bridge to the starting location.*

TRANSIT

Take the 236 or 237 Bus on Balboa Blvd. Disembark at the stop just south of the LA River (between Burbank Blvd. and Victory Blvd.).*

CAR

Exit the 405 Freeway at Burbank Blvd. in Van Nuys and go west on Burbank. Turn right on Balboa Ave. The starting place for the walk is just before the Balboa Blvd. Bridge over the LA River. Parking is available at the lot on the west side of the street, just south of the LA River.

Alternately, exit the 101 Freeway in Encino at Balboa Blvd., go north on Balboa, and follow the directions above.

*Bike/Transit Note: In the future, the Metro Orange Line will offer enhanced bike and transit access to the basin. At the time of this writing, the line was under construction and expected to open in late 2005. The Orange Line will connect with the North Hollywood Red Line Station, and will have stops at Balboa Blvd. and Woodley Ave. (just below Victory Blvd.). The project transforms an unused rail right-of-way into a bus rapid transitway and includes a bikeway extending from Warner Center to North Hollywood. To reach the start of this walk, exit the busway/bikeway at Balboa and proceed south to the LA River.

FUTURE PROJECTS IN THE AREA

LA River Headwaters Project: The county's Department of Public Works is planning a sculpture and small park to commemorate the river's headwaters at the confluence of Bell Creek and Arroyo Calabasas, adjacent to Canoga Park High School. The project began in 2003, and completion depends on when additional funding is available.

LA River Bike Path's West San Fernando Valley Segment: The city of LA is pursuing funding for a 2-mile bike path on the south side of the LA River from Mason Ave. to Van Alden Ave. This path is expected to be completed by early 2008, pending approval of funding. The project will be done in conjunction with city bridge rehabilitation projects at Mason, Vanowen Street, Winnetka Ave., and Tampa Ave.

Lush vegetation in the river near Balboa Blvd.

Sepulveda Basin

The Sepulveda Basin Recreation Area is one of LA's great parks. Its well-loved 2000 acres serve as a diverse Central Park in the middle of the San Fernando Valley. The basin features wildlife areas, paths for biking and jogging, playing fields, golf courses, a wastewater-treatment plant, and much more.

The basin is enclosed by the nearly 3-mile-long Sepulveda Dam, constructed by the Army Corps of Engineers in the 1930s and '40s. It is a good example of a multiuse facility, serving to protect the public from floods, while offering various public recreational and environmental amenities.

The basin is designed to flood. It detains storm water to prevent flooding in downstream areas. Every three to five years, the site floods during large storms and the roads are closed temporarily. Notice the gates (near the Burbank Blvd. entrance) that are used to block traffic from entering during floods. Afterward, the water is released, the basin dries up, and it reopens. This multiple-use storm-water detention model may be used at many sites along the LA River, resulting in enhanced flood protection and additional community benefits.

Although the LA River runs through the middle of the basin, it is largely anonymous. The Sepulveda Basin is also one of only three stretches of the river's main stem that has a soft bottom. Although the sides of the channel are reinforced with concrete, the bottom of the river here is unpaved. It looks and feels natural, though certainly not pristine, as it has been much straightened, deepened, reinforced with concrete sides, and then neglected and bombarded with trash carried by storm flows.

There are great opportunities here for future projects. This is a site where, with careful study, creative thinking, and thorough engineering, it should be possible to remove some concrete. The river through the Sepulveda Basin has minimal development alongside it; the Sepulveda Dam protects adjacent neighborhoods. It would be an excellent site to widen the river channel and restore riparian ecology. Some reinforcement and bank-stabilization would be necessary, but there are environmentally safe ways to do this that are aesthetically welcoming and effective in preventing flooding.

The LA River in Sepulveda Basin, downstream of Balboa Blvd.

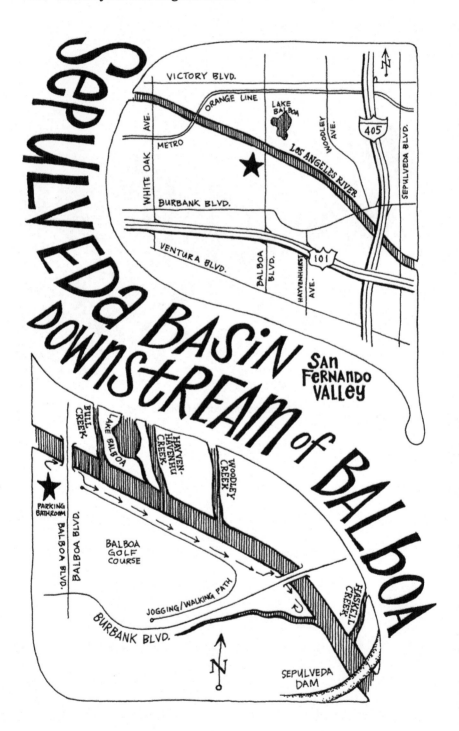

Walk 2

SEPULVEDA BASIN
Downstream of Balboa

HIGHLIGHTS

3 MILES

Similar to Walk 1 upstream, this walk travels downstream of Balboa Blvd. along a walking/running trail. The natural river bottom features tall trees and a large bird population. At the walk turnaround point, there is a small confluence and a view of the Sepulveda Dam. (For background on the Sepulveda Basin, see sidebar on page 34.)

Access Note: Although many people visit this area every day, this trip may include places that are not yet officially open to the public.

STARTING POINT

Parking lot on Balboa Blvd. directly south of the LA River (*Thomas Guide* p. 561, D1).

WALK DIRECTIONS

From the parking lot on Balboa, go north to the river. Walk down the concrete bike path and cross under the Balboa Blvd. Bridge. Where the bike path U-turns back to Balboa, continue downstream. Go through the entrance in the fence onto the wide dirt jogging path along the golf course. Continue walking downstream.

When the path turns to the right, continue straight ahead on the access road. Just before the Burbank Blvd. Bridge, turn left onto a dirt access road. Continue downstream beneath the bridge. Downstream of the bridge, foliage has been cleared to maximize river flows. The road becomes somewhat sandy as it peters out at the river's confluence with a small, unnamed creek that runs along the Hjelte Sports Center. Check out the view of Sepulveda Dam. Retrace your steps back to Balboa Blvd.

DIRECTIONS TO THE START

BIKE

The walk's starting point is located just off the parking lot on Balboa Blvd., on the Sepulveda Basin Bike Path. Getting there is an easy 7-mile ride from the Metro Red Line North Hollywood Station. From the station, bike west on Chandler Blvd., which is located directly across Lankershim Blvd. from the Metro station (Chandler is split into two one-way streets; take North Chandler to go west). Chandler, with an intermittent bike lane/route, is a pleasant ride. Continue directly west 4.2 miles until Chandler veers right and puts you on Van Nuys Blvd. Turn left onto Burbank Blvd. Cross over the 405 Freeway and Sepulveda Dam. Enter the Sepulveda Basin Bike Path on your right at the corner of Burbank Blvd. and Woodley Ave. Continue biking west, parallel to Burbank Blvd., and follow the path as it turns right at Balboa Blvd. At the LA River, take the right fork to go left under the Balboa Bridge to the starting location.*

TRANSIT

Take the 236 or 237 Bus on Balboa Blvd. Disembark at the stop just south of the LA River (between Burbank Blvd. and Victory Blvd.).*

CAR

Exit the 405 Freeway at Burbank Blvd. in Van Nuys and go west on Burbank. Turn right on Balboa Ave. The starting place for the walk is just before the Balboa Blvd. Bridge over the LA River. Parking is available at the lot on the west side of the street, just south of the LA River.

Alternately, exit the 101 Freeway in Encino at Balboa Blvd., go north on Balboa, and follow the directions above.

*Bike/Transit Note: In the future, the Metro Orange Line will offer enhanced bike and transit access to the basin. At the time of this writing, the line was under construction and expected to open in late 2005. The Orange Line will connect with the North Hollywood Red Line Station, and will have stops at Balboa Blvd. and Woodley Ave. (just below Victory Blvd.). The project transforms an unused rail right-of-way into a bus rapid transitway and includes a bikeway extending from Warner Center to North Hollywood. To reach the start of this walk, exit the busway/bikeway at Balboa and proceed south to the LA River.

The LA River tumbling over stones below Bull Creek

Signs of the Times

On this walk, you may notice the city of Los Angeles' bright blue LA River signs, installed in 2004. The signs feature the county's heron logo, which serves as a branding identity linking various features on the river across city and neighborhood boundaries.

The city's Department of Transportation installed these signs as a result of a motion by councilmembers Tom LaBonge and Ed P. Reyes. The signs are on all of the city's LA River bridges, from Owensmouth Ave. to Washington Blvd.

These signs are an important early step toward fostering river awareness. Later, as the greenway is implemented along the river, residents will recognize the river from more natural cues like sycamore and oak trees, river rock, and river-oriented public art.

It wasn't always this easy to get the city to post signs like these. FoLAR founder Lewis MacAdams tells a story about trying to go through the bureaucratic channels to get basic signs installed. He contacted LaBonge, who was then a council deputy, and LaBonge suggested they meet that Friday afternoon.

Their first stop was a liquor store, where they purchased a bottle of Jack Daniels. After that they visited the city's sign-making shop. LaBonge presented the liquor as a gift, and asked the staff if they could do him a favor and make up a half-dozen signs for the river. LaBonge and MacAdams drove out to the Glendale Narrows and installed the signs themselves.

Sepulveda Basin Wildlife Reserve

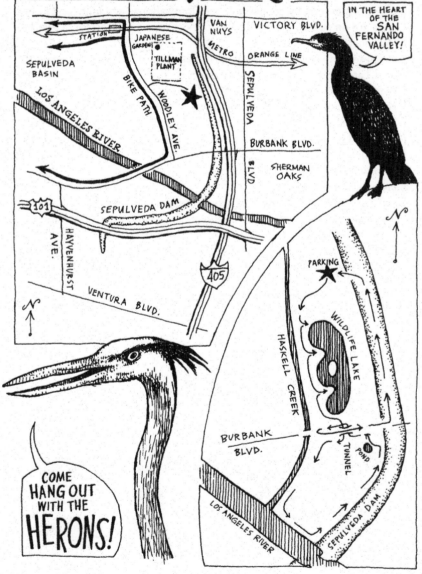

IN THE HEART OF THE SAN FERNANDO VALLEY!

COME HANG OUT WITH THE HERONS!

Walk 3

SEPULVEDA BASIN WILDLIFE RESERVE

HIGHLIGHTS

2.6 MILES

The Sepulveda Basin Wildlife Reserve is one of the few areas on the Los Angeles River specifically set aside for wildlife. In order to protect the wildlife, dogs are not allowed. The wildlife reserve is a 225-acre site within the larger, approximately 2000-acre park complex of the Sepulveda Basin. It is a joint project of the US Army Corps of Engineers and LA's Department of Recreation and Parks, partnering with community groups. The reserve features a lake with a bird-refuge island and extensive native plant re-vegetation. This walk features some of the best and most accessible bird-watching in the LA basin, informative inter-pretive signage, and a quiet green refuge from the bustle of its urban surroundings. Binoculars are recommended.

STARTING POINT

Sepulveda Basin Wildlife Reserve, off Woodley Ave. near Burbank Blvd. (*Thomas Guide* p. 561, G1).

WALK DIRECTIONS

Begin at the entry building next to the parking lot. This area includes ample parking, picnic areas, fields, bathrooms, a drinking fountain, and an amphitheater. Go through the mid-dle of the building, turn left, and then turn right to take the ramp down along the amphitheater and across the grass field. Enter the wilderness area through the gate on your left and head south on the walking path. (Feel free to leave a donation in the lock box here to help maintain and improve this park.)

On your right, at many points somewhat obscured by veg-etation, is Haskell Creek. This creek flows year round with reclaimed water from the Tillman Water Reclamation Plant (see sidebar, page 44).

Basic Birding on the Los Angeles River

Within urbanized Los Angeles, the best birding sites on the river are the soft-bottom areas. On the main stem of the river, this includes the Sepulveda Basin, the Glendale Narrows, and the Long Beach Estuary. For tributaries, soft-bottom areas include lower Compton Creek, Rio Hondo behind the Whittier Narrows Dam, Tujunga Wash behind the Hansen Dam, and the portion of the Arroyo Seco just downstream of the Rose Bowl. Even in the most degraded, concrete-covered areas of the river, there are birds. In these overly concreted areas, you frequently encounter killdeer, stilts, ducks, and hawks.

This brief listing, while not complete, should help novices get started identifying birds. The list contains some of the birds that I find most interesting—neither the most common nor the most obscure.

Great blue heron: The great blue heron is the biggest bird seen often in soft-bottomed areas of the river. A wonderful 3 to 4 feet tall, with elegant, mostly gray feathers, these birds feed on crayfish in the LA River. They are rather shy, flying away gracefully when humans come near.

Great egret/snowy egret: These two egrets—large white birds that are also in the heron family—are 2 to 3 feet tall. The great egret is a little taller, with black feet. The snowy egret is smaller, with yellow feet. The egrets are often mistakenly called cranes. Cranes fly with their necks extended; egrets (and herons) fly with their necks curled up.

Red-tailed hawk: Red-tailed hawks are frequently seen circling high above, and they are easy to identify by their copper-reddish tail feathers. Keen eyes will spot them perched on the all-too-ubiquitous power towers that line most of the lower river.

Turkey vulture: Similar to the red-tailed hawk, turkey vultures often circle high above. They are identifiable by their small heads and striking black and white undersides. Their small, featherless heads enable the birds to more easily eat the insides of dead animals.

Coot: Small black ducks with a white spot on the top of the bill, coots are very common.

Cormorant: Cormorants are a long-necked, black (to dark grayish-brown) water birds, standing 2 to 3 feet tall. Their feathers are not completely water-proof, so, after diving for food, they stand with their wings spread out to dry.

Killdeer: The killdeer is a small bird with a brown back, white belly, and distinctive black and white stripes around its neck. It's common to see killdeer running quickly away along concrete embankments of the LA River.

On your left, four short spur trails lead to wildlife-viewing areas. These viewing areas include helpful signs with information about birds, flooding, and more. These spots are excellent for checking out the many birds that frequent the refuge island. It's common to see cormorants, herons, egrets, and geese, and occasionally pelicans and owls. The observation areas are also good for just sitting quietly and listening to the birdcalls.

After checking out the viewing areas, continue walking south along the path. Cross the outlet for the lake (a spot where egrets frequently hang out), after which the path curves to the left. Go through the gate on your right and into the pedestrian tunnel under Burbank Blvd. At the end of the tunnel, continue through the gate, then bear right on the dirt path. The path curves left. Haskell Creek is again to your right.

The foliage opens up at the point where Haskell Creek empties into the Los Angeles River, with the Sepulveda Dam floodgates to your left. Although it's not the prettiest part of the river, the size of the channel and the dam give a sense of the powerful floodwaters that are held in abeyance here. This area is kept clear of vegetation to maximize its capacity. (Wheelchair users should double back to the start at this point.)

Continue along the river, downstream toward the dam. At the floodgates, the path turns left and continues along the base of the dam. Just before reaching Burbank Blvd., turn left on the path to view a pleasant wildlife pond. At the end of the pond path, turn left onto the path paralleling Burbank Blvd.

Turn right into the tunnel. At the end of the tunnel, take a sharp left onto the concrete path, just before the gate. On your left is a restoration project called Hummingbird Hill, which features flowering native shrubs planted to attract hummingbirds.

At the top of the ramp, turn left to head east along Burbank Blvd. Past the small parking lot, turn left. Go through the gate. Walk north along the top of the dam, with broad views of the basin, the freeway, and the San Fernando Valley. When you approach the large trees on your left, descend the unmarked diagonal path back down to the visitor center parking lot where you began.

This walk takes in many of the best features of the wildlife area, but there are additional paths to explore. As with nearly all sites along the river, the complexion of the wildlife changes with the seasons. In winter, you will see large flocks of Canada geese visiting for the warm weather.

FoLAR, the San Fernando Valley Audubon Society, the Sierra Club, the California Native Plant Society, and others frequently host guided walks, cleanups, and other volunteer events at the Sepulveda Basin. For schedules, call or check websites (see Resources section on page 303).

Reclaimed Water

Historically, the Los Angeles River's flows were greater in the winter and much lower in the summer. Some years, in some places on the river, the surface flow would dry up in hot summer months. Today, there is more water flowing year round in the LA River, due to reclaimed water discharged from wastewater treatment plants.

The largest volume wastewater treatment plant on the LA River is the Donald C. Tillman Water Reclamation Plant (Tillman WRP), located in the Sepulveda Basin, directly adjacent to the Sepulveda Basin Wildlife Reserve. Additional wastewater plants on the LA River system include Burbank WRP, Los Angeles–Glendale WRP (in North Atwater), and the Whittier Narrows WRP (on the Rio Hondo). The Tillman WRP provides reclaimed (or recycled) water for Balboa Lake, the Japanese Garden, and the two golf courses of the Sepulveda Basin, but it discharges the largest volume of water into the LA River—approximately 60 million gallons per day.

Wastewater plants receive sewage from our toilets, sinks, showers, and a few other sources. The plants clean the wastewater using various technologies that mimic natural processes, including settling, aeration/digestion, and filtration. This results in what is known as "terti-ary treated water," which is nearly as clean as drinking water.

It might seem disturbing to some that "sewage" is discharged into the LA River, but treated wastewater is generally relatively safe. Wastewater plant effluent is permitted and monitored to ensure that it is compatible with the ecosystem where it is discharged. Treated wastewater is a minor source of pollution, especially in comparison to dry-weather runoff and storm water entering the river through storm drains.

The large volume of treated wastewater in the LA River has a num-ber of effects on the river's ecology. One is that the river has a more consistent volume of water flowing year round than it had historically, with very little seasonal variation. This consistent wetness favors some non-native species, including invasive *Arundo donax* (a type of bamboo) and castor bean.

There are plans to increase the use of reclaimed water (not for drink-ing, but for landscaping, industrial, and other uses). This use is an impor-tant goal for the sustainability of the region because it will help reduce our dependence on the water we import from faraway watersheds. It also will mean that less of this water will be discharged into the LA River, therefore making the river somewhat drier than it is today (but proba-bly still wetter than it has been historically). This decrease will need to be done gradually and carefully to ensure that the habitat supported by the LA River is preserved and enhanced.

DIRECTIONS TO THE START

BIKE

There are approximately 10 miles of excellent bike path within the Sepulveda Basin, though the bike path is not necessarily useful for get-ting to the beginning of this walk. Currently, there's no off-ramp in the vicinity of the Wildlife Reserve.

The walk start is an easy, flat 7-mile ride from the Metro Red Line North Hollywood Station. From the station, bike west on Chandler Ave., which is located directly across Lankershim Blvd. from the Metro sta-tion. (Chandler is split into two one-way streets; go west on North Chandler.) Chandler, with bike lanes, is a very pleasant ride. Continue directly west 4.2 miles until Chandler veers right and puts you on Van Nuys Blvd. Turn left onto Burbank Blvd. After you cross the 405 Freeway and enter the Sepulveda Basin, turn right onto Woodley Ave.

continued on the next page

Directions to the Start, continued

Turn right at the second access road (look for the Sepulveda Basin Wildlife Reserve sign), then keep right and continue to the end of the access road. There are bike racks at the entrance gate below the amphitheater.*

TRANSIT

Take the Metro Bus 164 (Victory Blvd.) or 237 (Woodley Ave.) and exit at Victory and Woodley. Walk south on Woodley and turn left at the access road with the Sepulveda Basin Wildlife Reserve sign.*

CAR

Exit the 405 Freeway at Burbank Blvd. in Van Nuys and go west on Burbank Blvd. Turn right onto Woodley Ave. Turn right onto the second access road (look for the Sepulveda Basin Wildlife Reserve sign), then keep right and follow the signs to the end of the access road.

Alternately, exit the 101 Freeway in Encino at Balboa Blvd. Go north on Balboa Blvd. Turn right onto Burbank Blvd. Turn left onto Woodley Ave. Turn right at the second access road (look for the Sepulveda Basin Wildlife Reserve sign), then keep right and follow the signs to the end of the access road.

*Bike/Transit Note: In the future, the Metro Orange Line will offer enhanced bike and transit access to the basin. If the Orange Line busway/bikeway is open (expected late 2005), get off at Woodley Ave. and proceed south. Turn left at the access road.

The elegant central lake at Tillman's Japanese Garden

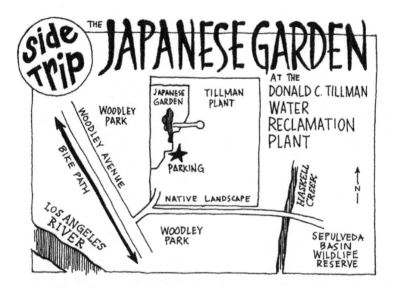

LOCATION AND INFORMATION

0.5 MILE

6100 Woodley Ave., Van Nuys, California 91406; 818-756-8166; www.thejapanesegarden.com. The garden is open Sunday through Thursday, 10 a.m. to 4 p.m., but it is frequently used for events, so call ahead. There is a $3 entry charge and hour-long guided tours are available by reservation. The garden is wheelchair accessible, except for the Plant Process Viewing Tower.

DESCRIPTION

Adjacent to the Sepulveda Basin Wildlife Reserve, on the grounds of the Donald C. Tillman Reclamation Plant, is an elegant 6.5-acre Japanese Garden. Officially called "Suiho-En Garden of Water and Fragrance," the garden was created in 1984 by the city of Los Angeles to showcase a positive aspect of reclaimed water.

The garden was designed by Dr. Kawana Kôichi, a former UCLA professor, in the Chisen-Kaiyushiki "wet garden with promenade" style, similar to gardens on the estates of 18th and 19th century Japanese feudal lords.

Numerous features include gates, stones marking forks in the road, gently curving strolling paths, exquisite ornamental landscaping, beautiful stone lanterns, ponds, a waterfall, and a central lake. Each of these elements is imbued with subtle traditional meaning, which you can learn more about on a guided tour or by reading the detailed booklet that you receive with admission. There's much more: boulders, bridges, a deer scare, a traditional boat landing, and even an authentically reconstructed Japanese teahouse.

River aficionados will want to check out the Plant Process Viewing Tower, located up a flight of stairs on the north end of the futuristic administration building. While certainly not as aesthetic as the garden, you get an impressive view of the 90-acre Tillman Water Reclamation Plant. Much of the water-purification processes are (thankfully) hidden from view, but you will see the bubbling aeration tanks. The water arrives here from the sewage of the residents and industries of Los Angeles, and then it is sanitized and much of it is released into the Los Angeles River.

While the garden is not really a natural area, it's well worth the price of admission. For naturalists, the gardens attract a good mix of bird life, including plenty of herons, egrets, and cormorants. It's also a quiet place for strolling or sitting and contemplating. Like the Los Angeles River

bridges, this garden, wet with treated wastewater, shows us that municipal infrastructure can be beautiful and welcoming.

In addition to its ornamental garden, the Tillman plant features an extensive native-landscaped berm on its south and east borders. Much of this project, officially titled Native Landscape of the Levee, is visible from the access road leading to the Sepulveda Basin Wildlife Area.

DIRECTIONS TO THE START

The Japanese Garden is located just east of Woodley Ave. on the same access road as the Sepulveda Wildlife Reserve. From the reserve, go east on the access road, and then turn right at the Y-intersection just before Woodley.

Wildlife viewing area in Sepulveda Basin Wildlife Reserve

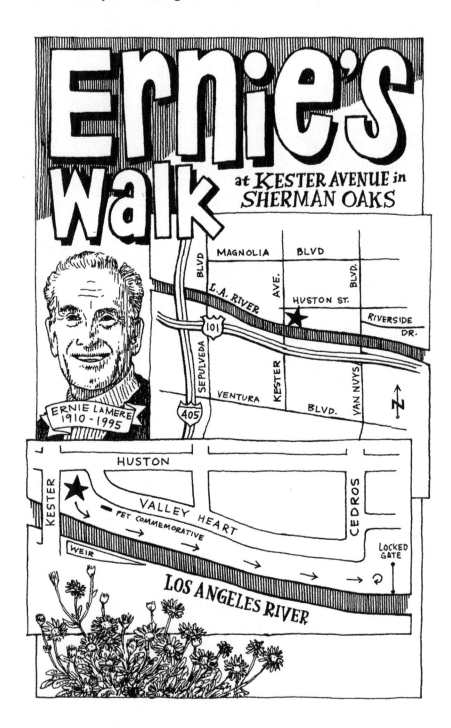

Walk 4

ERNIE'S WALK
Sherman Oaks

HIGHLIGHTS **0.6 MILE**

Ernie's Walk is the earliest community effort to revitalize the Los Angeles River. Begun by retired local resident Ernie La Mere in 1987, the formerly folksy garden site was refurbished by the county of Los Angeles in 2003. This walk traverses the popular 0.3-mile linear park, which features river-rock seating walls and native and non-native plantings along the concrete river channel.

STARTING POINT
Intersection of Huston Street and Valleyheart Drive in Sherman Oaks (*Thomas Guide* p. 561, J3).

WALK DIRECTIONS
Enter at the stairs or ramp by Kester Ave. and walk downstream along the river. Check out the assortment of native and non-native plants along the way. When, just past Cedros Ave., you get to the county's locked gate across your path, turn back and retrace your steps.

It's easy to find your way around Ernie's Walk. It's a small site and entirely linear, so take your time to explore. Those interested in the flood-protection engineering should take a look across the river at the weir (which runs parallel to the river from Kester for about 100 feet). These devices are placed at confluences to spread out large flows from tributaries, to prevent localized flooding.

In the 1980s, this stretch of river was strewn with weeds and plagued by illegal trash dumping. Retired local resident Ernie La Mere contacted various governmental agencies and prodded them until they finally came and cleared out the trash.

In 1987, Ernie was planting flowers in his own garden, so he took his extra plants and, without waiting for

---

The Bridges of San Fernando Valley

With small river parks opening in the Valley from Sherman Oaks to Studio City, the next step is linking them together. As you can see at the upstream terminus of Ernie's Walk, many east Valley bridges are obstacles to completing a continuous greenway.

The city is renovating many of the bridges through the Valley, and FoLAR and others have pressed for including appropriate bike and pedestrian access beneath all river bridge projects. Unfortunately, retrofitting these bridges ends up being much more expensive than creating the linear parks between the bridges.

---

permission, began planting them in the newly cleared river right-of-way. Soon, Ernie and a few neighbors planted a colorful assortment of flowers, trees, and shrubs. Ernie added benches, bulletin boards, "Boot Hill" (a mock graveyard with humorous epitaphs that later included some graves for deceased neighborhood pets), a deer crossing, and many more whimsical elements. A neighbor contributed a small sign declaring the site "Ernie's Walk." The walk became the initial site for the county's Adopt-a-Riverbank program in 1992.

When Ernie passed away in 1995, his grandson and other neighbors continued to maintain the site, though not with quite as much care as Ernie had. In 2003, the LA County Department of Public Works renovated the site. The county planted additional native landscaping, including more than a dozen cottonwood trees, and relocated many of Ernie's surviving plantings farther from the river in order to maintain clear maintenance

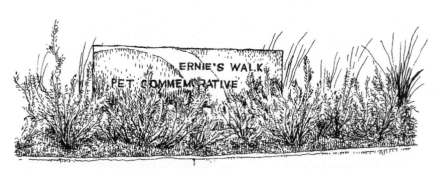

Pet commemorative marker at Ernie's Walk

vehicle access. The county also added river-rock retaining walls, stairs, ramps, and new fencing. In keeping with Ernie's tradition, the county added plenty of flowering plants. They removed the dilapidated wood tombstones and replaced them with an institutional concrete marker that cryptically states "Ernie's Walk Pet Commemorative" (visible from Valleyheart near the upstream entrance).

While the county mini-park, which opened in 2004, bears little resemblance to Ernie's creation, it's green and inviting. The natives are still getting themselves established and will continue to mature in the coming years. The site is well used by neighbors, though some lament that it's not quite as lush as it was when Ernie was around.

DIRECTIONS TO THE START

BIKE

There is no river bike path in this stretch. If riding from east of the site, take the convenient bike lanes on Riverside Drive. Follow Riverside to its end and turn right onto Van Nuys Blvd. Take the first left onto Huston Street and continue west to Valleyheart Drive. The entrance to Ernie's Walk is on your left. To combine a 5-mile bike ride with public transportation, take the Metro Red Line to the North Hollywood Station. Go west onto Chandler Blvd., left onto Hazeltine Ave., right onto Riverside Drive, and then follow the directions above.

TRANSIT

Take the Metro Red Line to Universal City Station. Board the Ventura Blvd. Rapid Bus (#750). Get off at Van Nuys Blvd. Walk west three long blocks. Turn right on Kester Ave. Ernie's Walk is on your right, just past the 101 Freeway. At 1 mile, the walk from the bus stop is longer than the walk along the river.

CAR

Exit the 101 Freeway at Van Nuys Blvd. Go north one block on Van Nuys and turn left onto Huston Street. Ernie's Walk is on your left where Huston intersects Valleyheart Drive (just before Kester Ave.). Convenient street parking is on either Huston or Valleyheart.

Ernie La Mere

At the entry to Ernie La Mere's modest home in Sherman Oaks, a sign with large, hand-painted letters welcomed visitors to "Shangri-la Villa." Ernie, a retired restaurant and hotel worker, called it a "paid-for, poor man's Shangri-la."

But Ernie's home and garden were rich. The site was filled with extensive gardens, idiosyncratic topiary sculptures, hidden rooms, and mysterious inventions. Nonetheless, the small lot wasn't enough to contain Ernie's energy, so he branched out to a quarter-mile stretch of the nearby Los Angeles River—and then the community shared in this wealth.

According to Ernie, the stretch along the river had been a dumping ground for 30 years. He made "a hundred phone calls" to the city, and when a crew finally arrived, it took them two days to clear trash that included mattresses, couches, refrigerators, and auto parts. Soon thereafter, Ernie began planting flowers. Initially, he would carry water from his home.

In its heyday in the early 1990s, this stretch, which neighbors dubbed "Ernie's Walk," was chock-full. Its imaginative feel was similar to other folk art installations such as Simon Rodia's Watts Towers and Howard Finster's Paradise Garden. A hedge of bright red geraniums lined the fence along the river channel. Throughout the site, flowering ornamentals thrived, including canna lilies, blackberry, and wisteria. Ernie also planted banana, pepper trees, and cactus.

Ernie placed various attractions throughout the site. "Boot Hill" had more than a dozen humorous wooden tombstones, including one that read, "Here lies Joe and the woman he didn't know." Ernie even shaped small mounds in front of the graves. A 6-foot inflatable Godzilla stood prisoner in its cage. Perhaps the cage protected Ernie's wooden sculptures of white-tailed mule deer at the nearby signed deer crossing. Keeping watch over these spectacles was a nude statue that Ernie called Lady Godiva. The American flag flew proudly above the community bulletin board.

Ernie built benches (under shade trees, of course) and regularly complimented them with magazines and fresh fruit grown in his backyard. For non-human visitors, he installed bird baths and doggie water dishes. There were various other decorations, mostly built from castaway junk that Ernie salvaged.

Ernie described this part of the river as the coolest spot in Sherman Oaks. He said that, due to the bend in the river, there was a constant cool breeze.

The mini-park brought neighbors together and attracted the attention of media, including the *Daily News*, *Los Angeles Times*, and even public television's Huell Howser. Ernie diligently maintained the site, which was sometimes damaged by vandals and, once, in 1992, by waters that over-topped the river.

Ernie was always a lively, generous, and gregarious person. Born on St. Patrick's Day in 1910, he celebrated this day in later years by dyeing his white hair a shocking shade of green.

As a youth, he had hoped to become a contractor or an engineer, but due to lack of opportunities during the Great Depression, he took a job as a busboy. His competence, enthusiasm, and hard work earned him promotions, and he soon became a sought-after maitre d', serving in this capacity at various restaurants around the United States. In the 1970s, he retired from the Sheraton Hotel in Waikiki and moved to Sherman Oaks.

He engaged anyone and everyone. In his 80s, he had more energy than most 20-year-olds. He took on many elaborate projects: remodeling his home, creating gardens and temporary Halloween installations in his yard, and reclaiming the riverbank at Ernie's Walk.

On June 24, 1995, Ernie La Mere died of kidney failure. His ashes were scatted along the river at the park he created. Unfortunately, even though more than a dozen neighbors continued Ernie's tradition, they were no match for his indefatigable energy. The park hasn't been the same since he passed away.

Nonetheless, Ernie's spirit lives on. He was a forerunner of FoLAR, the Village Gardeners, and other river revitalization movements that followed. His creation of community-built space is echoed by today's movements to reclaim public space, including Portland's City Repair.

When I visited the county mini-park in the spring of 2005, the county's native California alumroot plants were blooming bright red. I looked around for other traces of Ernie's folksy energy, but I could catch only a glimmer of it. I found myself hoping that, perhaps while the county's maintenance crews are looking the other way, someone might re-install Ernie's deer crossing sign.

Ernie La Mere
Photo courtesy of Joy Spain

LA RIVER VILLAGE GARDENS SHERMAN OAKS

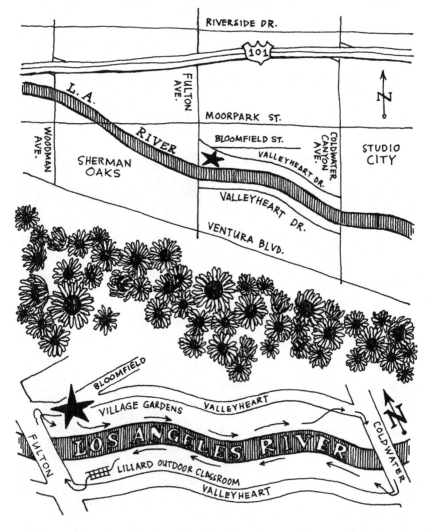

Walk 5

LOS ANGELES RIVER VILLAGE GARDENS
Sherman Oaks

HIGHLIGHTS

1.2 MILES

The Village Gardens, located in Sherman Oaks, is a short stretch of the LA River where one bank has been reclaimed by the neighbors and where the state has created a mini-park on the other bank, complete with an outdoor classroom. Despite the concrete channel, this is an enjoyable green and flowering stretch. A neighborhood group, the Village Gardeners, led the grassroots efforts to reclaim this stretch of the river, picking up trash and planting "whatever would grow," according to cofounder Annette Fuller. The site has a great feel; it's not the institutional uniformity found in many municipal projects. It feels like someone cares (or many someones care) about this area.

Access Note: Although many people visit this area every day, this trip may include places that are not yet officially open to the public.

STARTING POINT
LA River at Fulton Ave. (*Thomas Guide* p. 562, D5).

WALK DIRECTIONS
Enter the LA River right-of-way at the gate on the north side of the river, just east of Fulton (at the intersection of Bloomfield Street and Valleyheart Drive). Turn downstream (left) and walk along the river. The Village Gardeners have placed railroad ties to form a planter, and behind the ties are myriad flowering plants. On your right, creeping vines grow up the chain-link fence cascading down into the vertical channel.

The project thins out around Ethel Ave., but the Gardeners still keep this area neat. They pick up trash and provide trash cans and bags for dog walkers to clean up after their pets.

Continue walking until you approach the Coldwater Canyon Ave. Bridge (the first bridge you will encounter). You can walk up the ramp on your left to Valleyheart Drive, or take a steep footpath just past a large agave. Turn right and walk along the sidewalk on Valleyheart (north). At the corner, turn right on Coldwater and cross the bridge.

At the next corner, turn right at Valleyheart (south). Enter the river right-of-way along the gate. Continue walking upstream. There is a gate with a sign stating that trespassing and loitering are forbidden. People walk, jog, and garden here every day, so just enter easily to the right of the gate. Like many sites on the river, the signage hasn't caught up with the current usage.

Walk down the ramp and continue upstream. On your left, check out the mural, by artist Laurie Troja, that adorns a surface drain conveying runoff from the street into the river. On your right is a good view of the cascading plants growing on the railing.

Past the mural is a small park known as the Richard Lillard Outdoor Classroom. The park, completed in 2003, is a project of the Santa Monica Mountains Conservancy/Mountains Recreation & Conservation Authority (SMMC/MRCA), which worked with the Village Gardeners to plan and create the mini-park. Richard Lillard was a dedicated local environmentalist, author, and early proponent for preservation of open space in the Santa Monica Mountains.

Continue upstream, viewing the river-rock amphitheater followed by native plant landscaping. Contrast the state's approach on this bank with the community approach on the far side. They are both very good projects. The Village Gardens has a folksy feel, with a wide variety of plants that are beautiful, but some are not particularly well-suited to the Southern California climate. The SMMC/MRCA classroom park has a more institutional feel and a palette of only native plants.

Ascend the river-rock stairs and check out the interpretive panel on river history, which includes historic photographs of flooding in the San Fernando Valley.

Turn right (north) onto Fulton Ave. and cross the bridge. At the end of the bridge, descend the steps on your right to take in the last little piece of the Village Gardens. Ascend the ramp to return to the start.

DIRECTIONS TO THE START

BIKE

There is no river bikeway in this area at the present time. From the Metro Red Line, disembark at the North Hollywood Station. Bike west on Chandler Blvd. and turn left onto Fulton Ave. The walk begins on the near side of the Fulton Ave. Bridge over the LA River.

TRANSIT

Take the Metro Red Line and get off at Universal City. Board the Ventura Blvd. Rapid Bus (#750) and get off at Coldwater Canyon Ave. Walk one block north to the LA River at Coldwater and Valleyheart Drive. Turn left and walk upstream (west) along the LA River to Fulton Ave.

CAR

Exit the 101 Freeway at Coldwater Canyon Ave. in Sherman Oaks/Studio City. Go south on Coldwater Canyon and turn right onto Moorpark Street. Turn left onto Fulton Ave. and turn left again onto Valleyheart Drive. Street parking is available on Valleyheart or Bloomfield Street.

What's the Plan?

The LA River often serves as a sort of blank slate that attracts architects and urban designers with ideas to remake it. Even before FoLAR, various proposals have been floated for the LA River. Some of the more outlandish ones called for putting a freeway down the center of it, or buying all the land on both sides so the concrete could be removed. Some of these proposals come from the community; others are from academics. Many are collaborative; some reflect the vision of an individual. Some are nutty; others allow us to see possibilities for the future.

As of this writing, only one official plan governs the use and development of the river: That is the Los Angeles River Master Plan, which was adopted by the county in 1996 after much input from the surrounding cities, public agencies, and community groups.

The plan calls for improved public access, linear parks, habitat, and trails along the length of the Los Angeles River and the Tujunga Wash. The document has served as the basis for the greening, pocket parks, and bikeways that have been approved and built in the last decade.

The master plan isn't just a document that sits on the shelf. Through the planning process, the county initiated a stakeholder group, the LA River Master Plan Advisory Committee, which meets quarterly to work on plan implementation. These meetings are open to the public.

There are a number of overlapping planning processes underway, including the city of Los Angeles' ambitious Los Angeles River Revitalization Plan, Long Beach's River Link, and Compton's Compton Creek Regional Garden Park Plan.

Through the county's ongoing master plan processes, guidelines were developed to ensure consistent signage and landscaping. (For more information on signage, see page 39.) The county's Adopt-a-Riverbank program permits and supports local efforts to improve and maintain stretches of the river and its tributaries. If you're interested in organizing your neighbors to adopt a stretch of waterway in your community, contact the county at 800-675-4357.

The LA River Village Gardens, downstream of Fulton Ave. in Sherman Oaks

A POPULAR PLEASURE-GROUND

Walk 6

STUDIO CITY

HIGHLIGHTS

1.9 MILES

Studio City has two new, small, linear parks, each show-casing a slightly different approach to the revitalization of the LA River. Though the river channel is concrete, it's a great place to walk and check out the parks' native plants, public art, and river-rock walls, ramps, and benches. This stretch of the river is very popular with pedestrians, joggers, and folks walking dogs.

STARTING POINT

Laurelgrove Ave. Footbridge, intersection of Laurelgrove Ave. and Valleyheart Drive in Studio City (*Thomas Guide* p.562, F5).

WALK DIRECTIONS

At the south bank of the LA River on the Laurelgrove Ave. Footbridge, turn left and descend the ramp into the city of Los Angeles' generically named LA River Greenway Park. This small park, which opened in 2004, occupies the southern bank of the LA River for approximately 0.6 mile from Laurel Canyon Blvd. to Whitsett Ave. The park features extensive river-rock ramps (including a connection to the city's new Studio City parking structure), a series of clever rock seating areas, and native landscaping. To some river advocates, the park seems a bit heavy on infrastructure, with more hardscape, fences, and retaining walls than necessary. The park is nonetheless welcoming and enjoyable.

Public art, which will include an artistic bench and river poetry displays located at the tops of the ramps (near the parking structure), is set to be installed by late 2005. The River Project will be installing engravings of river poetry on large boulders at various points in the park, and adding a decorative gateway.

Continue walking downstream and ascend the ramp at the Laurel Canyon Blvd. Bridge (the first bridge you encounter). Turn left onto the sidewalk, crossing the bridge.

Turn right onto the crosswalk; watch out for oncoming traffic as you cross Laurel Canyon Blvd. Turn right on the sidewalk.

From the downstream side of the bridge, you get a good view of the weir on the south side of the river at Laurel Canyon Blvd. Weirs are placed at some river confluences with large storm drains. In this case, the structure drains the Laurel Canyon hillsides. The weir spreads out the tributary flow entering the river to prevent local flooding.

Turn left into the Great Toad Gate. You've just entered the also rather generically named Valleyheart Greenway (note that Valleyheart Drive parallels the LA River through the east San Fernando Valley), a joint project of Los Angeles County and the River Project (with initial funding from the California Costal Conservancy). This quarter-mile mini-park opened in 2004, with additional art features added in 2005.

Under the leadership of Melanie Winter and the River Project, the park was designed with input from students at the nearby Carpenter Ave. Elementary School. Students came up with ideas for the whimsical toad

Studio Stretch

From Studio City to Griffith Park, the Los Angeles River wends its way through five movie studios: CBS, Universal, Warner Brothers, Disney, and Dreamworks. In some cases, the studios occupy both sides of the river, which means FoLAR and other groups must work with these studios to develop a continuous greenway and bicycle path from the mountains to the sea. Many of the studios have been supportive of that effort.

There is a long and fascinating history of the Los Angeles River appearing in Hollywood movies. Many of us are familiar with scenes from *Terminator 2*, where Arnold Schwarzenegger is chased by a truck in the claustrophobic vertical channel walls of the river. Though he is shown entering the river in the San Fernando Valley, most of the chase was actually filmed in Ballona Creek. The movie *Grease*, with John Travolta and Olivia Newton-John, features a car rally filmed in the concrete canyon of the river through downtown (check out the historic bridges). Other films featuring the river include: *S.W.A.T., Repo Man, 187, Cannonball Run*, and *Terminator 3*.

Contemporary movies frequently feature the more graffiti-prone areas as dark dangerous lairs where murderers and thugs congregate and kill. This was not always the case. In the early days of Hollywood, the river, running through studio back lots, served as a wilderness setting for westerns. Perhaps if we restore and revitalize the LA River, it will once again be featured as an idyllic backdrop.

River-rock seating at the city's LA River Greenway Park in Studio City

gate and butterfly garden and bench, and the ideas were further refined by artists. The Great Toad Gate was designed by artist Lahni Baruck, based on a drawing by student Michael Harris.

Descend the ramp. Chose the high path or low path to continue walking downstream. Note that instead of asphalt, the county has used decomposed granite (fine rocks that resemble natural earth), a more permeable and environmentally friendly walking surface.

On your right is the Rattlesnake Wall, a river-rock retaining wall designed as a gigantic rattlesnake. The rocks are engraved with the names of students and others who worked on this park.

A few steps farther is the Butterfly Garden. The site features beds of various California native flowers, which attract butterflies. The various beds of the garden are in the shape and pattern of a butterfly's wing. Check out the beautiful Butterfly Bench. It's also designed by artist Lahni Baruck and includes a quote from Henry David Thoreau.

Continue downstream, and then ascend the ramp to Radford Ave. Turn left and walk across the Radford Ave. Bridge. If you look downstream from the bridge (into the CBS Studio Center), you can see the river water gathering into the low-flow channel. The low-flow channel in the middle of the river is provided to focus the water's gradual erosive power into a small area that is easier to maintain and repair.

From here, turn around and retrace your steps. When you get to the Laurelgrove Ave. Footbridge, you can continue under it to see the rest of the city park, which ends at Whitsett Ave.

FUTURE PROJECTS IN THE AREA

Sycamore Pocket Park: The River Project, a nonprofit dedicated to natural resource protection, conservation, and enhancement, plans to create a pocket park by 2007 at the northwest corner of Laurel Canyon Blvd. and Valleyheart Drive. The entryway will feature a large sycamore arch sculpture. For updates on this project, see www.theriverproject.org.

Additional City River Greenway Parks: In 1996, the city of Los Angeles voters approved a parks assessment ballot measure called Prop K, which, among many park projects, includes $10 million over 30 years for the creation of greenway projects in the east San Fernando Valley. The first phases involved developing a design scheme and building the initial park from Laurel Canyon to Whitsett. Additional phases of this project are in the planning process.

Lahni Baruck's Great Toad Gate at the county's Valleyheart Greenway Park in Studio City

DIRECTIONS TO THE START

BIKE

There is presently no river bikeway in this area. From the Metro Red Line, disembark at the Universal City Station and bike west on Campo De Cahuenga Way, crossing over the 101 Freeway. Turn right on Ventura Blvd. and turn right again on Laurel Grove Ave., which dead-ends at the park and footbridge.

For a less direct, very pleasant route on a street lined with great old oak trees, make a hard right onto the pedestrian way at the corner of Campo De Cahuenga and Ventura Blvd. This lets out on to a very short section of Riverton Ave. Turn left onto Bluffside Drive and turn right onto Vineland Ave. Cross the river and turn left onto Aqua Vista Street. Turn left onto Fair Ave., and then turn right onto Dilling Street. Once you pass Tujunga Ave., enjoy the wonderful canopy of tall old oak trees. Turn right onto Troost Ave., where you will see the Michelle Armitage's reused metal sculpture of a knight fighting a large foe. Turn left onto Chiquita Street and then left onto Colfax Ave.

As you cross the river, you can see the confluence of the Los Angeles River and the Tujunga Wash on your right. Turn right into the alley (before Ventura Blvd.), cross Radford Ave., and continue straight on Ventura Place. Cross Laurel Canyon Blvd. and ride upstream (in the paved river right-of-way) to the footbridge.

TRANSIT

Take the Metro Red Line to the Universal City Station and follow the signs toward the Rapid Bus. Board the Ventura Boulevard Rapid (#750). Get off at Laurel Canyon Blvd. and walk one block north to the LA River. Turn left and walk west (upstream) along the LA River to the Laurelgrove Ave. Footbridge.

CAR

Exit the 101 Freeway at Laurel Canyon Blvd. in Studio City and go south on Laurel Canyon. Turn right onto Moorpark Street and left onto Laurelgrove Ave. Proceed two blocks to the end of Laurelgrove at Valleyheart Drive. Street parking is available on Laurelgrove or Valleyheart.

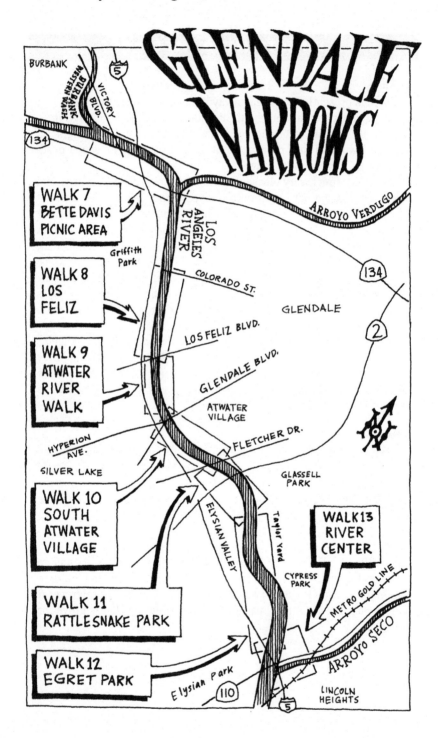

GLENDALE NARROWS

BURBANK

BURBANK WESTERN WASH

5

VICTORY BLVD.

134

WALK 7
BETTE DAVIS
PICNIC AREA

Griffith
Park

LOS ANGELES RIVER

ARROYO VERDUGO

WALK 8
LOS
FELIZ

COLORADO ST.

GLENDALE

134

WALK 9
ATWATER
RIVER
WALK

LOS FELIZ BLVD.

GLENDALE BLVD.

2

ATWATER
VILLAGE

HYPERION AVE.

FLETCHER DR.

SILVER LAKE

GLASSELL
PARK

WALK 10
SOUTH
ATWATER
VILLAGE

ELYSIAN VALLEY

Taylor Yard

WALK 13
RIVER
CENTER

CYPRESS
PARK

METRO GOLD LINE

WALK 11
RATTLESNAKE PARK

WALK 12
EGRET PARK

Elysian Park

110

5

ARROYO SECO

LINCOLN
HEIGHTS

The Glendale Narrows is my favorite area of the Los Angeles River. While it's not pristine, it is the longest soft-bottom area. It's where people visit and say, "Wow! It really is a river." It also has enjoyed the lion's share of recent improvements, including a dozen small parks, hundreds of trees, the LA River Center, and Taylor Yard State Park (due to open in 2006).

The Glendale Narrows extends approximately 8 miles from the north end of Griffith Park (where it borders the city of Glendale), to the confluence with the Arroyo Seco (near Dodger Stadium). In the Glendale Narrows, the river travels through various residential neighborhoods including Los Feliz, Atwater Village, Elysian Valley, and Cypress Park.

The hydrology of the area gives this stretch of river its unique character. Water travels underground through the San Fernando Valley and is pinched by the Santa Monica Mountains and the Verdugo Hills, forcing the underground water to the surface. Throughout the Glendale Narrows in winter and spring, especially soon after rainfall, you will see small springs where underground water is bubbling up into the river. These springs resemble drinking fountains.

Due to water pushing up from underneath, this area has never been fully covered by concrete. The channel was deepened and the sides were armored, but the stream itself retains a soft, earthen bottom. This soft bottom supports plenty of wetland habitat, hence the area is home to birds, trees, and other natural life.

Walk 7

BETTE DAVIS PICNIC AREA
Griffin Park

HIGHLIGHTS

2.1 MILES

This park is named after the film star who reportedly lived in one of the large houses along Rancho Ave., across from the park. This walk is in the upstream end of the Glendale Narrows, which is my favorite stretch of the LA River because it retains a soft, earthen bottom. It is home to birds, trees, turtles, lizards, a great historic bridge, a stretch of the Glendale Narrows section of the LA River Bike Path, and a pleasant picnic area with tall sycamores and oaks.

STARTING POINT

Bette Davis Picnic Area, intersection of Riverside Drive, Victory Blvd., and Sonora Ave. (*Thomas Guide* p. 563, J3).

WALK DIRECTIONS

Begin at the intersection of Riverside Drive, Victory Blvd., and Sonora Ave. If you arrived and parked on the upstream (west) side of Victory and Riverside, cross to the east side and walk along Riverside to the Riverside Drive Bridge. This is one of at least five Riverside Drive Bridges in the area (three over the LA River), so it's generally called Riverside/Zoo or Riverside/Victory. Completed in 1938, this beautiful Merrill Butler bridge is one of the later examples, smaller and somewhat more streamlined than those downstream. The ornamentation below the lighting standards is best viewed from the bike path.

At the end of the bridge, turn left onto the bike path. Note that the bikeway is a shared bike/pedestrian facility, so please walk to one side to allow bicyclists to pass. The soft-bottom channel on your left features tall willow trees and plentiful birds. Walk downstream on the bike path, crossing beneath the 5 Freeway and along the Ferrarro Soccer Fields. Note the native California sycamore and oak trees on your right, which were planted by North East Trees (NET), a nonprofit dedicated to urban forestry and watershed restoration.

As the river and bikeway turn south, the channel walls become vertical, and the riverbed is paved for a short stretch. Beneath the 134 Freeway, the channel widens at its confluence with the Arroyo Verdugo (also called the Verdugo Wash), which is Spanish for Hangman's Wash. The name doesn't refer to any unfortunate incident; it is the last name of one of the early families of the region.

The Arroyo Verdugo watershed drains most of the city of Glendale. It is a relatively steep tributary, historically known for excellent steelhead trout fishing until it was confined to a concrete channel in the 1950s.

Here, you'll see the sharpest corner in the 51-mile river. The river is leaving its east-west trajectory through the San Fernando Valley and making a right turn into the coastal plain. On a clear day, you get a good view of the distant downtown Los Angeles skyline.

For a 2-mile walk, turn around beneath the 134 Freeway. For a longer walk, follow the bikeway downstream to Los Feliz Blvd. (3.1 miles from the start) and beyond (see page 207 for information on this bikeway).

Retrace your steps to the end of the bike path at the Riverside Drive Bridge. At this point, the dangerous part begins as you try to cross the street next to the freeway off-ramp. The safest way is to turn left toward Griffith Park. Watching out for cars, turn right to cross Riverside at Zoo Drive, and then turn right on Riverside, walking back toward the river.

DIRECTIONS TO THE START

BIKE

The start is at the upstream end of the Glendale Narrows LA River Bike Path.

TRANSIT

Take Metro Bus 96. Get off at the corner of Zoo Drive and Riverside Drive. Walk north to the bridge.

CAR

Exit the 5 Freeway in Glendale at Western Ave. and go southwest on Western. Turn left on Victory Blvd. In three blocks you will see the Bette Davis Picnic Area, located at the corner of Victory, Sonora Ave., and Riverside Drive (at this point Victory becomes Riverside). Park on Riverside Drive (south/west side only) either straight ahead on your right, or turn right onto Riverside and park along the park on your left.

FUTURE PROJECTS IN THE AREA

Headworks: The city of LA's Department of Water and Power is working with the US Army Corps of Engineers to create a riverside park as part of an underground reservoir project on the Headworks site located between Forest Lawn Drive and the 134 Freeway. For more information on this project, see www.spl.usace.army.mil/headworks/laheadsworks.htm.

Glendale Narrows River Walk Project: The city of Glendale is planning a riverside linear park on the north side of the river. This park will extend downstream from Bette Davis Picnic Area for approximately a half mile. It is due to be completed by 2007.

LA River Bike Path Phase 4: The city of LA is pursuing funding for extending the bike path upstream at least to Barham Blvd. The project will include undercrossings at the Riverside Drive Bridge and the 134 Freeway.

Cross the freeway off-ramp. A bike path undercrossing eventually will make this easier, but that appears to be a few years away.

Now cross the bridge and go through the first gap in the low fence on your left to descend the sloped footpath into Bette Davis Picnic Area. Walk upstream about 50 yards and enter the river right-of-way by turning left at an equestrian ramp. The ramp is unmarked but recognizable by its uneven cobblestones. At the river, turn right and walk upstream on the asphalt maintenance road.

The turnaround point is where the soft-bottom river ends, about a half mile upstream from Riverside Drive. Retrace your steps back to Bette Davis Picnic Area.

Historically, in this area, the riverbed formed the border between the city of Los Angeles' Griffith Park and the city of Glendale. When the course of the river was straightened, a small remnant of LA land was stranded on the north side of the river; this land became Bette Davis Picnic Area. Originally, Griffith Park—at 4000 acres, one of the largest urban parks in the US—included more than 3 miles of riverfront. This important habitat linkage was severed in the 1950s with the construction of the 5 and 134 freeways (mostly atop what had been Riverside Drive).

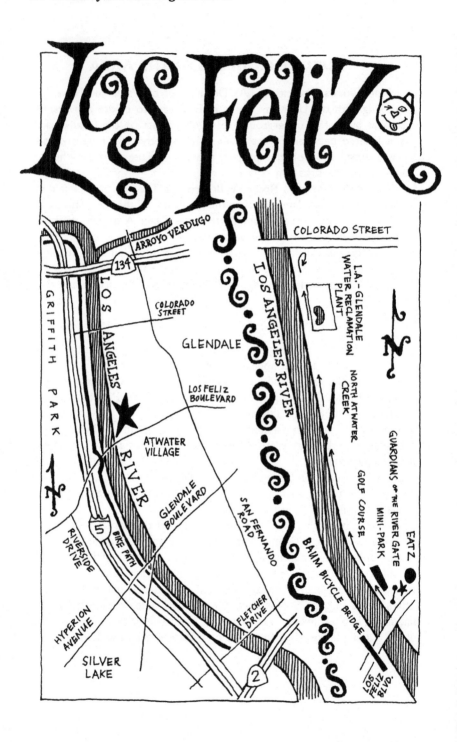

Walk 8

LOS FELIZ
North Atwater

DESCRIPTION
2.6 MILES

With its pocket parks, bike paths, public art, and the only riverside café in LA, Los Feliz is an excellent place for experiencing the LA River. This soft-bottom stretch is popular with walkers, runners, and even dogs and horses. The walk features the infamous river cats, painted by Leo Limón on storm drain outlets, and views of the downtown skyline.

Access Note: Although many people visit this area every day, this trip may include places that are not yet officially open to the public.

STARTING POINT

Eatz Café, 3207 Los Feliz Blvd., Atwater Village (*Thomas Guide* p. 594, C1, adjacent to the Los Feliz Municipal Golf Course).

WALK DIRECTIONS

Take the sidewalk west from Eatz toward the river. On your right, enter the river right-of-way through the beautiful, welcoming Guardians of the River Gate. The gate, created by artist Michael Amescua depicts various river flora and fauna. Can you find a bear, a butterfly, a deer, a duck, three fish, a heron and three other birds, a lizard, a mountain lion, a rabbit, four snakes, a turtle, two worms, and a magic half-bird, half-fish creature?

Continue walking upstream. Note the beautiful circular stonework, native vegetation, decorative bench, and picnic area. They are all part of a 1999 mini-park created by the nonprofit group North East Trees (NET). The park was funded and is maintained by the Santa Monica Mountains Conservancy/Mountains Recreation and Conservation Authority (SMMC/MRCA). Try out the equestrian-themed artistic bench (also by Amescua). At the small picnic area, check out the signs telling part of the story of the De Anza expedition and the beginnings of the Rancho Los Feliz.

River Cats

If you spend time on the LA River, you're likely to run into Leo Limón. He's that smiling goateed artist who rides that cruiser bicycle real slow.

Limón is an artist who is well known for painting cats on the, well, cat-shaped ends of storm drain outlets. These outlets are circular with two triangular hinges at the top. For more than 30 years, Limón has painted various cats, smiling, winking, lipsticked, fanged, and much more. Other artists paint river cats now and then, but Limón has done the most for the longest time.

In addition to the cats, Limón does fine art paintings, prints, graphics, and drawings. He frequently draws on themes and imagery from the LA River.

For more of his artwork, see www.chicanoart.org, or pedal your beach cruiser down to Fletcher Drive (Walk 11) and see the bicycle-themed benches Limón designed. He contributed designs for FoLAR's 1993 and 2004 annual river cleanup T-shirts. His 12-color lithograph, *Buenos Dias, LA*, depicts the LA River from Atwater to Long Beach and is available on the FoLAR website, www.folar.org.

From here, you have a good view of the soft-bottom river and the historic Los Feliz Blvd. Bridge, called the "Tropico Bridge" when it opened in 1925. It was damaged in the floods of 1938 and soon thereafter reworked. Its ornamental concrete railing was replaced with the bland metal railing you see today. From the upstream deck, attached to the elongated piers below, you can see the Army Corps of Engineers plaque, dated 1938. Across the river is the Alex Baum Bicycle Bridge over Los Feliz Blvd. For more information on that bridge, see Walk 9.

Continue walking upstream on the access road. On your right is an equestrian neighborhood. Horses ford the river to get into Griffith Park, located on your left across the river and the 5 Freeway. Equestrians are hoping to eliminate the slippery crossing by constructing an equestrian/pedestrian bridge.

On your right, just past the stables, is a remnant riparian area known as North Atwater Creek. I have heard a couple of different theories about the history of this creek. It may have been a historic creek tributary, or it may have been one of the braided channels of the river itself, before the river was straightened and deepened. In any case, the site, though dry much of the year, supports wetland vegetation and is a good site for future restoration projects. You can get a better look at the creek by taking the path on your right, which leads to North Atwater Park. However, the seasonal creek area itself is fenced off and inaccessible.

As you continue walking upstream, you will see on your right a large pond. It is part of the Los Angeles-Glendale Water Reclamation Plant, a city of Los Angeles wastewater treatment plant that discharges recycled water into the river. (See the sidebar on page 44 for additional information on wastewater and the river.)

The turnaround point for the walk is at Colorado Blvd. It is possible to walk under the bridge and continue upstream another half mile, but the area is somewhat uninviting.

When you turn around, check out the view of the downtown Los Angeles skyline, visible over the hills of Silver Lake. Retrace your steps to the starting point.

If you want to continue walking, cross Los Feliz (either at Glenfeliz or at the bicycle bridge) and do Walk 9. If you're stopping here, grab a bite at Eatz Café, a dependable diner-style eatery with outdoor seating under tall sycamore trees. (It has played host to many informal FoLAR meetings.) Public restrooms are located at the municipal golf course.

DIRECTIONS TO THE START

BIKE

There is easy bicycle access from the Glendale Narrows section of the LA River Bike Path. Exit on the north (upstream) side of the Alex Baum Bridge at Los Feliz Blvd. Ride east on the sidewalk, cross the river, and stop at Eatz, the first establishment you'll see.

TRANSIT

Take Metro Bus 180 or 181, which run from Hollywood to Pasadena (with an easy Metro Red Line connection at the Hollywood/Western Station). Get off the bus at the intersection of Los Feliz Blvd. and Glenfeliz Blvd.

CAR

Take the 5 Freeway, exit at Los Feliz Blvd., and head east on Los Feliz. Cross under the bike bridge, over the river, and find street parking on Los Feliz Blvd. or adjacent neighborhood streets (Glenfeliz Blvd. or Garden Ave.). Limited parking is available in the lot at Eatz.

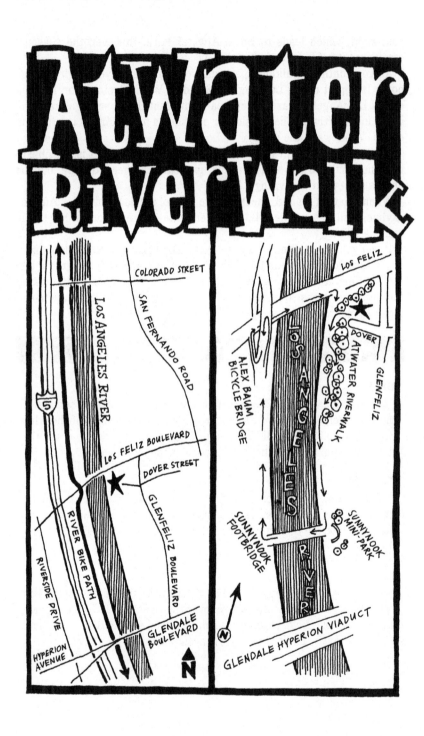

Walk 9

ATWATER RIVER WALK

HIGHLIGHTS

I MILE

Atwater River Walk is one of the first and largest pocket parks along the soft-bottom Glendale Narrows. Cottonwood and sycamore trees planted there in the mid-1990s are getting nice and tall. The walk features pocket parks with native vegetation and even a unique yoga course, as well as excellent views from bicycle and pedestrian bridges.

Access Note: Although many people visit this area every day, this trip may include places that are not yet officially open to the public.

STARTING POINT

Atwater River Walk, Dover Street entrance (near the intersection of Dover Street and Legion Lane), Atwater Village (*Thomas Guide* p. 594, D1).

WALK DIRECTIONS

Walk downstream. On your left is a small park called Atwater River Walk. You can go into the park through the paths on your left, or just walk on the asphalt access road for excellent views of the soft bottom river.

The park features what I suspect is LA's only yoga stretch par course. The park and yoga course were built by North East Trees (NET), a nonprofit dedicated to urban forestry and watershed restoration. Atwater River Walk also features extensive native planting, a dry streambed, and benches.

The park itself was started in 1995 by a group of Atwater Village neighbors, who planted a small flowering garden in the downstream end of the park. Soon thereafter, NET proposed a fitness course. When some nearby residents expressed fears that gang members might use the fitness course to become stronger, NET modified the fitness course to a yoga course. The five-station yoga course features various stretching poses (be sure to try pavana muktasana, or "the sycamore") and breathing exercises, as well as quotes by Nelson Mandela, Helen Keller, and others.

Continue walking downstream and turn right onto the Sunnynook Footbridge. It's unmarked but easily recognizable as the only pedestrian bridge in this area. On your left at the base of the bridge, you'll notice another NET mini-park with an artistic bench by Brett Goldstone and semicircular river-rock retaining wall.

The bridge is an excellent place to look over the river as it riffles and pools below your feet. Also, check out the view (downstream) of the historic Glendale-Hyperion Viaduct. (For information on this bridge, see Walk 10.)

Continue to the southeast end of the footbridge and turn right onto the river bikeway. Share the path with bikes.

Ascend the ramp up to the top of the Alex Baum Bicycle Bridge, which was completed in 2002. The bridge, a project of the city of Los Angeles Department of Transportation, is an important gap closure, making the bikeway more effective and enjoyable for cyclists commuting along the river. The bridge features large bicycle wheels and bicycle wheel motifs in the railing designed by artist Paul Hobson. The bridge is named after the tireless bicycle advocate Alex Baum, who chaired the city's Bicycle Advisory Committee for more than 20 years. The bridge offers excellent views of the river.

At this point, if you want to walk more, continue across the bike bridge, turn left at the bottom of the ramp, and turn left again at Los Feliz to reach the start of Walk 8. Otherwise, retrace your steps halfway back down the bridge ramp. Make a sharp right turn. Descend, turn right, and cross the Los Feliz Blvd. Bridge (see Walk 8 for information on this bridge). At the end of the bridge, turn right onto the asphalt access road. Greet the wise old tall sycamore trees. Continue downstream to the starting location.

The Baum Bicycle Bridge over Los Feliz Blvd.

View of the LA River downstream of Los Feliz Blvd. in Atwater Village

DIRECTIONS TO THE START

BIKE

There is easy bicycle access from the Glendale Narrows section of the LA River Bike Path. Exit on the south (downstream) side of the Alex Baum Bridge at Los Feliz Blvd. and ride east. Cross the river and turn right onto the access road at the end of the bridge.

TRANSIT

Take Metro Bus 180 or 181, which run from Hollywood to Pasadena (with an easy Metro Red Line connection to the Hollywood/Western Station). Get off the bus at the intersection of Los Feliz Blvd. and Glenfeliz Blvd. Walk west to the river, then turn left onto the access road before the bridge.

CAR

Take the 5 Freeway. Exit at Los Feliz Blvd. and head east. Cross under the bike bridge, over the river, and turn right onto Glenfeliz. Turn right onto Dover Street. Go two blocks to the end of Dover and park on Dover or Legion Lane.

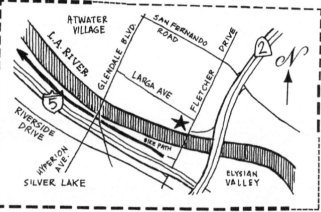

Walk 10

SOUTH ATWATER VILLAGE

HIGHLIGHTS

1.6 MILES

This walk features an excellent soft-bottom stretch of river, historic bridges, mini-parks, native plantings, and Brett Goldstone's dramatic Water with Rocks Gate.

Access Note: Although many people visit this area every day, this trip may include places that are not yet officially open to the public.

STARTING POINT

Water with Rocks Gate, northwest corner of Fletcher Drive and the LA River (*Thomas Guide* p. 594, E3).

WALK DIRECTIONS

Before beginning the walk, take a moment to look behind you at the stonescaped Fletcher Drive Median Islands, created by nonprofit forestry group North East Trees (NET). These traffic islands used to be impermeable asphalt, but NET de-paved them and added river rock, native succulents, and a barely visible "river" of broken windshield glass.

Also nearby is the commemorative plaque on the Fletcher Drive Bridge, one of Merrill Butler's finest. The bridge was completed in 1927, declared Los Angeles Historic-Cultural Monument #322 in 1987, and seismically retrofitted in 1992. The other bronze plaque on this part of the bridge, a smaller HCM plaque, is painted over.

Walk through the Water with Rocks Gate, which was created by sculptor Brett Goldstone. The gate depicts the river waters gradually building, from quiet to high flood stage, flowing into downtown skyscrapers. Surrounding the gate is a mini-park where NET planted native vegetation. Turn left just behind the gate to see another Goldstone piece, a funky bench made of curved metal and a large boulder.

Walk upstream. Look back to your left to get a long view of the Fletcher Bridge. Proceed along the asphalt access road at the top of the levee. As you walk along the river, you will see two small areas on your right that were planted by

Brett Goldstone's River Sculpture

Brett Goldstone is a Los Angeles-based sculptor originally from New Zealand. Prior to his official, permanently installed gates, fences, and benches on the LA River, he was known for site-specific temporary works, including a 30-foot-long rolling portable metal and rope suspension bridge sometimes sighted over the LA River.

Goldstone's Great Heron Gate is located at the southeast corner, where Fletcher meets the LA River. The gate was dedicated on April 22, 1999, at the Earth Day Celebration kickoff for FoLAR's 10th Annual La Gran Limpieza Great LA River Cleanup. The Great Heron Gate became the first gate that invites people to the river, instead of keeping them away. FoLAR commissioned the gate with funding from the Mountains Recreation and Conservation Authority (MRCA). The scenery on the gate represents the river from the mountainous upper Tujunga Wash, filled with willow trees (on the left), to the skyscrapers of downtown (on the right). Can you spot two great blue herons, an egret, cattails, and a frog?

Goldstone's Rocks and Water Gate is located at the northwest corner, where Fletcher meets the LA River. It was commissioned and installed by North East Trees, and was dedicated on Earth Day 2001. It depicts the gentle waters of the river to the left, gradually building to powerful baroque flood-stage waters on the right, where they crash against the puny manmade buildings. Can you spot the helicopter?

Other Goldstone works are featured at Sunnynook Footbridge Pocket Park (Walk 9), the new LA River Bicycle Park (Walk 11), Steelhead Park (Walk 12), Elysian Park (Walk 14's side trip), and on the San Gabriel River at the back of the Whittier Narrows Nature Center (Walk 24's side trip.)

Brett Goldstone's Water with Rocks Gate

NET. The first is called Silver Lake Meadow, the second is Petite Meadow (both named after the streets that end into them, both unmarked).

Continue walking upstream. Ahead of you is the Glendale-Hyperion Bridge. Completed in 1927, it was named the Victory Memorial Viaduct, in honor of the veterans of World War I. Merrill Butler called it "an architectural jewel in a landscaped setting."

The sylvan setting has been much degraded by the paving of the river and the onset of the 5 Freeway. Although its original railing has been covered in concrete, the massive bridge, with its austere octagonal pylons, still looks impressive. In 1976, it was designated LA's Historic-Cultural Monument #164.

There are empty platforms at the downstream end of the bridge's piers. These platforms historically supported the Red Car commuter rail line. The trains are gone, but the Friends of Atwater Village are planning to commemorate them with murals on the piers.

On your right is another NET mini-park, now known as the Red Car River Park. The small park features native trees, a seating wall, and circle stage made of broken concrete.

Turn back and retrace your steps to the start of the walk.

DIRECTIONS TO THE START

BIKE

There is easy access across the river from the downstream end of the Glendale Narrows section of the LA River Bike Path. Cross the river on Fletcher Drive.

TRANSIT

Take Metro Bus 603 from Pico-Union to Glendale. Get off at Fletcher and Ripple Street and cross the river.

CAR

Exit the southbound 5 Freeway at Fletcher Drive (there's no Fletcher exit on the northbound 5) and go left (north) on Fletcher. Cross the river, turn left onto Larga Ave., and park. Walk back to the river and look for the gate on your right.

Alternately, exit the southbound 2 Freeway at Fletcher (there's no Fletcher exit on the northbound 2 either). Go right on Fletcher at the end of the off-ramp. Turn left onto Larga Ave. and park.

Alternately, exit the 2 Freeway at San Fernando Road. Go northwest on San Fernando one block. Turn left on Fletcher, turn right onto Larga Ave., and park.

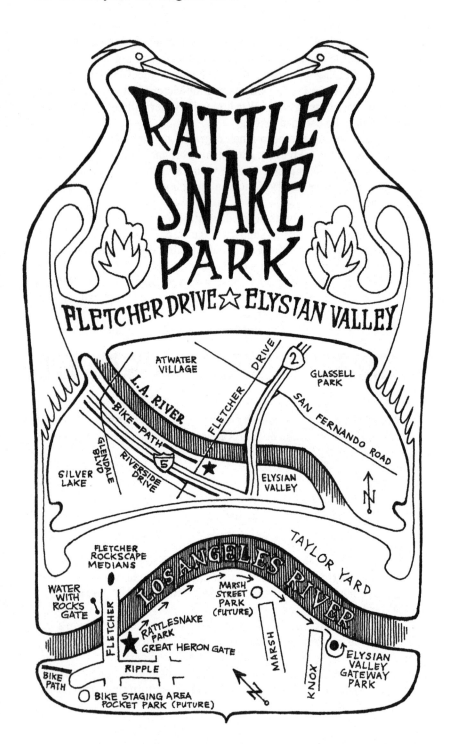

Walk 11

RATTLESNAKE PARK
Elysian Valley

HIGHLIGHTS **1.6 MILES**

Rattlesnake Park, opened in 1997 and maintained by the state's Santa Monica Mountains Conservancy/Mountains Recreation and Conservation Authority (SMMC/MRCA), is an excellent place to begin exploring the LA River. The walk features a pocket park with native trees, plants, and benches—and you'll also see the magnificent Great Heron Gate sculpture and the historic Fletcher Drive Bridge. Downstream, on the west riverbank to Elysian Valley Gateway Park, you'll visit the earliest of the string of pocket parks in the Glendale Narrows.

Access Note: Although many people visit this area every day, this trip may include places that are not yet officially open to the public.

STARTING POINT

Rattlesnake Park, Fletcher Drive and the LA River (*Thomas Guide* p. 594, E-3).

WALK DIRECTIONS

Before you begin this walk, take a moment to check out sculptor Brett Goldstone's Great Heron Gate (see sidebar accompanying Walk 10). Pass through the gate's door and read FoLAR founder Lewis MacAdams' river poetry, which is etched in metal atop the river stone bollard. Descend the river rock steps to your left into Rattlesnake Park.

When North East Trees (NET), which designed and constructed this park in 1997, began clearing this formerly vacant, trash-ridden site, they discovered a small nest of rattlesnakes. The snakes, indigenous fauna to the LA River but very rare these days, were relocated to Elysian Park.

Park designer Lynne Dwyer incorporated a subtle snake motif in the stonework at the park: Notice the curving river-rock wall with a rattle-tail upstream and snake's head drinking fountain on the downstream end. Stay away from the slippery wet surface below the storm drain at Fletcher.

The Art of the River

Rivers throughout the world have provided inspiration for various artistic endeavors, and the mighty LA has inspired its own loose creative school—photographers, poets, visual artists, muralists, sculptors, performance artists, and even opera singers have graced its stark banks. The Arroyo Arts Collective and others have staged extensive art installations along the river and the Arroyo Seco.

FoLAR was founded by poet and journalist Lewis MacAdams. In 1985, MacAdams and two friends staged a symbolic performance art piece entitled "Friends of the Los Angeles River." This unheralded spectacle gradually led to the formation of a nonprofit advocacy organization and the ongoing transformation of the river that you see today.

MacAdams has published three volumes of Los Angeles River-themed poetry; look for his compiled *The River: Books One, Two & Three,* published by Blue Press (2005). Other poets, including Gary Snyder, Buddy Roberts, and many more, have been inspired to publish poetry about the river.

MacAdams ends his poem "To Artesia" with the following encouragement:

"... the river
is a rigorous mistress,
but when you tickle her
with your deeds, you can hear her laughter
from beneath her concrete corset."

Walk downstream. As you leave the pocket park, take a moment to look back at the beautiful 1927 Fletcher Drive Bridge. For more information on the Fletcher Drive Bridge, see Walk 10.

This stretch of river is the setting for a scene in Janet Fitch's best-selling novel *White Oleander.* Fitch's protagonist, Astrid, "rested her arms on the damp concrete railing.... The water flowed through its big concrete embankments, the bottom covered with decades of silt and boulders and trees. It was returning to its wild state despite the massive sloped shore, a secret river. A tall white bird fished among the rocks, standing on one leg like in a Japanese woodcut." Unfortunately, this scene was omitted from the movie. Over the course of the novel, Astrid's moves follow the course of the Los Angeles River from the upper watershed of the Tujunga Wash to the house on Ripple Street in Elysian Valley. I wonder if a sequel would find Astrid moving downtown, then on to Long Beach.

Walk along the river in the shade of the sycamores and cottonwoods, all planted by NET in the late 1990s. You are walking on an old, unimproved county flood-control easement access road, which has an uneven surface at points—watch your step.

Continue under the 2 Freeway. To your left is a deeper section of the river, where I've often seen locals fishing. The river does support fish, including two threatened species called the Santa Ana sucker and the Arroyo chub. On your right, currently a large, gray-walled building at the end of Marsh Street is the future site of a 5.5-acre riverside park. The property was acquired in 2001 by the SMMC/MRCA, which is working with the community to design the park. An initial portion of the new Marsh Street Park is expected to open in 2006. (For more information on Marsh Street Park and other SMMC/MRCA parks, see www.lamountains.com.)

Continue walking downstream until you reach Elysian Valley Gateway Park, just over a half mile from the 2 Freeway. Enter through an unmarked chain-link gate on your right. Gateway Park, which opened in 1995, is the earliest of the Glendale Narrows pocket parks. Designed by NET's Lynne Dwyer, the park retained existing non-native trees and NET added native landscaping, picnic benches, and a drinking fountain. Get a drink of water, and then return back the way you came. If you want to walk farther at this point, continue downstream (see Walk 12.)

When you return to Fletcher, there are a few more sights to see nearby. Go through the heron gate and turn left. Cross Ripple at the crosswalk, then cross to the upstream side of Fletcher. Continue walking upstream on what is now Crystal Street. On your left is the LA River Bicycle Park, which opened in July 2005. The site was a vacant area around the footing of the LA City Department of Water and Power's transmission towers. The pocket park features a bike staging area with maps showing suggested bike trips. There's also native landscaping, river rock, a Brett Goldstone heron sculpture, benches designed by Leo Limón, and five parking spaces.

Cross the river at Fletcher to check out another great Goldstone Gate (see Walk 10.)

Elysian Valley Gateway Park

DIRECTIONS TO THE START

BIKE

The start is across the street from the downstream end of the Glendale Narrows section of the LA River Bike Path. Park your bike at Rattlesnake Park.

TRANSIT

Take Metro Bus 603 from Pico-Union to Glendale. Get off at Fletcher Drive and Ripple Street and look for the heron gate—you can't miss it.

CAR

Exit the southbound 5 Freeway at Fletcher (there's no Fletcher exit on the northbound 5). Go left (north) on Fletcher for one block. Parking is either to the right or left on Ripple. Five spaces are available to the left at the LA River Bicycle Park. There's usually plenty of street parking on Clearwater Street, one block to the right.

Alternately, exit the southbound 2 Freeway at Fletcher (there's no Fletcher exit on the northbound 2). Go left at the end of the off-ramp, cross the river, and follow the directions above for parking.

Alternately, exit the 2 Freeway at San Fernando Road. Go northwest on San Fernando for one block and turn left onto Fletcher. Cross the river and follow above directions for parking.

FUTURE PROJECT IN THE AREA

LA River Bike Path Phase 1C: The city of LA received funding to extend the bike path downstream through Elysian Valley. The project, expected to begin construction in 2006, will include an undercrossing at Fletcher Drive.

River-rock stairway at Rattlesnake Park

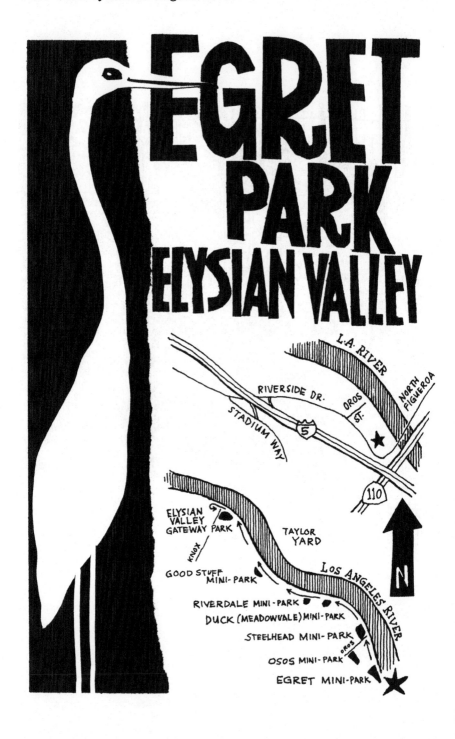

Walk 12

EGRET PARK
Elysian Valley

HIGHLIGHTS

3.4 MILES

From Egret Park, located at the downstream end of the scenic Glendale Narrows, you can observe the contrast in the river where the soft bottom ends and miles of concrete begin. This walk features seven pocket parks, native planting, and scenic soft-bottom river. This is one of the most appealing and natural stretches along the entire river.

Access Note: Although many people visit this area every day, this trip may include places that are not yet officially open to the public.

STARTING POINT

Egret Park, on Riverside Drive, one block southeast of the intersection of Riverside and Oros Street, Elysian Valley (*Thomas Guide* p. 594, H6).

WALK DIRECTIONS

Start at Egret Park, a triangle-shaped pocket park designed by Lynne Dwyer. The park marks the downstream end of Elysian Valley and the last of the soft-bottomed Glendale Narrows. The formerly barren spot was transformed into a mini-park by North East Trees (NET) in 1997. The park, maintained by the Santa Monica Mountains Conservancy/Mountains Recreation and Conservation Authority (SMMC/MRCA), features interpretive signs with information about native birds, plants, and the Native American history of the area.

Painted on the far side of river is the *Anza Mural* by Frank Romero. The piece commemorates the 1775-76 Juan Bautista de Anza expedition, incorporating iconography based on Tongva symbols for mountains, river, and dolphins. (See sidebar for more on the Anza expedition.)

Walk upstream (away from the freeway) along the access road. Watch out for bicyclists.

The Anza Trail

As you walk along the river through the Glendale Narrows, you will notice occasional small trail markers commemorating the Juan Bautista de Anza National Historic Trail. The Anza Trail is a federally recognized historic trail, administered by the National Park Service.

In 1775 and 1776, Juan Bautista de Anza, a soldier of New Spain, led an expedition from Sonora, Mexico, to San Francisco. The expedition helped to secure Spanish colonization and control of the West Coast (then known as Alta California) and to establish the presidio and port at present-day San Francisco.

The expedition consisted of 38 soldiers and their families—198 people in all. They traveled 1400 miles along the Gulf of California, southern Arizona, and up the California coast. Like other expeditions throughout the Americas, Anza relied heavily on routes already well established by the local indigenous peoples.

On February 21, 1776, Anza recorded in his diary that he departed from the Mission San Gabriel and crossed the Rio Porciúncula, today's Los Angeles River. The expedition's chaplain, Father Pedro Font, described the Los Angeles River as carrying plenty of water, though it "spreads out and is lost a little in the plains before reaching the sea." Father Font added that the river area was *"muy verde y florida"*—very green with plentiful flowers. That day, the expedition continued upstream along the river to the El Portezuelo, a pass between hills. The site corresponds to today's Cahuenga Pass (where the 101 Freeway passes from Hollywood to the San Fernando Valley), with the campsite along the river near present-day Universal Studios.

On your left in about a tenth of a mile is Steelhead Park, also a collaboration of NET and the SMMC/MRCA. Steelhead Park features a fence designed by Brett Goldstone with silhouettes of steelhead trout. Steelhead were plentiful in the Los Angeles River until it was paved with concrete in the middle of the last century. FoLAR founder Lewis MacAdams is fond of stating that we will know that FoLAR's job is done when the steelhead return to the river.

Steelhead, a mini-park, features a small outdoor classroom constructed from reused broken concrete and interpretive signs about the Juan Bautista de Anza expedition. The park is designed to collect rainwater, which soaks into a small yarrow meadow in the middle.

Continue walking upstream through one of the nicest areas of the entire river. The water meanders from one side of the channel to the other. Ducks, coots, swallows, and other birds make their homes here. Keep an eye on the old access road, as it does have some dips and bumps. On your left are sycamores and cottonwoods planted by NET in the late 1990s.

There are a number of pocket parks along this section; all are collaborations of NET and SMMC/MRCA. At 0.6 mile, the end of Meadowvale Street has been converted into Duck Park, which features an artistic bench, native vegetation, and decorative stonework. Can you spot the throne?

Just past Meadowvale is Riverdale Park, a well-used site with benches overlooking the river and river-rock stairs connecting to the end of Riverdale Street. Farther along (even with Eads Street, though only accessible from the river) is a small park informally known as Good Stuff Park. It's named for the frequent aroma of fresh-baked bread wafting over the area from commercial bakeries nearby.

At mile 1.7 (recognizable by a large eucalyptus tree on your left), is Elysian Valley Gateway Park (see Walk 11), one of the earliest pocket parks along the river. This is the turnaround point for this walk. Retrace your footsteps to the start. If you want to continue upstream, follow the directions from Walk 11.

Near the starting point, at the corner of Oros Street and Riverside Drive, is one more NET and SMMC/MRCA park project called Osos Park. The pocket park features native trees and plants, and life-sized silhouette sculptures (designed by Michael Amescua) of native fauna that would have inhabited the area historically, including grizzly bear and deer. To get to Osos Park, exit the river at Steelhead Park and walk southeast on Oros Street to Blake Street.

DIRECTIONS TO THE START

BIKE

The start is located at the downstream end of Elysian Valley, reachable by bicycle via the access road downstream of the Glendale Narrows stretch of the LA River Bike Path. Take the access road downstream from Fletcher Drive. Bike parking is available at Egret Park.

TRANSIT

Take Metro Bus 96 and get off at the corner of Riverside Drive and Elmgrove Street. Walk three blocks southeast on Riverside to Egret Park.

CAR

Exit the 5 Freeway at Stadium Way/Riverside Drive in Elysian Valley and go south/east on Riverside Drive. Turn left at Oros Street and park. Walk south/east on Riverside Drive to Egret Park, located just past Barclay Street.

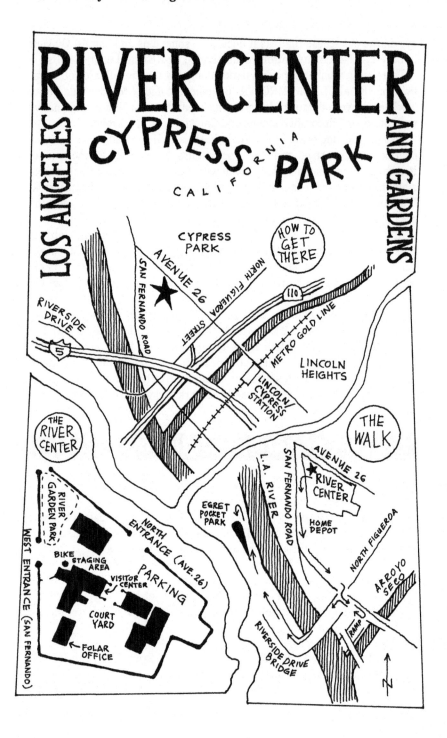

Walk 13

RIVER CENTER
Cypress Park

HIGHLIGHTS

1.3 MILES

The Los Angeles River Center and Gardens is the head-
quarters for many governmental agencies and nonprofits—
including FoLAR—who are working on LA River
revitalization. The River Center, which features lush landscaping, fountains, and a mini-park, is open every day from
7 a.m. to 9 p.m. The visitor center—a small river museum
featuring dioramas of river flora and fauna and interpretive
panels about river history, flooding, and wildlife—is open
weekdays from 9 a.m. to 5 p.m. and is closed on state holidays. The walk is largely on city streets from the River
Center to two river access points. The walk showcases two
very different faces of the river: the all-concrete access
ramp at the historic confluence of the LA River and the
Arroyo Seco, and the southern tip of the scenic soft-bottom
Glendale Narrows.

STARTING POINT

Los Angeles River Center and Gardens, 570 West Ave. 26,
Cypress Park (*Thomas Guide* page 594, J6).

WALK DIRECTIONS

Enter the main gates of the Los Angeles River Center and
Gardens, near the large ficus tree.

This site was formerly Lawry's California Center, one of
the earliest examples of the corporate campus. The
Spanish-style complex looks historical, but the buildings
date back to the 1950s and 1970s. Lawry's hosted a very
popular restaurant, boasting 600,000 visitors annually. The
restaurant closed and the site was due to be demolished for
the construction of a Home Depot in the 1990s. But thanks
to the work of the community and local elected officials, a
compromise was reached to preserve the best portions of

FUTURE PROJECT IN THE AREA

Taylor Yard: This is the most important site for the restoration of the Los Angeles River. A Taylor Yard walk is not included in this book because the area is not officially open to the public at this time.

Taylor Yard is a 248-acre former Southern Pacific (SP) rail yard, with nearly 3 miles of living riverfront. The yard was established in the 1920s and named for the largest business in the area at that time: Taylor Milling. In the 1950s, Taylor Yard was a full classification yard with more than 10,000 employees—a majority of whom commuted on foot, mainly from adjacent Cypress Park. SP gradually shifted the yard's functions to West Colton, leaving much of the site derelict and contaminated.

Taylor Yard is the site of river advocates' greatest victory to date. FoLAR, in coalition with other community groups, sued to block planned industrial development. The legal victory led the way for California State Parks to purchase 40 acres in 2001 and to purchase an additional 18 acres in 2003, with more anticipated.

Construction is underway for a mixed-use park that will feature active recreation and passive habitat. The park will be jointly managed by State Parks and the city's Department of Recreation and Parks. Keep an eye out for the grand opening, expected in 2006.

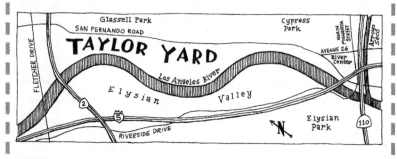

the site, which were purchased by the state's Santa Monica Mountains Conservancy/Mountains Recreation and Conservation Authority (SMMC/MRCA). Today, it's a popular place for weddings and other events (book early because it fills up).

Through the main gates, through the doors on your right (adjacent to the small fountain) is the visitor center. Explore the visitor center, and then go through the large, open wooden doors to check out the main courtyard. The courtyard features a large fountain and colorful flowering plants. FoLAR's offices are on the far right; if you visit during business

The historic confluence of the LA River and the Arroyo Seco, as viewed from the San Fernando Road Bridge

hours, check out the FoLAR and North East Trees (NET) displays in the hallway called the "idea room." Say hello to the FoLAR staff, and ask them how you can get involved in restoring the river.

Exit the courtyard to the right of where you entered and pass into another, smaller courtyard. Continue through an arched doorway on the far side and exit toward the parking lot. On your right is the center's bicycle staging area, featuring a bicycle work stand, tools, and a pump. There is a bathroom and drinking fountain (including a doggie dish) in this area that remains open even when events prevent access to the interior of the River Center. There is also an interpretive panel about the nearby historic confluence.

Walk across the parking lot to the River Garden Park, which features a small lawn area, native plantings, picnic benches and tables, and a clever water feature that is modeled after the Los Angeles River. Follow the path upstream and check out the beautiful mosaics at the mini-river's headwaters. Retrace your steps to where you entered the mini-park, then exit the River Center through the fence on your right.

Turn left onto the sidewalk of San Fernando Road. Across the street from you is the tail end of Taylor Yard (see accompanying sidebar). Across the tracks and behind the Metrolink maintenance building is the river, not yet visible. Continue walking past Home Depot. Turn left (east) at the first corner, where San Fernando Road turns east. Cross San Fernando Road at Figueroa/Riverside, and continue east on the south side of San Fernando.

Look up at the Figueroa Street Viaduct. This 59-foot-wide, 803-foot-long viaduct with art deco ornamentation was completed in 1936. At the time it was constructed, the 200-foot girder river span was the longest of its type in the nation. The structure was planned in the late 1920s to connect the downtown portion of Figueroa Street with what was then Dayton Ave. (now renamed North Figueroa). In the late '30s, this central portion of Figueroa became the Pasadena Freeway, the first freeway in the west.

Just after walking under the Pasadena Freeway, you arrive at the confluence of the Los Angeles River and the Arroyo Seco (pronounced Uh-ROY-oh SAY-co, which means "dry creek" in Spanish). This confluence figures prominently in the earliest written account of the Los Angeles region. As Blake Gumprecht tells the story in *The Los Angeles River: Its Life, Death, and Possible Re-birth*: In 1769, the Portolá expedition's Father Juan Crespi described the Los Angeles River as a "good sized, full flowing river... with very good water, pure and fresh." Crespi described the beds of the LA River and the Arroyo Seco as being "very well lined with large trees, sycamores, willows, cottonwoods, and very large live oaks," as well as sage and wild roses.

It was the beauty and plentiful nature of this site (already well known to our indigenous residents) that appealed to the Spanish. As a result, they settled nearby today's El Pueblo or Olvera Street. Infused with water, flora, and fauna from the river, that backwater outpost grew into the thriving metropolis that Los Angeles is today, so we can say that we are here due to this confluence.

Today, the site serves as a confluence of imposing infrastructure—freeways, railroads, utility power lines, bridges, and concrete levees. FoLAR and others have pushed for establishing a confluence park here to commemorate the historic significance of the site, and to restore the spot to, in the words of Father Crespi, a "very lush and pleasing spot in every respect." The SMMC/MRCA has received funding for the first phase of this project, which will include a fountain located at what is today an empty lot between San Fernando Road and Home Depot.

North entry to the LA River Center

You can view the confluence by looking to your right from the 1913 San Fernando Road Bridge over the Arroyo Seco. On rainy days, the Los Angeles Fire Department's special Swift Water Rescue Unit can be found here, ready with jet skis, ropes, nets, and other accoutrements, poised to try to rescue anyone trapped in the river's deadly storm flows.

Walk back (west) along the south sidewalk of San Fernando Road. Cross Figueroa/Riverside and turn left onto the far/upstream sidewalk of the Riverside Drive Bridge (one of at least five Riverside Drive bridges, so it's generally known as Riverside/Figueroa). The 60-foot-wide, 200-foot-long gracefully curving Riverside/Figueroa Bridge features ornate concrete railing and lampposts.

The first modern bridge at this site, known as the Riverside–Dayton Viaduct, was completed in 1929 and featured a large, elegant arch over the LA River. Twice, the 1929 bridge was severely damaged by landslides: first in November 1937 and then again in the floods of March 1938. It was also subsequently re-worked with the armoring of the river and the introduction of the 110 and 5 freeways. In the repair work after the 1938 floods, the high central arch was demolished and replaced with a much less aesthetic girder truss underbelly.

Looking to your right from the bridge, you will see the downstream end of the soft-bottom Glendale Narrows. Directly ahead of you (across the on-ramp connecting the 5 and 110 freeways) is the steep hillside of Elysian Park, the city of Los Angeles' first and oldest park (see Walk 14's side trip.)

Walk across the river, turning right as the bridge curves. Descend the sidewalk into Elysian Valley. Compare the graceless bulk of the 5 Freeway bridge with that of the historic 110 Freeway. Enjoy the shade of native trees planted by NET on your right as you enter Egret Park (see Walk 12).

If you wish to continue walking, see Walk 12, which begins at Egret Park. Otherwise, retrace your steps back to the River Center.

DIRECTIONS TO THE START

BIKE

There is easy access from the Metro Gold Line (see Transit below). From the LA River Bike Path, continue downstream from Fletcher Drive on the access road. At Egret Park, exit the bikeway and turn left to continue downstream on Riverside Drive. Cross the river and take the first left onto San Fernando Road. Take the first right to stay on San Fernando. Enter the River Center at its side entrance, on your right past Home Depot.

TRANSIT

Take the Metro Gold Line to the Lincoln Heights/Cypress Park (Ave. 26) Station. Transit riders should note the LA River-themed artwork at this station. Artist Cheri Gaulke's 2003 installation, *Water Street: River of Dreams*, features a sculpture of a Tongva (Native American) woman gathering water, a dry riverbed, river rock, sycamore trees, and panels with river stories, including part of a poem by FoLAR founder Lewis MacAdams. Exiting the station, turn left (west, toward the 110 Freeway) and walk on Ave. 26. Go below the freeway, cross the historic 1925/1939 Ave. 26 Bridge over the Arroyo Seco. Cross Figueroa Street; the River Center is on your left.

CAR

From the 110 Freeway northbound, exit at Figueroa (first exit after the 5 Freeway, on the left side). Head north on Figueroa and make the first left at Ave. 26. The River Center is on your left.

From the 110 southbound, exit at Ave. 26. Turn right on Ave. 26, cross Figueroa, and find the River Center on your left.

From the 5 Freeway northbound, exit at Figueroa/Ave. 26 (on the off-ramp to the 110 north). Turn left on Ave. 26, cross Figueroa, and find the River Center on your left.

From the 5 Freeway southbound, exit at Stadium Way and turn right onto Stadium. Take the first right, onto Riverside Drive, which crosses the river and becomes Figueroa. Turn left at Ave. 26. The River Center is on your left.

There is ample parking at the River Center. Occasionally, for large weddings or other events, the lot can fill, in which case there is street parking on Ave. 26 or San Fernando Road.

Flooding and Concrete

It's difficult to imagine now, but for most of recorded history, the Los Angeles River has flooded every 10 to 20 years. The flooding is a result of the region's climate and geography, though the amount of damage caused by floods is affected by patterns of development.

The Los Angeles basin is a mostly flat alluvial plain surrounded by relatively steep (and still growing) mountains. Our rainy season is concentrated between October and May, with the heaviest falls in the foothills. This regime results in rivers that carry a lot of sediment but don't carve deeply into the landscape. During heavy rains, the rivers used to jump out of their shallow beds and take new courses.

From 1815 to 1825, the LA River actually changed its mouth from San Pedro Bay (Long Beach) to Santa Monica Bay. It basically took a right turn just south of present-day downtown Los Angeles, approximately following Washington Blvd., and emptied into the Pacific Ocean through what is today Ballona Creek.

Of course, the natural dynamic character of our rivers is not entirely compatible with extensive human development of the historic floodplain, and, over the years, a number of parties suggested ways to keep people and structures out of harm's way. One such idea, in the 1930 Olmsted-Bartholomew Plan, advocated the public purchase of river-adjacent lands for the creation of parkways that would serve dual purposes: recreation and flood protection. Due to a Depression-era lack of funds and other factors, the region failed to muster the needed vision and vigor to implement the 1930 plan.

In 1934 and 1938, the region experienced its most devastating floods. The 1934 flood was worst in Montrose and La Cañada, the foothill communities of the upper Arroyo Verdugo. Not only does water flow rapidly off these steep mountainsides, it brings with it tons of debris. On Picken's Canyon Creek, at the intersection of Rosemont and Fairway avenues, there is a historic marker commemorating the victims of "The Great Flood of 1934." The American Legion Post, where people had gathered to take refuge from the storm, was at this site. Shortly after midnight on New Year's Day, storm flows demolished the Legion Hall, killing 12 people.

The 1938 flood washed away more than 20 bridges, took numerous lives, and caused tens of millions of dollars in damage (nearly a billion in today's dollars). From historic photographs, we can see that when the river overflowed, it didn't merely leak some water off to the side; it actually reasserted its natural meander, doubling back across the channel and breaking through the levees in multiple places.

Soon thereafter, the Los Angeles County Flood Control District worked with the US Army Corps of Engineers to prevent future flooding. At a cost of approximately $5 billion (in today's dollars), the Corps straightened and deepened the river, reinforcing its levees and making many other changes throughout the systems of tributaries and drainages. The river has not flooded since 1938 (though in 1969 it came close, depositing debris on the top of the levee near Wardlow Road in Long Beach).

Today, opinions worldwide are changing about the effectiveness of using concrete to keep rivers from flooding. In many places, concreting and damming rivers has reduced the risk of floods in the short run, but not necessarily in the long run. While the infrastructure of such systems confines the waters for most storms, enabling development of previously flood-prone areas, big rains can overwhelm the capacity of the systems, and the damage can be catastrophic.

As impermeable development spreads throughout the local watersheds, more water is dumped into the river systems more rapidly, increasing the potential for flooding. To solve this problem of increased runoff, many engineers propose increasingly dramatic interventions such as higher walls and more concrete. This sort of channelization supports increased development, which in turn leads to more channelization—creating a vicious cycle that degrades the health of the river.

In LA, FoLAR and others press for flood-control solutions that will also improve the health of the watershed. These include low-tech solutions such as planting more trees, paving less, and including swales in the landscapes, and high-tech solutions like computer-coordinated cisterns and infiltration basins. (To find out how to join these efforts, see page 317.)

Damage from 1938 flood at the confluence of the LA River and Arroyo Seco

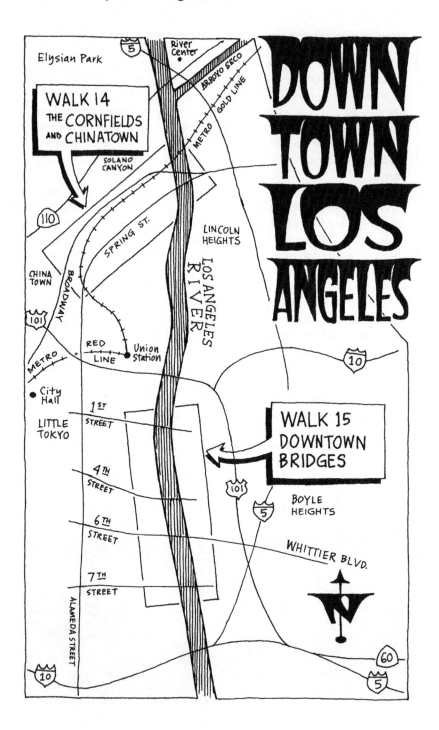

In recent years, the character of downtown Los Angeles has been changing. Large numbers of underutilized buildings have been renovated and reopened as loft housing, and these new river-area residents take their places alongside the longer-term river communities of Lincoln Heights, Boyle Heights, Solano Canyon, William Mead Housing, Chinatown, and Little Tokyo.

Downtown may be lacking in green space, but it has bridges! There are more than a dozen wonderful historic bridges, many among the most beautiful in the world. Walk 15 features four of downtown's finest bridges .

Railroad tracks line both sides of the river through nearly all of downtown LA. The tracks are an obstacle to river restoration and revitalization because they create a barrier between communities and the river. FoLAR would like to see the city of Los Angeles investigate the feasibility of consolidating the downtown tracks and either relocating them underground or elevating them to facilitate river revitalization.

Large railyards (including the Cornfields Yard, Midway Yard, Taylor Yard, and Mission Road Yard) historically have been important job centers, though their bulk separated communities from each other. Much of the rail activity at these sites has been relocated, presenting opportunities for the reuse of these sites. Some of the process is already well underway at the Cornfields and Taylor Yards, and other yards will play important roles in the future.

Downtown is a difficult area for river restoration but important for connecting with our rich history and in creating livable communities for our future.

THE CORNFIELDS AND CHINATOWN

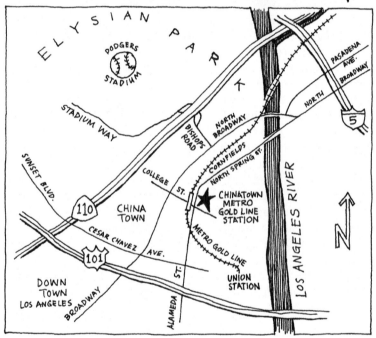

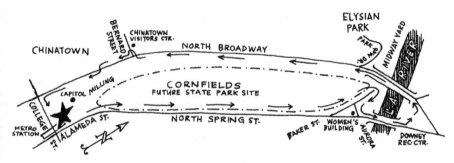

Walk 14

CORNFIELDS AND CHINATOWN

HIGHLIGHTS

2.3 MILES

The Cornfields is a highly visible and important historic site for the region. The former rail yard was slated for warehouse construction, but in the late 1990s, FoLAR and the Chinatown Yards Alliance successfully led a campaign to halt the development. California State Parks has purchased the site to develop a park commemorating its cultural and natural history. The process of planning, funding, and building the new park is a expected to take many years, but interim portions of the park should be open in 2006. This walk goes around the future park, touring an area rich in cultural and historic heritage. Please note that these directions were written prior to the park's construction. If the park is complete when you visit, you can either follow these directions or look for the entry point into the new park and explore there.

STARTING POINT

Chinatown Metro Gold Line Station, corner of Alameda Street/North Spring Street at College Street, Chinatown Los Angeles (*Thomas Guide* p. 634, G2).

WALK DIRECTIONS

From the upper level of the Metro Gold Line Chinatown Station, there is an excellent panoramic view. Go to the north (Pasadena) end of the station. The Cornfields Yard, a flat, banana-shaped 32-acre former rail yard connecting Chinatown with the LA River, is to the right of the Metro tracks.

The river is difficult to see, but it's there below the arches of the North Broadway Bridge at the far end of the Cornfields. In the late 1990s, FoLAR and other groups successfully sued to stop a planned industrial development here. In 2001, California State Parks purchased the site and formed a community advisory committee to develop a plan for the park.

From the Metro station, to the left of the Cornfields, you can also see the hills of Elysian Park (see the side trip this walk). Behind the row of palm trees is Dodger Stadium. Farther left is Chinatown, and the downtown skyline, including Los Angeles City Hall, is behind you.

Directly west of the Metro station is Capitol Milling. At the time of its closure in 1999, Capitol Milling was the oldest continually operating business in the city of Los Angeles. The initial building on the site dates to 1831. The original mill was powered by water from the LA River, delivered via the Zanja Madre (see sidebar, page 117). This business went through incarnations as Stearns Mill, Eagle Mills, and, in 1883, Capitol Milling. The site is now slated to become mixed-use downtown loft living.

From the station platform, descend to the ground level and walk left (north, toward the Cornfields) onto Alameda, which turns slightly to the right and becomes North Spring Street. Walk along the perimeter fence, with the Cornfields on your left. Between Sotello Street and Mesnager Street on your right (across the street) is a small historic marker acknowledging this site as the historic River Station Terminus of the Southern Pacific Railroad established in 1876. The entire Cornfields site, called the River Station Area, is designated as Los Angeles Historic-Cultural Monument #82.

Continue walking north on North Spring and veer left onto Baker Street. Walk to the end of Baker and look up at the magnificent North Broadway Bridge. When it opened in 1911, this bridge was called the Buena Vista Viaduct. The bridge, which featured a newly invented open spandrel arch (instead of a fully filled solid arch, there is space between the arches and the roadway), was technologically innovative for its day. It had the longest concrete arch in California when it was built. The bridge predates Merrill Butler's tenure as city bridge engineer. It was designed by architect Alfred F. Rosenheim, though it is generally credited to Homer Hamlin, who served as the Los Angeles city engineer from 1906 to 1917.

Angels Walk LA information stanchion

In 1998 through 2000, the city of Los Angeles did a fantastic job of retrofitting, rebuilding, and reinforcing the bridge. This included restoring long-lost ornamental features such as the four decorative pylon pedestals at the ends of the bridge. You may be able to spot cliff swallows that form earthen nests on the underside of the bridge.

Directly ahead of you, at 1800 Baker Street, is what is historically known as Midway Yard. These yards are currently temporarily serving as the maintenance yards for the Metro Gold Line. In the future, when the Gold Line has been extended to the east San Gabriel Valley, Metro plans to relocate the maintenance yards to the eastern end of the line, freeing up this important site to connect Elysian Park with the LA River Greenway.

At this point, you're very close to the river, but it's not easily accessible due to railroad tracks that line both sides of the channel through much of downtown. The tracks are active, with dozens of Amtrak and Metrolink trains daily. FoLAR has called for Los Angeles to study the long-term feasibility of consolidating, raising, and/or building underground portions of the railroad tracks, in order to reconnect downtown with the river.

Walk south (away from the river) on Baker Street. Take the first left onto Aurora Street (unmarked). On your right, the three-story red brick building at 1727 North Spring Street, is the Woman's Building. Established in 1975, the Woman's Building was an important space for feminist art, hosting groundbreaking gallery and workshop projects for many years. It still serves as artist studio space.

Turn left on North Spring and ascend the North Spring Street Bridge. This bridge was constructed in 1927 to relieve crowding on the North Broadway Bridge. It was designed by Major John C. Shaw, Los Angeles city engineer from 1925 to 1930, although Merrill Butler's name also appears on the plaque (on your left at the far end of the bridge). Restoration in 1992 included repair and replacement of railings and lighting. Check out the views of the North Broadway Bridge to your left, and the Main Street Bridge to your right.

Just past the end of the bridge, turn left onto the stairway into Downey Recreation Center, cross the site, and ascend the steps on the far side. Turn left onto North Broadway.

As you cross the North Broadway Bridge, you encounter views of the North Main Street Bridge, the Cornfields, and the downtown skyline. The views are especially nice from the large central belvedere (viewing platform).

Continue walking south on North Broadway. An historical marker across the street describes the 1769 Portolá Expedition (see Walk 13). The marker is located at the entrance to Elysian Park (see side trip).

Continue walking south. On your right, across the street at 1039 and 1051 North Broadway, respectively, are St. Peter's Church and Casa Italiana. The area that is known today as Chinatown has many layers of history. Prior to its 1938 inauguration as "New Chinatown," it had been home to waves of immigrants from Mexico, Croatia, and Italy. Los Angeles' Chinese communities were relocated to the current site to make way for the construction of Union Station.

Turn right on Bernard Street. Check out the information stanchion in front of the Chinatown Heritage and Visitors Center (411 Bernard Street; 323-222-0856; open Sundays 12 p.m. to 4 p.m.). This stanchion is one of 15 on a self-guided walking tour of Chinatown. It's a project of Angels Walk LA and provides valuable historical information, including a section on the Cornfields and the Zanja Madre.

If you're up for it, you can do the entire 1.9-mile Chinatown walking tour (follow directions on the stanchions), or you can just check out the five stanchions on your way back to the starting point. Return to North Broadway and turn right (south). At Chinatown's East Gate, turn left onto the crosswalk. Turn right to continue south on the east side of the street. Turn left onto College Street to return to the starting point.

DIRECTIONS TO THE START

BIKE
There is no river bike path in this area. Consider biking to a Metro Gold Line station and bringing your bike on board.

TRANSIT
Take the Metro Gold Line to the Chinatown Station.

CAR
Exit the 110 Freeway at North Hill Street in Chinatown. (This exit is on the left for the southbound 110.) The exit puts you southbound on Hill. Turn left on College Street and left again on Alameda Street (which becomes North Spring Street). If the park is open (interim use expected to open in 2006), turn left and park in the park's lot. If the park is not yet open, street parking is available on Alameda/North Spring or College.

Alternately, exit the 5 Freeway at Pasadena Ave. in Lincoln Heights. Turn southwest (toward downtown) on Pasadena Ave., which merges into North Broadway just before the LA River. Continue on Broadway into Chinatown, turn left on College Street, and follow the directions above.

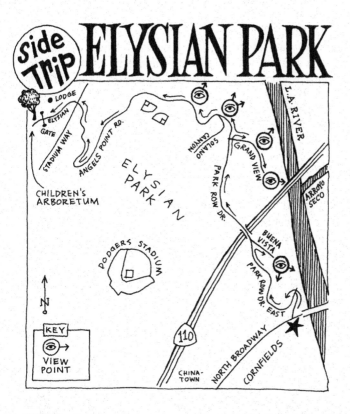

NOTE

This side trip is different than others in this book. It is a 3-mile, one-way tour of six sites in Elysian Park. While it is walkable, at 6 miles round trip, it's probably best experienced by bicycle or car. The directions on page 116 take you to the starting location, with additional directions to navigate to subsequent sites.

LOCATION AND INFORMATION

This trip begins in Elysian Park (835 Academy Road, Los Angeles) at Buena Vista Hill, at the end of Buena Vista Drive (*Thomas Guide* p. 634, H1). For more information about the park, call 213-847-0926, or visit www.laparks.org/dos/parks/facility/elysianPk.htm. This side trip showcases LA's first and oldest park, established in 1886 and now managed by the city's Department of Recreation and Parks. At 575 acres, it's the city's second largest park (after Griffith Park). The northeast edge of Elysian Park offers fantastic views of the Los

6 MILES

Angeles River, from Taylor Yard to the Arroyo Seco confluence to downtown Los Angeles. Over the years, the park's natural setting has been encroached upon by the addition of freeways, Dodger Stadium (and its enormous parking lot), and other development. Only through the diligent efforts of community activists has the park been preserved.

This side trip includes only a few river-related highlights within the greater park: five viewpoints and a walk through the Children's Arboretum. The six sites, described below, are spread out over about 3 hilly miles.

BUENA VISTA HILL

Walk east on the asphalt path from the parking lot. Where the path levels off, you'll find an overlook area where the nonprofit urban forestry organization North East Trees (NET) added native plantings, stonework, and interpretive signs identifying historic buildings. This project differs somewhat from NET's river parks; the stones are not river rock, but the sandstone found in the Elysian Park. The artistic benches are by sculptor Brett Goldstone, who is responsible for many of artistic gates along the river (see page 84). From the overlook, you have excellent views of Lincoln Heights and the surrounding Ascot Hills, including the river as it passes beneath the North Broadway and North Spring Street bridges. Retrace your steps to the parking lot.

Directions from Buena Vista Hill to Point Grandview: Take Buena Vista Drive back down the hill. Continue west onto Park Row Drive and cross the 1941 Park Row Drive Bridge (over the 110 Freeway). The bridge has an unremarkable railing, with a large arch below (best viewed from near Elysian Reservoir). Park Row Drive ascends, curves to

North East Trees' eucalyptus stump thrones in Elysian Park's Children's Arboretum

the right, then levels off. Look for a way-finding sign on your right and follow the directions for Point Grandview. Just past the sign, take the first road on your right, Grand View Drive, to access Point Grandview. For a few years, the park road has been damaged, so a barrier gate is across it with a sign stating ROAD CLOSED TO THRU TRAFFIC. The locked gate here prevents car access, but bicycles and pedestrians can easily go around the gate. If the gate is in the way, park here and walk around the gate, then proceed about a third of a mile on Grand View Drive to Point Grandview.

POINT GRANDVIEW

This steep lookout is developed with parking, a small picnic area, and rows of palm trees. It features views of the confluence area, including the LA River, the Arroyo Seco, the River Center, and freeways.

Directions from Point Grandview to additional viewpoints and to Children's Arboretum: From Point Grandview, go west about a quarter mile on Grand View Drive to where the view north opens up again. This unnamed, undeveloped area features a wide view of soft-bottom river through Elysian Valley, Cypress Park, and Mount Washington. Continue west back to the (generally gated) intersection, then turn right (north) onto Grand View Drive. At the intersection of Grand View Drive and Park Row, the view opens up along a low stone wall, with more excellent views of the river through the Glendale Narrows. Continue west; Grand View Drive becomes Angel's Point Road. On your right, just before the baseball fields is another undeveloped vista point, good for viewing all of Taylor Yard.

Continue west on Angel's Point Road. Pass the baseball fields and Angel's Point. The road curves to the right and descends. Go straight across Stadium Way, where Angel's Point Road becomes Elysian Park Road. The road curves to the left. If you're driving, turn left at Grace Simons Lodge and park. You're in Chavez Ravine Arboretum. The Children's Arboretum (unmarked) is on the right, just past the gate across Elysian Park Road.

CHAVEZ RAVINE ARBORETUM—CHILDREN'S ARBORETUM

The Chavez Ravine Arboretum is located on the west side of Stadium Way both north and south of Elysian Park Drive. It contains many old and large trees from various parts of the world, most with labels denoting their species. This is the city's oldest botanical garden, begun in 1893 by the Los Angeles Horticultural Society, with continued planting through the 1920s. It has been designated Los Angeles City Historical-Cultural Monument #48.

The small Children's Arboretum is located on the west side of the site. The children's area features a weaving path up a small hillside peppered with interpretive signs describing the trees and plants. In 2003, NET worked on this area, adding native plants, refurbishing trails, and creating two fun thrones out of old eucalyptus stumps.

DIRECTIONS TO THE START

BIKE

There is no bike path in this area and the park is hilly. From the Metro Gold Line, disembark at Chinatown Station. Go west on College Street. Turn right on to North Broadway and turn left on Park Row Drive East (just before the North Broadway Bridge). Take the first left to stay on Park Row Drive and continue uphill. Turn sharply right at Buena Vista Drive (just before the bridge over the Pasadena Freeway).

TRANSIT

This side trip is long and hilly and therefore best suited for bicycling or driving. From the Metro Gold Line Chinatown Station, follow the bicycle directions above.

CAR

Exit the 5 Freeway at Pasadena Ave. in Lincoln Heights and go south on Pasadena, which merges onto North Broadway at the bridge. Turn right onto Park Row Drive East (just after the North Broadway Bridge). Take the first left to stay on Park Row Drive and continue uphill. Turn sharply right at Buena Vista Drive (just before the bridge over the Pasadena Freeway).

Alternately, exit the 110 Freeway at Stadium Way. Keep right and do not enter Dodger Stadium. Turn right onto Stadium Way, which merges onto Bishops Road. Turn left onto North Broadway and left again onto Park Row Drive East (just before the North Broadway Bridge). Take the first left to stay on Park Row Drive and continue uphill. Turn sharply right at Buena Vista Drive (just before the bridge over the Pasadena Freeway).

Park at the small lot at the end of the road.

North East Trees' interpretive signage at Buena Vista Hill in Elysian Park

The Zanja Madre

For more than a hundred years, the Los Angeles River was the only source of water for the young pueblo of Los Angeles. The river water met the domestic needs of the populace and also served the extensive agriculture that characterized early Los Angeles. The pueblo was surrounded by orchards and vineyards. The water was brought to the pueblo through an elaborate series of zanjas. The largest central zanja was called the Zanja Madre (pronounced ZAHN-ha MAH-dray, Spanish for mother ditch).

The Zanja Madre was initially an earthen ditch flowing through the present-day Cornfields site along the base of the bluffs, approximately where the Gold Line tracks are. The ditch was lined with bricks, and later was covered over with a brick arch. In 2000, a pair of amateur archeologists, led by Craig Howell, uncovered an existing remnant of the Zanja Madre, said to date from the 1850s or 1860s. This occurred near Capitol Mills, in an area currently inaccessible to the public.

DOWNTOWN BRIDGES

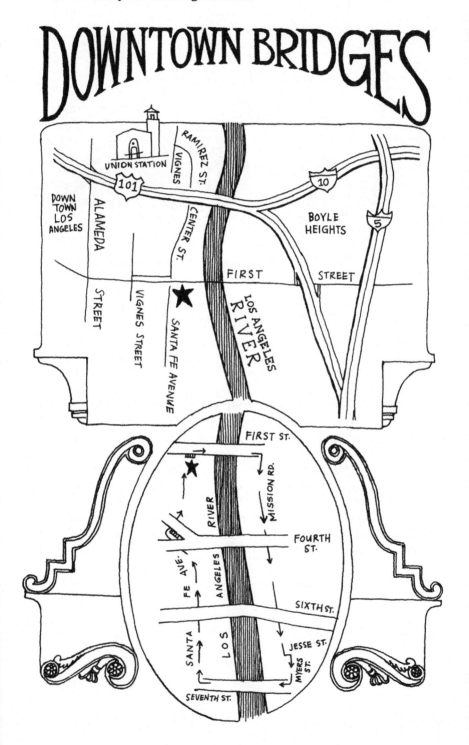

Walk 15

DOWNTOWN BRIDGES

HIGHLIGHTS   **2.5 MILES**

The beauty of the Los Angeles River through downtown
derives not from its natural wonders, but from its urban
ones. This walk features four of the more than a dozen
prominent historic bridges dating from 1910 to 1932. These
bridges are monuments to civic pride, featuring graceful
arches and a variety of intricate ornamental details, all
demonstrating that public infrastructure can be lasting,
beautiful, and functional. Please note that this walk is best
enjoyed on weekends, when the weekday truck traffic is
absent from this industrial area.

STARTING POINT

First Street Bridge stairs, First Street and Santa Fe Ave.,
downtown Los Angeles (*Thomas Guide* p. 634, H4).

WALK DIRECTIONS

Ascend the stairs to the deck of the First Street Bridge, turn
right, and walk east over the LA River.

This bridge, completed in 1929, was designed by Merrill
Butler, the person most responsible for LA's historic
bridges. The bridge bears a bronze plaque with a dedication
to the memory of Henry G. Parker, who was an assistant
city engineer in charge of bridge building. In 1909, at age
40, he drowned while supervising repairs to flood gates of
the city's outfall sewer near Redondo Beach.

Looking downstream, to your right, is an excellent view
of the Fourth Street Bridge. In 1931, this bridge replaced
the last remaining wooden bridge downtown. It features
gothic-style detailing. Note that these historic downtown
bridges were designed to be seen from many vantage points.
Ornate railing, lighting, columns, and overlook areas are
seen up-close by pedestrians and other surface traffic.
Graceful arches below provide appeal for those at a distance, including train passengers.

At the ends of nearly all the bridges are bronze plaques commemorating the completion of the bridge and the names of elected officials and lead city staff responsible for their construction. Note the plaque across the street on your left as you approach Mission Road.

Turn right onto Mission and walk south through this industrial area. Directly ahead you will see the Fourth Street Bridge, now with a closer view of the gothic motif in its railing.

Continue walking below the bridge and look up at the 1932 Sixth Street Bridge. At 3600 feet long, it was the longest concrete bridge in California in its day. Unlike the other downtown bridges with concrete arches, the Sixth Street Bridge uses two riveted steel arches. The arches are visible to your right and are best viewed later in the walk from the deck of the Seventh Street Bridge.

At the corner of Mission and Jesse Street, to your right is the Seventh Street Bridge, originally built in 1910 as a nearly at-grade trolley bridge. In 1927, under the guidance of Merrill Butler, a new bridge was constructed as an additional layer atop the existing bridge. This stacking is easiest to see from this side view.

Turn left at Jesse, where you get a good view of the large pylons at the east end of the Sixth Street Bridge. Take the first right, unmarked, at Meyers Street.

Turn right onto Seventh Street and note the antique plaque on your right. Ascend the bridge. From the central bridge deck, to your right, are good views of the Sixth Street Bridge. Descend to Santa Fe Ave.

At 710 Santa Fe Ave., visible to your left from the corner of Santa Fe and Sixth, is a modest old fire station. Engine Company No.17 is no longer in public service, but this pleasant building is another good example of lasting aesthetic public infrastructure.

Turn right onto Santa Fe and walk north, again viewing and passing below the Sixth Street Bridge.

Continue north. Near Santa Fe and Palmetto Street, you'll find more good views: looking back at the Sixth Street Bridge and ahead at the Fourth Street Bridge.

Santa Fe veers left. Go under the initial spur of the Y-shaped Fourth Street Bridge. On your right, just before you go under the main stem of the bridge, ascend the stairway. Check out the gothic ornamentation up close, as well as the little-used pedestrian seating areas atop the bridge. If you have time, walk out over the river and see the elaborate porticos, and even more views of the Sixth Street Bridge. Walk back and descend the stairs.

Continue north on Santa Fe and walk under the main stem of the Fourth Street Bridge. On your left is a quarter-mile-long former freight depot that now serves as the campus of the Southern California Institute of

Architecture (SCI-Arc). The freight depot building was constructed in 1907 and is one of the earliest local examples of reinforced concrete buildings. SCI-Arc is one of LA's premiere architecture schools and is an ally in the task of re-envisioning the Los Angeles River.

Continue north to the starting point.

DIRECTIONS TO THE START

BIKE

No river bike path exists in this section of the LA River. You can take your bicycle on the Metro Red Line or Gold Line, Amtrak, or Metrolink, and disembark at Union Station. Follow transit directions below.

TRANSIT

Take the Metro Red Line or Gold Line, Amtrak, or Metrolink to Union Station. From there, it's a 0.6-mile walk through a very industrial area. Go to the east end of the station by following signs TO BUSES or to Patsaouras Transit Plaza (also known as Gateway Plaza). When you get to the large lobby, go upstairs to the bus area. Walk east through the transit plaza and continue east down the exit ramp to cross Vignes Street. Proceed east on Ramirez Street, which turns right and crosses below the 101 Freeway, where it becomes Center Street. Continue south on Center. At Banning Street (a block before the already visible First Street Bridge), take Santa Fe Ave., which splits off to the right. Take the stairs located on the south side of the bridge.

CAR

Exit the 101 Freeway at Alameda Street in downtown Los Angeles and go south on Alameda. Turn left on First Street. Just before the bridge, at the intersection of First and Vignes Street, turn left, then immediately turn right onto the First Street frontage road, directly north of the bridge. Turn right on Santa Fe Ave. and cross under the bridge. Street parking is available on Santa Fe.

Merrill Butler's Sixth Street Bridge over the Los Angeles River

Merrill Butler and the Bridges of Los Angeles

Merrill Butler was born in upstate New York in 1891. He graduated from the old Los Angeles Polytechnic High School, but he never attended college. Instead, he learned civil engineering via a correspondence course. He served as the city of Los Angeles' engineer for bridges and structures (later called engineer of design) from 1923 to 1961. He passed away in 1963 and is buried at Forest Lawn Cemetery in Glendale.

While a few extant bridges predate his era (including the marvelous Buena Vista Viaduct or North Broadway Bridge, designed by Homer Hamlin and Alfred F. Rosenheim; see Walk 14), Merrill Butler is widely acknowledged as the guiding force behind the design and construction of nearly all of this city's marvelous historic bridges.

At least nine historic bridges over the LA River are attributed to Butler. His impressive work can also be found over the Arroyo Seco and many other crossings in central parts of Los Angeles (see pages 265 to 291 for a selected listing of historic bridges not included in this walk).

Los Angeles' iconic bridges grew out of the late 19th century City Beautiful tradition, when monumental public works were developed in order to uplift the character of urban residents.

In 1924, LA voters approved the $2 million Viaduct Bond Act, which levied a tax to fund the city's ambitious program to upgrade and modernize its bridges. Butler began in the beaux arts tradition that dominated US public architecture at the time. Beaux arts is an architectural style that draws from various European traditions, including Roman imperial, Italian renaissance, and late 19th century Parisian neo-baroque. This style can be seen in the Butler's more ornate earlier bridges, including the 1926 Cesar Chavez Ave. Bridge (originally the Macy Street Viaduct) and the 1925 Olympic Blvd. Bridge (originally the Ninth Street Viaduct).

Butler's later bridges are also spectacular but slightly more streamlined, more modern. Examples include the 1938 Riverside Drive Bridge (at Zoo Drive; see Walk 7) and the 1930 Washington Blvd. Bridge. All the bridges reflect a consistency of purpose and vision. Individual bridges display thematic variations from the gothic patterns of the Fourth Street Viaduct to the Spanish colonial style of the Chavez Bridge.

Each bridge features its own unique lighting standards that compliment the individual design. Many of the bridges feature seating areas, belvederes (overlook areas), and even fixtures for overhead wires for streetcars (look for these on the Seventh Street Bridge and others). These touches hark back to an age when walking and transit played a more important role in the lives of Angelenos. The detail accorded to the

continued on the next page

Merrill Butler, continued

design of public infrastructure waned when the car emerged and began to dominate our landscape.

Merrill Butler's bridges eliminated river and rail crossings to enable the city to grow. The expansion literally paved the way for the highway era. Most automobile traffic is now focused onto freeways, allowing the bridges to lapse into obscurity. Butler was aware of this dilemma; in an April 18, 1938, *Los Angeles Times* article, he states: "It is difficult for the average motorist to realize how much relief of traffic congestion has been provided… the volume of traffic in the city appears to increase faster than outlets can be built. The result is that automobile traffic still is congested… especially during the morning and evening rush hours." The article tries to put a positive spin on the exigencies of high-speed city traffic, but, even in the midst of the Great Depression, it ends up telling the now-familiar tale that extensive road building wasn't quite the solution to gridlock.

In 1934, the Board of Public Works appointed Butler to serve briefly as city engineer, while longtime city engineer Lloyd Aldrich was in Washington. Throughout his career, Butler gave talks and presentations about various aspects of bridge building and maintenance. He continued to oversee the city engineering design division until his retirement in

Merrill Butler's gothic-style 1931 Fourth Street Bridge

1961. In his later years, he was chiefly known for shepherding the creation of the Hyperion Sewage Treatment Plant.

As a result of the 1989 Loma Prieta and 1994 Northridge earthquakes, the city was faced with ensuring the seismic integrity of the bridges. Some recommended that the antique bridges be replaced with standard CalTrans bridges (historic bridge railings cannot be crash-tested at 70 miles per hour).

Fortunately, the city Bureau of Engineering, under the leadership of Clark Robins and others, embarked upon an ambitious program of rehabilitating and reinforcing the bridges. In many cases, the retrofit projects tore down and reassembled bridges in place (generally a half-bridge at a time, so traffic could continue). Many of these projects restored original features that had been damaged or removed many years earlier.

In an October 2000 *Los Angeles Times Magazine* article, James Ricci quoted Merrill Butler Jr., saying, "My father was as modest a man as you would ever meet ... In his opinion, being a civil servant was a very noble profession. He was proud of working for the city. His ethics were unassailable."

Merrill Butler serves as an example for those of us who strive to make our river and our city beautiful. His amazing bridges stand as monumental legacies.

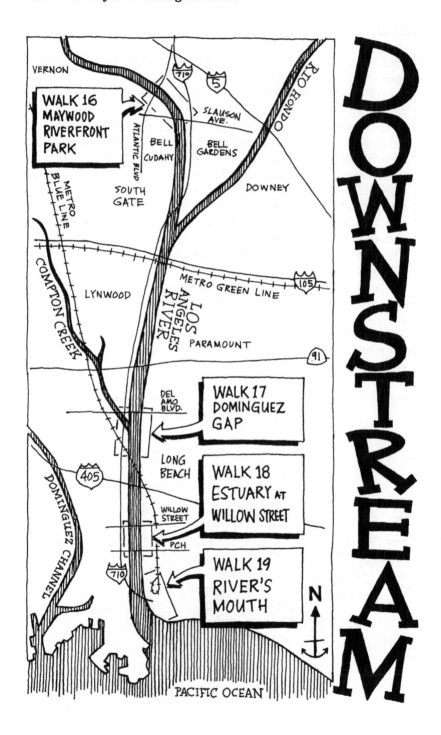

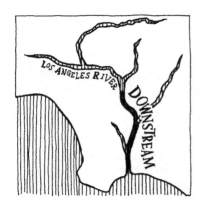

The complexion of the LA River varies as it leaves the city of Los Angeles and wends its way through Vernon, Bell, Commerce, Maywood, Bell Gardens, Cudahy, South Gate, Lynwood, Paramount, Compton, and Long Beach. For the purposes of this book, I call the walks along this stretch of river "downstream."

It may not be apparent to others, but people in Long Beach know the connection between all of these locations. Each year, storms bring trash and other debris down the river and into the San Pedro Bay. And each year, tons of this trash wash up on the beaches of Long Beach.

From Vernon to Long Beach, the river is most characterized by a broad concrete channel, with very little natural riparian ecosystem remaining. This concrete is abutted by industrial areas, and, for most of its length, the 710 Freeway, with its large amounts of truck traffic serving the ports.

Blessedly, the concrete does end—at the estuary just below Willow Street in Long Beach (see Walk 18)—and that's one of the nicest spots on the entire river. This is where the river's freshwater mingles with the ocean's saltwater to create a unique ecosystem. Another bright spot is that the downstream area has the river's longest bike path, stretching 17 miles from Atlantic Blvd. in Vernon to the Pacific Ocean in Long Beach.

The efforts to reclaim the Los Angeles River in this area are varied and challenging. A few cities have completed river greenway-related projects, including pocket parks in Maywood, Bell Gardens, and Long Beach; tree-planting in Cudahy; a bikeway staging area in South Gate; and channel wall murals in Paramount. Many more projects are in various stages of planning, acquisition, and remediation.

Though people in all of these communities walk and bike along the river every day, it's somewhat challenging to build a vocal constituency for restoration because it's hard to see the vast concrete channel as a "real" river. Residents tend to refer to the river just as "flood control" or, worse, "the sewer" or "aguas negras." Restoration in this area is difficult but not impossible. Change will be incremental, starting with river-adjacent greenways connecting along bike paths. This will allow for a change in perception of the river as a barren area into a green amenity for the community. Many of these majority Latino and African American communities have been neglected and underserved. Most are harmed by toxics in the air, ground, and water. The renewal of the river is an important component of achieving environmental justice for residential communities in this area.

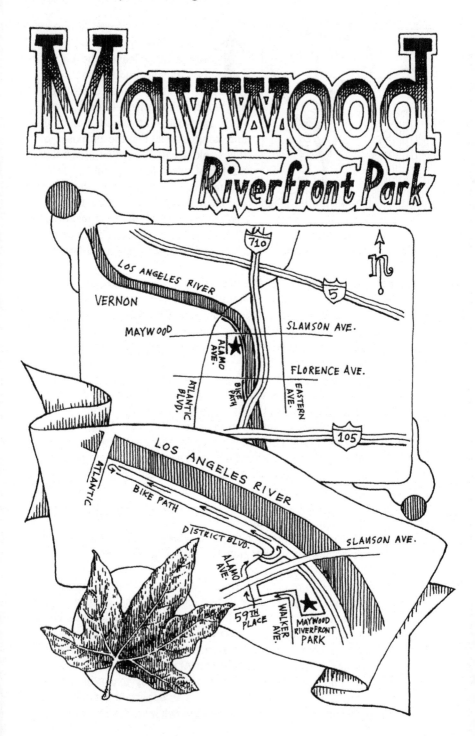

Maywood Riverfront Park

Walk 16

MAYWOOD RIVERFRONT PARK

2.1 MILES

HIGHLIGHTS

This walk, through Maywood Riverfront Park, features an industrial face of the Los Angeles River. There is not much in the way of nature, but there is a stark beauty in the vast concrete channel. While this walk is not recommended to introduce newcomers to the river, it's important to become familiar with the challenges facing those who would restore the river and bring amenities to underserved areas.

STARTING POINT

Maywood Riverfront Park, Walker Ave. and 59th Place, Maywood (*Thomas Guide* p. 675, F6).

WALK DIRECTIONS

The walk begins at Maywood Riverfront Park, which, when complete in 2006, will occupy 7.3 acres. With nearly 30,000 people in just over a square mile, Maywood is said to be the most densely populated city west of the Mississippi River. Its working class neighborhoods are impacted by their proximity to air pollution from the adjacent industrial areas and the truck-heavy 710 Freeway. This park will more than double the city's existing 5.8 acres of parkland.

This river park has been championed by the city of Maywood, the Trust for Public Land, FoLAR, and others. Unfortunately, this site suffered from chemical contamination, which has held up the construction of this park.

If it is complete, walk through the park to access the South County LA River Bike Trail along the east side of the park. Walk upstream (left). If the park is not yet complete, access the river by walking west on 59th Place. Turn right onto Alamo Ave., cross Slauson Ave., and turn right on the frontage road directly north of (and adjacent to) Slauson. Enter the South County bikeway through the gates on your right just before the frontage road turns left.

Note the stone pillar bikeway entry points. In the late 1990s, the county installed about a dozen of these entryways at access points along the bikeway. The stonework enhances the bikeway and is much nicer than the stark poles and chain-link fence it replaced, but the access points still need more enhancing to match the welcome of similar access-point enhancements constructed by North East Trees (NET) in the Glendale Narrows area. Some have suggested the need for a "South East Trees" to work with the southeast cities and the county on improving this area by adding native plants, artwork, and signage.

Turn left to walk upstream on the bikeway. (Watch for bicyclists!) Just upstream of Slauson, you enter the "exclusively industrial since 1905" city of Vernon. Vernon is approximately 5 square miles with less than 150 official residents. By day, the city boasts a workforce of more than 55,000. In 1996, the *Los Angeles Times* called Vernon "a city unlike any other in Los Angeles County... almost treeless... no parks, no movie theaters, no bookstores." Vernon contains 3.5 miles of riverfront, among the most challenging areas for future restoration. (For much more information on exploring this unique industrial city, see the LA Conservancy's 1997 publication, *Cruising Industrial Los Angeles.*)

The river in this area fans out nearly to its full downstream width. It's a vast expanse of concrete, and the flow is confined mainly to the narrow, central, low-flow channel. The area is most "natural" during the late summer and early fall when sediment has been deposited and low-lying vegetation grows on artificial sandbars.

Walk upstream to the turnaround point, where the bikeway ends at the historic 1931 Atlantic Blvd. Bridge.

The 1931 Atlantic Blvd. Bridge over the LA River in the city of Vernon

DIRECTIONS TO THE START

BIKE

The walk starting point is easily accessed from the South County LA River Bike Trail, which runs on the west bank of the LA River from the Atlantic Blvd. to Imperial Highway (from the city of Vernon to the cities of Compton and Paramount). To reach the walk starting place, exit the South County bikeway at Slauson Ave., the first bridge downstream of Atlantic. The unmarked exit is on the upstream side of Slauson. As you exit at Slauson, go left (west) on the frontage road adjacent to Slauson. Turn left onto Alamo Ave., cross Slauson, then turn left onto 59th Place. The park will be on your right at the end of 59th. The site is also easily accessed from the Metro Blue Line Slauson Station. From there, ride east on Slauson to Alamo Ave. Turn right onto Alamo, and then turn left on 59th.

TRANSIT

Take the Metro Blue Line to the Slauson Station. Take Metro Bus 108 or 358 eastbound on Slauson to Alamo Ave. (immediately before the LA River and the 710 Freeway). Walk south on Alamo, then east on 59th Place.

CAR

Exit the 710 Freeway at Atlantic Blvd. in Vernon/Bell (just south of the intersection of the 5 Freeway). Go south on Atlantic and turn left on Slauson Ave. Turn right on Alamo Ave. and then left on 59th Place. Find street parking on Walker Ave. or 59th. If park construction is complete (expected in 2006), turn left off 59th to enter the parking lot.

Alternately, exit the 710 Freeway at Florence Ave. in Bell/Bell Gardens and go east on Florence. Turn left on Eastern Ave., left on Slauson Ave., and left again on Alamo Ave. Turn left on 59th Place. Find street parking on Walker Ave. or 59th. If park construction is complete (expected in 2006), turn left off 59th to enter the parking lot.

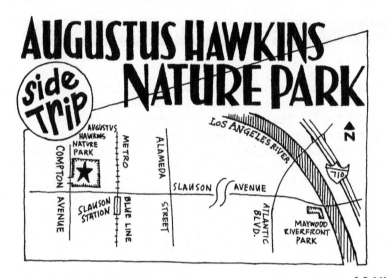

AUGUSTUS HAWKINS NATURE PARK

0.3 MILE

LOCATION AND INFORMATION

Augustus Hawkins Nature Park, 5790 Compton Ave. (at Slauson) in South Los Angeles (*Thomas Guide* p. 674, F-5). Just 4 miles west of Maywood Riverfront Park, this 8.5-acre park features strolling paths, picnic areas, native vegetation, public art, and a visitor center. The park opened in 2001 and is a very popular family hangout in this park-poor area. Augustus Hawkins Nature Park was initially a project of the Santa Monica Mountains Conservancy/Mountains Recreation and Conservation Authority (SMMC/MRCA), which transitioned management of the park to the city of Los Angeles in 2005. For more information about this park, call 323-585-3205, or visit www.laparks.org/dos/parks/facility/theAugustusFawkinsNaturalPk.htm.

DESCRIPTION

You might begin your visit at the Evan Frankel Discovery Center, which is designed to echo the appearance of nearby craftsman homes. The center features interpretive displays about nature and environmental issues.

After visiting the center, you can explore the walking paths throughout the park. Check out mosaics, cactus gardens, extensive native trees and shrubs, and the beautiful decorative perimeter fencing with panels featuring native animal motifs. The park has an excellent mix between a more conventional central field area designed for picnicking and play, and native vegetation around its perimeter designed for strolling and for supporting habitat.

DIRECTIONS TO THE START

BIKE

From Maywood Riverfront Park, experienced cyclists preferring the most direct route can ride west on Slauson and turn right on Compton Ave. Those less comfortable riding on busy streets may ride south on Walker Ave., then turn right (west) on Randolph Street. Continue west as Randolph jogs slightly to the left at Maywood Ave. Randolph turns to the right and intersects Slauson. Go left (west) on Slauson for three blocks, turn right on Compton, and turn right again into the park.

TRANSIT

The park is located three short blocks directly west of the Metro Blue Line Slauson Station. It is visible from the platform.

CAR

Exit the 710 Freeway at Atlantic Blvd. in Vernon/Bell (just south of the intersection of the 5 Freeway) and go south on Atlantic. Turn right on Slauson Ave., right on Compton Ave., and enter the parking lot on the right.

Rock and mosaic amphitheater at Augustus Hawkins Nature Park

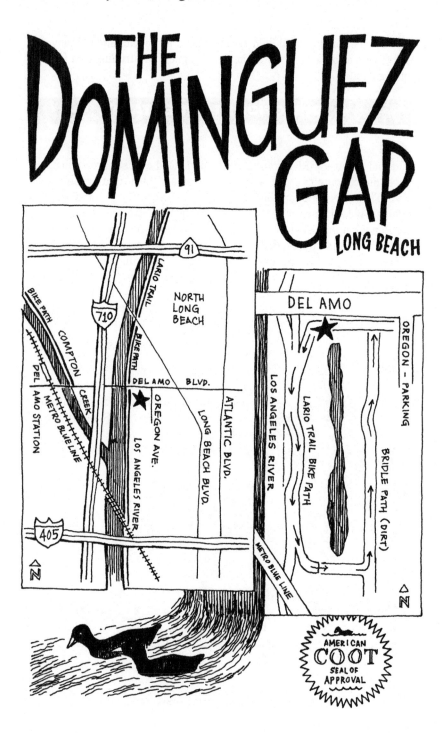

Walk 17

DOMINGUEZ GAP
North Long Beach

HIGHLIGHTS

1.9 MILES

The Dominguez Gap is an area in North Long Beach where two side-channel wetlands parallel the Los Angeles River from just upstream of the 405 Freeway to upstream of Compton Creek. This walk showcases only the 30-acre east basin. A similar 14-acre basin exists on the west side of the river, but it's difficult to access. Though the river itself is contained in a concrete-lined channel, the wetlands support seasonal bird populations. It is generally better seen at the wetter times of the year, winter through early summer.

STARTING POINT

West Del Amo Blvd. and the LA River (*Thomas Guide* p. 765, C4).

WALK DIRECTIONS

Enter the river right-of way at the bike path entrance along Del Amo Blvd. and follow the Lario Bike Trail along the top of the levee, walking downstream.

As you head downstream, you'll notice the vast concrete expanse of the river on your right and the parallel wetlands on your left. At the top of the levee, you can get a good look at the not-so-good-looking Los Angeles County Drainage Area Project: parapet walls built in the late 1990s to increase flood-protection capacity in the downstream stretches of the river.

As you continue walking downstream, look across the river to your right to see the LA River's heavily armored confluence with Compton Creek. For an up-close-and-personal look at the confluence, see Walk 27.

Pass below the railroad bridge and along the pumping station. Just before the Metro Blue Line bridge, turn left on an asphalt access road. The road turns into a bridle trail, which turns left and loops back to the start of the walk.

DIRECTIONS TO THE START

BIKE

Take the Lario Bike Trail to Del Amo Blvd. in North Long Beach.

TRANSIT

Take the Metro Blue Line to the Del Amo Station. Walk three long blocks east, under the 710 Freeway and over the LA River.

CAR

Exit the 710 Freeway at Del Amo Blvd. in North Long Beach and go east on Del Amo. Cross the LA River, turn right on Oregon Ave., and park on the street.

FUTURE PROJECT IN THE AREA

Dominguez Gap Wetlands Multiuse Project: The LA County Department of Public Works, working with the city of Long Beach, the Lower Los Angeles and San Gabriel Rivers and Mountains Conservancy (RMC), and the California Coastal Conservancy, is planning to restore wetland habitat in this area. The project, scheduled for completion in early 2007, proposes to divert water from the LA River into the upstream end of the Dominguez Gap, with the water re-entering the river at the downstream end. The project will include riparian habitat, vegetated islands and slopes, and walking trails.

Wetlands of the Dominguez Gap in North Long Beach

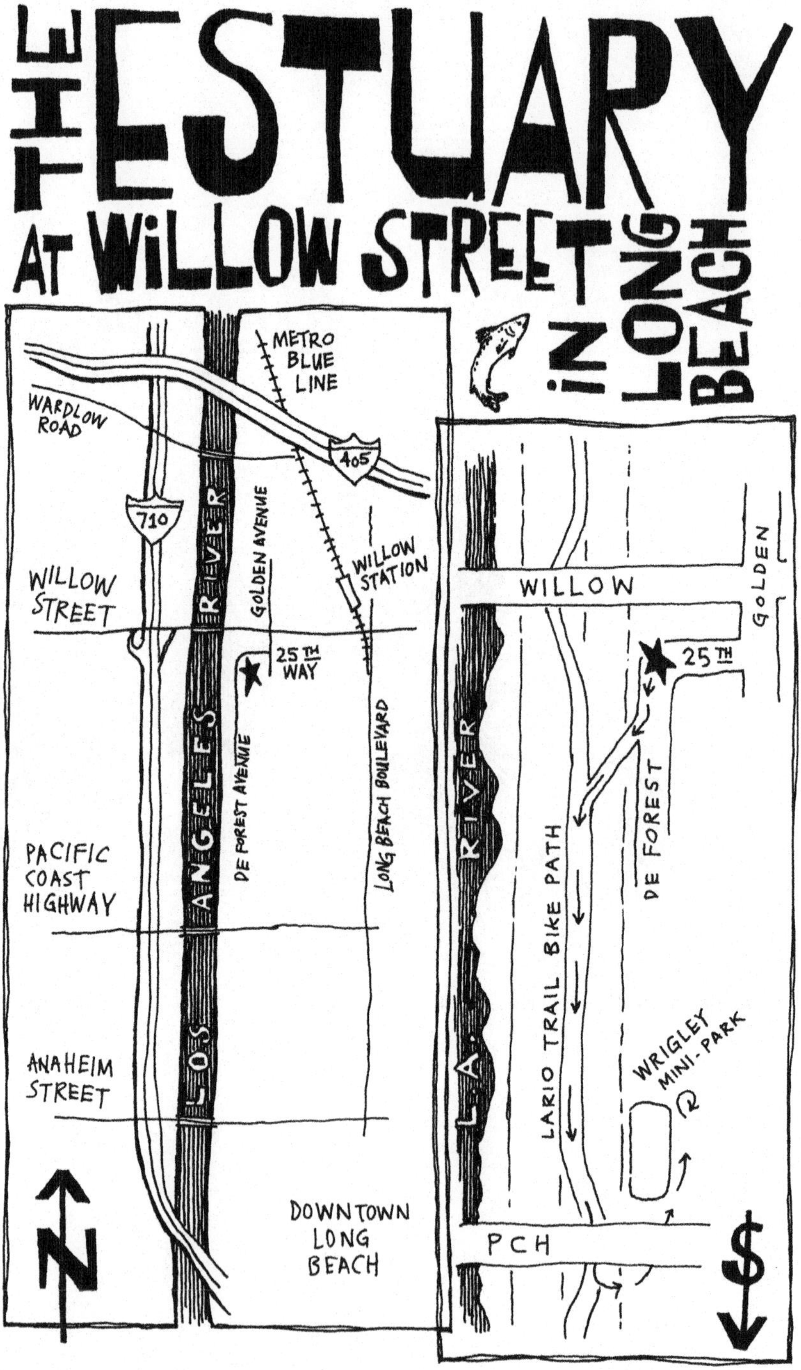

THE ESTUARY AT WILLOW STREET IN LONG BEACH

WARDLOW ROAD

METRO BLUE LINE

405

710

GOLDEN AVENUE

WILLOW STATION

WILLOW STREET

LOS ANGELES RIVER

25TH WAY

DE FOREST AVENUE

LONG BEACH BOULEVARD

PACIFIC COAST HIGHWAY

ANAHEIM STREET

DOWNTOWN LONG BEACH

N

WILLOW

GOLDEN

25TH

L.A. RIVER

LARIO TRAIL BIKE PATH

DE FOREST

WRIGLEY MINI-PARK

PCH

$

Walk 18

ESTUARY AT WILLOW STREET
Long Beach

HIGHLIGHTS

2 MILES

This walk begins where the concrete ends. Below Willow Street in Long Beach, the river has an earthen bottom with sides reinforced by boulder riprap levees. The walk features native plantings, pocket parks, and good bird-watching.

STARTING POINT

DeForest Ave. at 25th Way in Long Beach (*Thomas Guide* p. 795, C3).

WALK DIRECTIONS

Walk south on DeForest Ave. On your right, near 25th Street (not 25th Way), is an access ramp that ascends the levee wall. The outer levee wall is planted with native shrubs and trees, as part of the Los Angeles County Drainage Area (LACDA) project, which raised the height of the walls in the late 1990s.

Look out over the estuary. This is where the moving freshwater of the river meets the tidal-influenced saltwater of the sea. It's a unique area ecologically, with flora and fauna not found elsewhere. The river gurgles an audible sigh of relief here as it finally outruns the more than 20 uninterrupted miles of concrete bottom extending from downtown Los Angeles to Willow Street. You see plentiful bird life here—ducks, cormorants, egrets, herons, and more.

Turn left on the bike path and walk downstream. Make room for bicyclists! On your left is a neighborhood called Wrigley, which was one of the only areas where homeowners joined FoLAR's historic 1995 lawsuit against the county. The county, working with the US Army Corps of Engineers (USACE), had planned to raise the levee walls as part of the LACDA project. FoLAR and its allies advocated for more ecological alternatives.

While FoLAR's lawsuit did not stop the project, some aspects of the project were softened. The plan initially called for 6- to 10-foot walls separating the community from the river. The walls were added in some areas, but, in this stretch, the county instead raised the levee top, without actual walls. The agency also included native plantings on the outer side of the levees. The lawsuit was settled in 1996, resulting in the formation of the Los Angeles and San Gabriel Rivers Watershed Council, a group that has brought together stakeholders to educate the public and plan steps toward healthier rivers and watersheds.

Continue walking downstream to the Pacific Coast Highway Bridge, where the bikeway descends. Exit through the access point in the fence and turn left to check out the Wrigley Property Maintenance Landscape Project, a pocket park created and maintained by the Wrigley Homeowners Association. The park features native plants and trees and a picnic area.

Turn around here and retrace your steps upstream for a 2-mile round-trip walk. If you want a longer walk, head downstream below the bridge. The path continues all the way to Golden Shore Marine Reserve (see Walk 19), about 3 miles below Willow.

You may also wish to continue your walk north of Willow. Continue upstream on the bike path as it dips beneath the 1946 Willow Street Bridge. It's not a showy historic bridge, but the lighting standards are antique and quite pleasant. Also, look for cliff-swallows' mud nests attached to the underside of the bridge.

As you ascend back to the top of the levee upstream of Willow, you will notice a series of long, rectangular concrete boxes atop the concrete river

Tall trees in the LA River estuary near Pacific Coast Highway

bottom, just upstream of Willow. These devices serve as baffles, creating turbulence that causes high flows to spread out to the full channel width as it widens at this point. Also note the bulb-shaped devices on the upstream end of the piers of the Willow Street Bridge. They serve the same function.

One perhaps unintended consequence of the baffles on the channel floor is the increased deposition of sediment. The baffles cause the moving water to slow down; this releases dirt that the river is carrying. This sediment builds up on the channel floor over time, creating sandbars. The sandbars grow vegetation and host relatively large numbers of birds, especially for a concrete-bottom area. The best time of year to visit this area is late summer or early fall, as the county's Flood Control District clears the sediment in late September or early October, prior to the rainy season.

Retrace your steps to the access point below Willow.

DIRECTIONS TO THE START

BIKE

The walk starting point is easily accessed from the Lario Bike Trail, which runs on the east bank of the LA River from the Rio Hondo to the ocean (South Gate to Long Beach). Exit the bikeway at Willow Street; the exit ramp is located a couple blocks south of the undercrossing at Willow. It is easily to recognize because this is where the river transitions from concrete bottom to earthen bottom.

TRANSIT

Take the Metro Blue Line to the Willow Station in Long Beach. From there, walk south on Long Beach Blvd. to Willow Street. Walk west on Willow about 0.75 mile and turn left on Golden Ave. Turn right on 25th Way. Alternately, take the Long Beach Transit Bus #102 west on Willow. Get off at Golden, walk one block south on Golden, and then turn right onto 25th Way.

CAR

Exit the 710 Freeway at Willow Street in Long Beach. Go east on Willow Street. Turn right at the first signal onto Golden Ave., and then take an immediate right onto 25th Way. Continue on 25th Way two blocks to DeForest Ave. Convenient street parking is on 25th or DeForest.

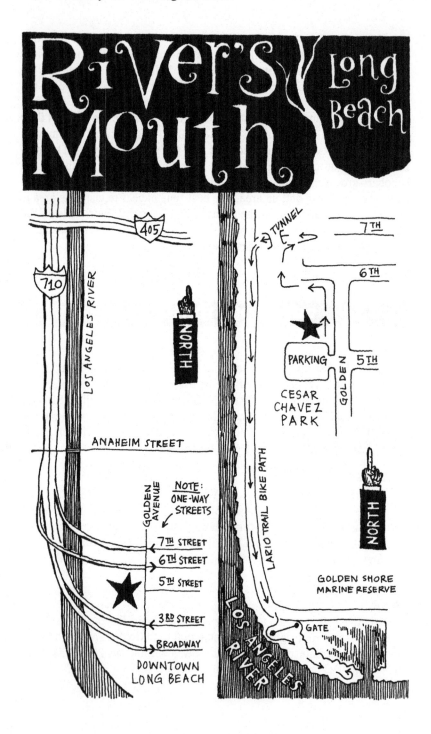

River's Mouth — Long Beach

405

710

LOS ANGELES RIVER

NORTH

TUNNEL

7TH

6TH

PARKING

GOLDEN

5TH

CESAR CHAVEZ PARK

ANAHEIM STREET

GOLDEN AVENUE

NOTE: ONE-WAY STREETS

LARIO TRAIL BIKE PATH

NORTH

7TH STREET

6TH STREET

5TH STREET

3RD STREET

BROADWAY

DOWNTOWN LONG BEACH

GOLDEN SHORE MARINE RESERVE

LOS ANGELES RIVER

GATE

Walk 19

RIVER'S MOUTH
Long Beach

HIGHLIGHTS   **2.2 MILES**

The Los Angeles River empties into the Pacific Ocean at the
Port of Long Beach. This walk features the new Cesar
Chavez Park and the Golden Shore Marine Reserve—a
restored tidal wetland area. Cesar Chavez Park serves the
population-dense communities on the west side of downtown Long Beach. Its bathroom and community center
buildings echo the craftsman style common to historic
homes in the adjacent neighborhood. The walk follows the
riprap embankments of the river, where it becomes very
tidal. The area features good bird-watching and cool ocean
breezes.

STARTING POINT

Cesar Chavez Park, 401 Golden Ave. in Long Beach (*Thomas
Guide* p. 795, C7).

WALK DIRECTIONS

Walk north on Golden. At the north end of the park, across
from the *Long Beach History* mural by Art Mortimer, turn left
onto West Sixth Street. Turn right onto San Francisco Ave.
and cross under the Sixth Street off-ramp. Follow San
Francisco as it turns to the right. Make a U-turn sharply to
the left onto the extension of Seventh Street and descend
into the tunnel below the 710 Freeway.

Ascend and enter the river right-of-way via the bikeway
on-ramp. You are now on the Lario Bike Trail, which is
shared by bicyclists and pedestrians. Look out over the
wide, riprapped mouth of the Los Angeles River, which is
nearly entirely tidal in this estuary area. Pelicans and seag-
ulls are common here.

Turn left on the bike path and walk downstream. Note the
native shrubs planted on the outside of the levee walls (on
your left) as part of the Los Angeles County Drainage Area

project in the late 1990s. These attract various birds, including golden finches.

On your right, during dry-weather months, you can observe a trash boom, designed to prevent floating trash from making its way to Long Beach's beaches. During wet weather, the boom will break and wash out to sea, so it is used only during dry weather. With its largely urbanized watershed, the Los Angeles River delivers tons of trash onto our beaches. Help prevent this by reducing your use of disposables, putting trash in its place, picking up trash in your neighborhood, and volunteering at FoLAR's annual La Gran Limpieza—the Great LA River Cleanup, held at multiple sites each May.

Continue walking downstream. The bike trail turns left at the Golden Shore Marine Reserve, which was established in the late 1990s as mitigation for wetlands destroyed by development of the nearby Rainbow Harbor. The site is set aside for wildlife; humans and dogs should keep out of the lowland portions of the site. The wetlands are home to various shorebirds. View them by turning left and walking along the perimeter of the site.

From the eastern end of the site, looking across the river, you see the historic Queen Mary, sometimes called "the toothpick in the mouth of the LA River." The historic Queen Mary was launched in 1934 and crossed the Atlantic more that a thousand times before coming to rest in Long Beach in 1967.

Turn around here and retrace your steps, walking on the bike path back to Chavez Park. If you're up for a longer walk, continue along the Long Beach Shoreline Bike Path (see Bikeway 4's side trip). The path weaves through the Catalina Cruises terminal and along Shoreline Park as the estuary debouches into Long Beach Harbor. You can visit the Aquarium of the Pacific or get a bite to eat a bit farther on at Shoreline Village.

DIRECTIONS TO THE START

BIKE

The walk begins near the downstream end of the Lario Bike Trail, which runs on the east bank of the LA River from the Rio Hondo to the ocean (from South Gate to Long Beach). To reach the walk starting point, exit the trail just south of where it crosses under the 710 Freeway (at approximately Seventh Street) in downtown Long Beach. Take the unnamed access road, which crosses under the 710 Freeway. At the top of the access road, make a sharp right U-turn and continue on the road, turning left where it becomes Golden Ave. at Chavez Park.

TRANSIT

Take the Metro Blue Line to its southern terminus at Long Beach Transit Plaza. Walk west one block to Pacific Ave. Turn right, walk two blocks to Third Street. Walk approximately 10 blocks west on Third Street to Golden Ave.

CAR

Exit the 710 Freeway south at Sixth Street in Long Beach (this exit is on the left, just before downtown Long Beach). Take the first right, at the end of the off-ramp, onto Magnolia Ave. Turn left onto Fifth Street and cross Golden Ave. into Cesar Chavez Park. Very convenient free parking is located in the park's lot or along Golden Ave.

Ocean Blvd. Bridge over the mouth of the LA River in Long Beach

Restored wetland thicket along the Arroyo Seco in Lower Arroyo Seco Nature Park in Pasadena

TRIBUTARIES

Within the urban LA Basin, there are more than two dozen named tributaries of the Los Angeles River, and many more than that exist as numbered storm drains, waiting to be rediscovered, re-named, or re-remembered. Each tributary has its own set of tributaries and sub-watershed. All of this forms an intricate, interconnected fractal that is the Los Angeles River Watershed.

I have to confess that, for many years, I have had an unnecessary chau-vinism for the main stem of the river. But recently it has become more clear to me that, in many cases, the tributaries actually offer better oppor-tunities for more immediate and radical restoration. Restoring tributaries will be critical in creating the conditions for restoration of the river, both for the continuity of species and for the connecting of river efforts into communities throughout the watershed.

This section features only a small taste of all the good walks that can be taken on a few of the major tributaries. These tributary walks feature some of the most natural areas in the urbanized portion of the watershed. They include soft-bottom stretches of the Tujunga Wash, Arroyo Seco, Rio Hondo, and Compton Creek.

These tributaries, with the exception of Compton Creek, extend into the forested upper watershed. These upper tributary areas offer some of the greatest nature hikes in the region. (I have not attempted to catalogue them here. However, many of these natural areas are described in local hiking guidebooks, such as Jerry Schad's *Afoot & Afield in Los Angeles County,* available from Wilderness Press.)

Many of the upper watershed tributaries are threatened by inappropri-ate development. If we are to restore the river to health, we must care for and protect the tributaries that feed the river.

Descriptions of each featured tributary proceeds its walks. The overall map of the tributaries is on pages viii and ix.

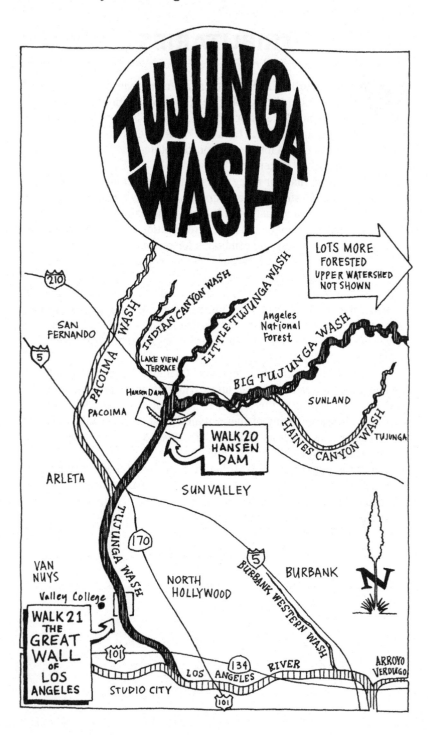

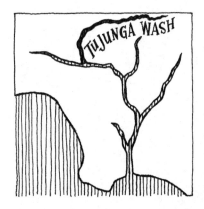

The Tujunga Wash originates in the San Gabriel Mountains north and east of Sunland/Tujunga. It flows through Hansen Dam, downstream of which it becomes a concrete box channel. From north to south, it flows through the San Fernando Valley communities of Sun Valley, Arleta, Panorama City, Van Nuys, and North Hollywood before its confluence with the LA River in Studio City. The confluence is on the CBS Studio Center lot, visible from the Colfax Ave. Bridge over the LA River.

Historically, the Tujunga Wash, like most LA waterways, was a broad, braided channel. You can get a sense of this in the unchannelized areas above Hansen Dam. Coming out of the relatively steep San Gabriels, the wash is flashy, going from a small trickle to a thunderous flow very quickly.

The lower Tujunga Wash has relatively large, vacant right-of-ways on both sides, making it conducive to greenway, parkway, bikeway, and restoration projects.

There are a number of efforts afoot to restore and revitalize the Tujunga Wash and its watershed. It is included in LA County's 1996 Los Angeles River Master Plan, and restoration projects are planned by the county's Department of Public Works, the Santa Monica Mountains Conservancy/Mountains Recreation and Conservation Authority, Tree People, The River Project, and others. Other important Tujunga Wash watershed efforts have focused on protecting critical areas from inappropriate development.

Two walks are inadequate to represent the entirety of the Tujunga Wash, so please consider this a sample to whet your appetite for future projects and walks.

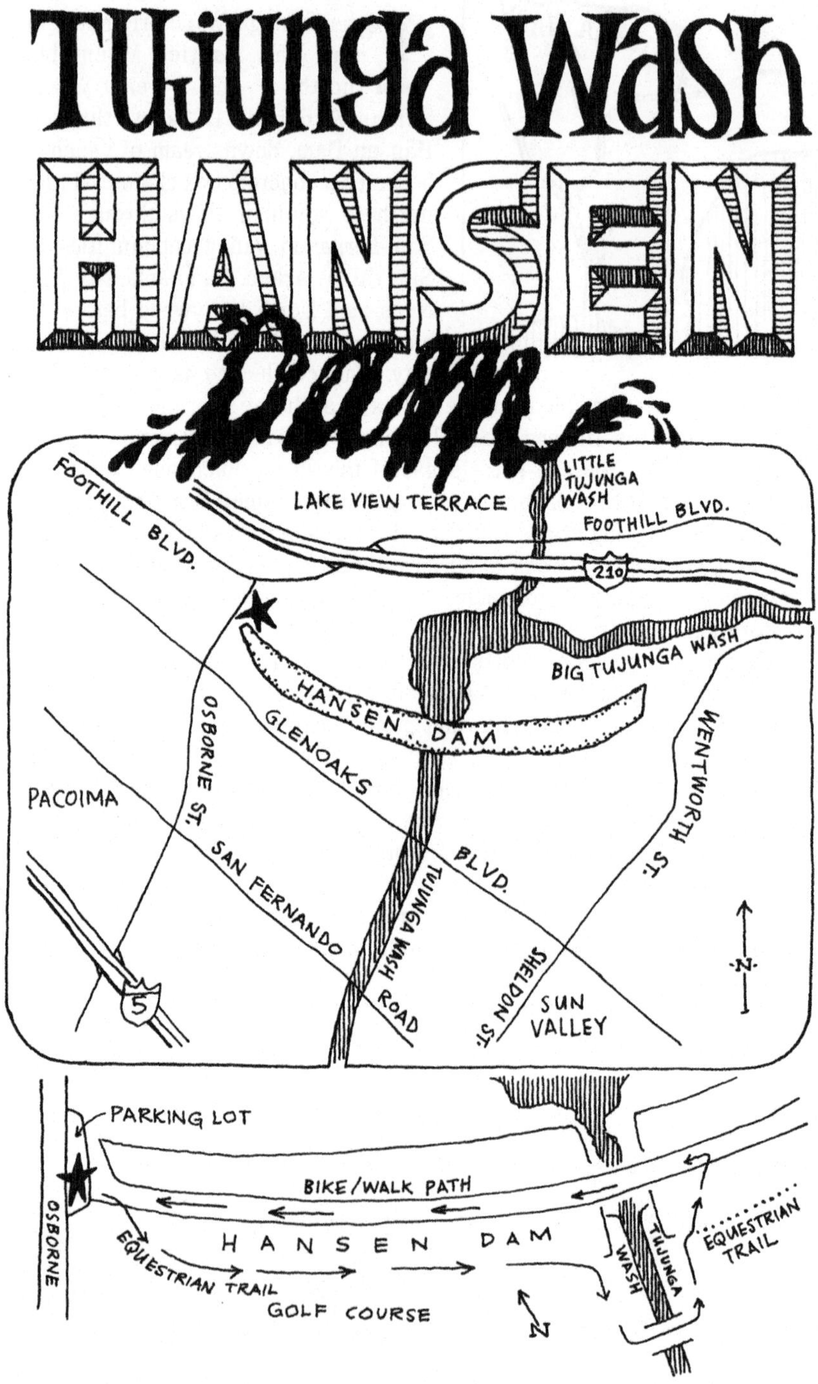

TUJUNGA WASH
HANSEN DAM

FOOTHILL BLVD.

LAKE VIEW TERRACE

LITTLE TUJUNGA WASH

FOOTHILL BLVD.

210

HANSEN DAM

BIG TUJUNGA WASH

OSBORNE ST.

GLENOAKS

PACOIMA

SAN FERNANDO

TUJUNGA WASH ROAD

BLVD.

SHELDON ST.

WENTWORTH ST.

SUN VALLEY

·N·

5

PARKING LOT

BIKE/WALK PATH

OSBORNE

H A N S E N   D A M

EQUESTRIAN TRAIL

GOLF COURSE

TUJUNGA WASH

EQUESTRIAN TRAIL

N

Walk 20

HANSEN DAM
Lake View Terrace

HIGHLIGHTS **2.5 MILES**

Hansen Dam is a very popular place for pedestrians, runners, equestrians, and bicyclists—a sort of beach bike path
for the families of the north San Fernando Valley. The dam's
massive size is an indicator of the power of the broad
Tujunga Wash as it descends from the steep San Gabriel
Mountains into the San Fernando Valley. Most folks walk
along the top of the dam, which offers cool breezes and
panoramic views of the San Fernando Valley. I prefer to
start out on the equestrian trail below the front of the dam,
and return along the top. Wheelchair users will want to
remain on the even surface atop the dam.

STARTING POINT

Hansen Dam parking lot on Osborne Street near Glenoaks
Blvd., Lake View Terrace (*Thomas Guide* p. 502, F2).

WALK DIRECTIONS

From the parking lot, go through the gate onto the top of
the dam. Immediately to the right, at the sign marked BRI-
DLE TRAIL—NO VEHICLES ALLOWED, descend onto the trail in
front of the dam, which is shared by pedestrians and equestrians. It's slightly steep at first but soon levels out as it
turns to the left. This area features largely native alluvial
scrub vegetation, including plenty of the distinctive yucca
known as Our Lord's candle, seen blooming here in the late
spring. This brush serves as home to rabbits, lizards, and
other critters.

Continue along the trail with the dam above to the left
and the golf course below to the right. When you approach
the main stem of the Tujunga Wash spilling though the center of Hansen Dam, stay on the trail as it turns right (downstream) and descends. Cross the wash at the unnamed golf
course bridge and continue to follow the trail as it curves

left (upstream) and ascends. The trail turns right and levels out again. At this point, ascend to the top of Hansen Dam via the footpath on your left. At the top of the dam, turn left.

Check out the impressive views. On clear days, you can see the Santa Monica Mountains ringing the far side of the valley from Universal City to Calabasas.

Walk across the spillway and return to the starting point.

DIRECTIONS TO THE START

BIKE

Follow the convenient bike lanes on Glenoaks Blvd. to Osborne Street.

TRANSIT

Take Metro Bus 92 on Glenoaks Blvd. to Osborne Street. Turn right (uphill) onto Osborne and look to your right for the starting point at the crest of the dam.

CAR

Take the 210 Freeway and exit at Foothill Blvd. in Lakeview Terrace. Go west on Foothill and turn left (south) onto Osborne Street. The parking area is accessible only from northbound Osbourne, so drive past the dam and make the next U-turn. Park in the lot on your left.

Alternately, take the 5 Freeway to Osborne Street in Arleta and go northeast on Osborne. The parking lot is on the right at the crest of the dam, just past Glenoaks Blvd.

Our Lord's candle in bloom at Hansen Dam

TUJUNGA WASH
The GREAT WALL
of LOS ANGELES
The LONGEST MURAL in SOUTHERN CALIFORNIA!

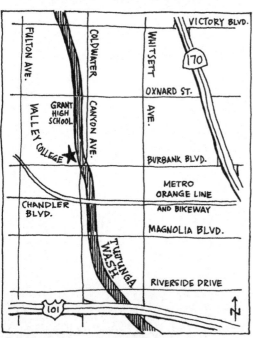

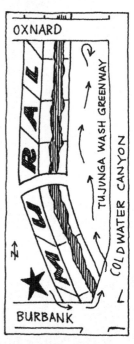

NORTH HOLLYWOOD

Walk 21

THE GREAT WALL
OF LOS ANGELES
North Hollywood

HIGHLIGHTS

I MILE

This walk features the grassy, tree-lined Tujunga Wash Greenway. It also showcases LA's longest mural, *The Great Wall of Los Angeles*, painted on the concrete wall of the Tujunga Wash, which runs alongside Los Angeles Valley College.

STARTING POINT

Intersection of Burbank Blvd. and Coldwater Canyon Ave., in North Hollywood adjacent to Los Angeles Valley College (*Thomas Guide* p. 562, E1).

WALK DIRECTIONS

Enter the Tujunga Wash Greenway from Coldwater Canyon Blvd., just north of Burbank Blvd. (on the east side of the wash). Walk upstream/north and look into the channel on your left to check out Los Angeles' longest and one of its finest murals, *The Great Wall of Los Angeles.*

This half-mile-long mural is the work of Judith Baca and hundreds of collaborators, including well-known local artists Eva Cockcroft and Patssi Valdez. Judith Baca is one of the founders of the Social and Public Art Resource Center (SPARC), LA's leading nonprofit mural organization. She is responsible for thousands of thought-provoking murals throughout Los Angeles.

Great Wall was painted in five sections dating from 1976, 1978, 1980, 1981, and 1983. It depicts the history of the Los Angeles area from 20,000 BC to the present day. It showcases many neglected historical incidents important to us all and especially to LA's communities of color, including the internment of Japanese-Americans during WWII, the destruction of Chavez Ravine, and various Civil Rights struggles.

To Mural or Not to Mural?

There are many murals, official and unofficial, on the concrete walls of the LA River system. These range from the extensive *Great Wall of Los Angeles*, to the *Anza Mural* at Egret Park (see Walk 12), to Adel Rakhshani's turtles, sharks, and killer whales (located in the city of Paramount at Rosecrans Ave., Compton Blvd./Somerset Blvd., and Alondra Blvd.), to some incredible "graf-art" in downtown's concrete canyon.

There is an ongoing debate as to whether murals should be allowed on the walls of the river. Few people are fans of the stark, sterile concrete walls, and some would like to see the concrete removed.

Often, when a mural is painted on a wall, the wall becomes a beautiful cultural resource, generally worthy of preservation. As a result, mural walls can make it more difficult to remove the concrete. Many river advocates have discouraged murals in locations where concrete removal appears to have good potential in the near term.

Paul Robeson, as depicted on The Great Wall

The mural is showing a few signs of wear, but it still looks great. The city's Cultural Affairs Department is seeking funding to restore and enhance this monumental piece of art.

When you reach Oxnard Street, you're at the turn-around point for the walk. Look across Oxnard to see if the Santa Monica Mountains Conservancy/Mountain Recreation and Conservation Authority (SMMC/MRCA) has completed the Tujunga Wash Demonstration Project, which will landscape both sides of the wash, from Oxnard to Victory Blvd. (a little over half a mile). The project is slated to include a side stream somewhat similar to Pasadena's Lower Arroyo Seco Nature Park (see Walk 22). The park should open in 2006. If it looks like it's open, cross Oxnard and check it out.

You can return to the start via paths on either side of the Tujunga Wash, but there is no mural to view on the other side.

DIRECTIONS TO THE START

BIKE

Officially, there is a very short section of bike path along the Tujunga Wash from Chandler Blvd. to Oxnard Street. It's short, discontinuous, circuitous, and, below Burbank Blvd., the width is better suited to pedestrians.

From the Metro Red Line North Hollywood Station, bike west on Chandler Blvd. and turn right (north) on Coldwater Canyon Ave. (or enter the bike path at the corner of Chandler and Coldwater). Go north one block and cross Coldwater Canyon Ave. and Burbank Blvd.

TRANSIT

Take the Metro Red Line to the North Hollywood Station, and then take the Metro bus line 156 to Los Angeles Valley College.

CAR

Exit the 101 Freeway at Coldwater Canyon Ave. in Studio City and go north on Coldwater. Turn left on Burbank Blvd., then make an immediate right into LA Valley College. Park on the access road that runs between the college and the Tujunga Wash (or, on most weekends, you can park in the college's parking lot along Burbank Blvd.).

Alternately, exit the 170 Freeway at Burbank Blvd. and go west on Burbank. Immediately past Coldwater, turn right into LA Valley College.

Tujunga Wash along Valley College

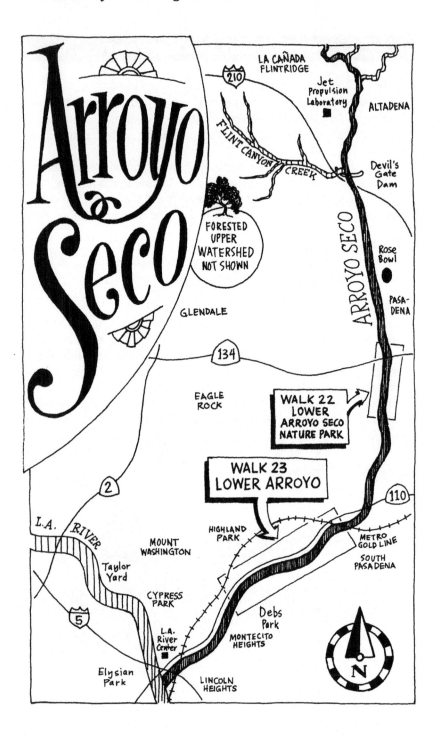

Arroyo Seco

LA CAÑADA FLINTRIDGE

Jet Propulsion Laboratory ■

ALTADENA

FLINT CANYON CREEK

Devil's Gate Dam

FORESTED UPPER WATERSHED NOT SHOWN

ARROYO SECO

Rose Bowl ●

PASADENA

GLENDALE

134

EAGLE ROCK

WALK 22 LOWER ARROYO SECO NATURE PARK

WALK 23 LOWER ARROYO

110

HIGHLAND PARK

METRO GOLD LINE

SOUTH PASADENA

L.A. RIVER

MOUNT WASHINGTON

Taylor Yard

CYPRESS PARK

Debs Park

5

L.A. River Center ■

MONTECITO HEIGHTS

Elysian Park

LINCOLN HEIGHTS

N

2

Tongva people called this tributary Hahamongna, which translates to "place of flowing waters and fruitful valley." The early Spanish expeditions had a very different perception of the same place and renamed it the Arroyo Seco, or "dry creek."

In the early 20th century, President Teddy Roosevelt was so taken with the beauty of the Arroyo that he recommended that it be preserved as a national park. Though part of the corridor was preserved through the creation of a string of parks, the major public investment there was the first freeway in the west. The Arroyo Seco Parkway, more commonly known as the Pasadena Freeway (or just the 110 Freeway), opened on December 30, 1940. Proponents promoted the parkway as a way to access the natural beauty of the Arroyo, but others (including myself) think the freeway was a step in the wrong direction.

The headwaters of the Arroyo Seco are in the forests of the San Gabriel Mountains. The tributary emerges into the Raymond Basin (where Pasadena sits) near Jet Propulsion Laboratory. It cruises past the Rose Bowl, then skirts South Pasadena before flowing through the Los Angeles communities of Garvanza, Hermon, Highland Park, Montecito Heights, Lincoln Heights, and Cypress Park. The Arroyo Seco joins the LA River just around the corner from downtown LA. This historic confluence (see Walk 13) was described in the earliest written accounts of the region.

In 1920, the Arroyo was severed by Devil's Gate Dam, located just upstream of the Rose Bowl. The stretch of the Arroyo below the dam was channelized by Works Progress Administration (WPA) workers in the 1930s. A couple short sections of channel remain unlined soft bottom, including a short stretch (see Walk 22) in Pasadena just upstream of Colorado Blvd.

There are many groups working to restore and revitalize the Arroyo. Among community groups, North East Trees (NET) and the Arroyo Seco Foundation have been in the lead. Their governmental partners include the LA County Department of Public Works, the US Army Corps of Engineers, the Santa Monica Mountains Conservancy/Mountains Recreation and Conservation Authority (SMMC/MRCA), and the cities of Pasadena, South Pasadena, and Los Angeles.

Arroyo Seco
Lower Arroyo Seco
Nature Park
Pasadena Calif.

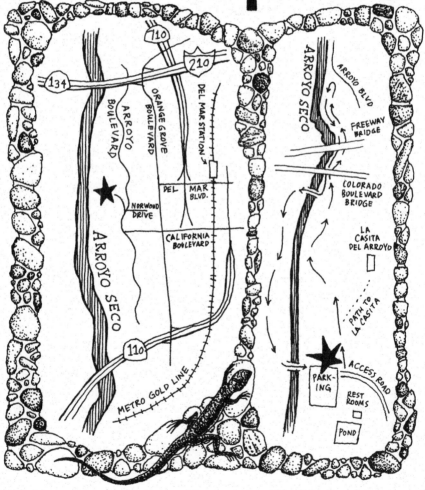

Walk 22

LOWER ARROYO SECO NATURE PARK
Pasadena

HIGHLIGHTS

The city of Pasadena's Lower Arroyo Seco Nature Park features an innovative wetlands restoration project. Water from the concrete Arroyo Seco channel is diverted into a series of parallel side streams, which are now lushly vegetated and provide excellent bird habitat. This walk also includes a secluded, unpaved stretch of the Arroyo below the historic Colorado Blvd. Bridge and the 134 Freeway. Warning: This park has poison oak. Stay on trails and avoid it.

1.3 MILES

STARTING POINT

Lower Arroyo Seco Nature Park, entrance on Arroyo Blvd. at Norwood Drive, Pasadena (*Thomas Guide* p. 565, F6).

WALK DIRECTIONS

Walk to the northeast corner of the parking area and head left (north) onto the unmarked trail at the point where the paved ramp of the entry road ends. The side streams are running alongside this trail, on your left, but, due to thick vegetation, they are difficult to see in some areas.

On your right, there is a trail that veers off and ramps uphill to La Casita del Arroyo (see side trip). Continue straight ahead. The path veers left, going close to the concrete channel of the Arroyo, then veers right again. On your right, in the midst of great oak and sycamore trees, you can see remnants of river-rock retaining walls built in the 1930s by workers of the Works Progress Administration.

At approximately 0.3 mile, you encounter the magnificent Colorado Blvd. Bridge. This is the only local bridge listed on the National Register of Historic Places. It opened in 1913 and was retrofitted and reopened in 1993. This bridge is directly above a much more modest low bridge, still visible today. You can often spot cliff swallows' mud nests on the underside of the bridge.

Wetlands Restoration

Pasadena's Lower Arroyo Seco Nature Park features extensive streams and wetlands alongside the concrete channel of the Arroyo Seco. In this innovative wetlands restoration project, water is diverted from the main channel of the Arroyo via pipes fed from an existing upstream dam. The water flows on the surface for approximately half a mile and then re-enters the concrete box channel.

This type of side stream is one model for riparian restoration in the Los Angeles River system. The project, completed in 1997 by the city of Pasadena with help from Browning Ferris Industries, has succeeded in creating lush wetland thickets, with vegetation so dense that in some places it's difficult to see the water. The streams also provide superb habitat for birds and help improve water quality.

Some watershed advocates look forward to the day when restoration means moving beyond the side streams and losing the box channel itself.

Continue walking upstream and ascend the sloped path. At the top of the dam, you overlook a small impoundment area. You can see the intake holes for the side streams on either side of the small dam.

This portion of the Arroyo Seco is soft-bottom. The city of Pasadena is currently working to restore natural habitat in this area by removing exotic plants and reintroducing native vegetation.

Yarrow in bloom at La Casita del Arroyo

Veer right to continue along the path. Cross below the 134 Freeway. Just past the freeway, largely obscured by ivy is the 1927 Arroyo Blvd. Bridge. The trail ends at Arroyo Blvd. near Holly Street. From this point, visible just upstream is the 1925 Linda Vista Bridge and the Rose Bowl.

Turn around and retrace your steps to the bottom of the slope below the Colorado Street Bridge. Just below the dam, turn right and cross the Arroyo on the pedestrian bridge. From this bridge, and along the subsequent path, look up along the west ridgeline to see the "Wayne Manor" house, which was used for the 1960s Batman television series.

Continue downstream on the path to the west side of the Arroyo. When the path veers right, turn left and cross the Arroyo. Looking upstream and downstream from the pedestrian bridge, you can see water draining from the wetlands back into the concrete channel of the Arroyo. Directly ahead of you is the parking lot.

DIRECTIONS TO THE START

BIKE

There is no bike path along the Arroyo Seco, but Arroyo Blvd. is a designated bike route and a pleasant ride. There is easy bike access from the Metro Gold Line Del Mar Station; follow transit directions below.

TRANSIT

It's a bit of a walk (1.4 miles), but mainly through old Pasadena neighborhoods with big, beautiful houses. Take the Metro Gold Line to the Del Mar Station in Pasadena. Turn right (west) onto Del Mar Blvd., cross and turn left onto Orange Grove Blvd. Turn right on Arbor Street, left onto Arroyo Blvd., and look for the park entry on your right across from Norwood Drive. Walk down the entry road to the bottom of the hill.

CAR

Exit the 134 Freeway at Orange Grove Blvd. in Pasadena and go south on Orange Grove. Turn right onto California Blvd. and right again onto Arroyo Blvd. The park entrance is on the left, just before Norwood Drive. Look for the three-tier LOWER ARROYO PARK sign. Plenty of parking is available at the bottom of the hill.

Alternately, take the 110 Freeway north until its end and continue north on Arroyo Seco Parkway. Turn left onto California Blvd. When California ends, turn right onto Arroyo Blvd. and look for the park entrance on the left, just before Norwood Drive.

View of the Colorado Blvd. Bridge from Pasadena's Lower Arroyo Seco Nature Park

LOCATION AND INFORMATION

0.2 MILE

177 S. Arroyo Blvd., Pasadena (*Thomas Guide* p. 565, F5). For more information, call 626-744-7275.

DESCRIPTION

La Casita del Arroyo is a funky little meeting house constructed in the 1930s primarily for the purpose of putting Pasadena's unemployed back to work. Noted local architect Myron Hunt designed it. He also oversaw its construction, which relied almost entirely on reused materials from local sources (a practice that has been rediscovered in green-building circles). Stones were brought up from the Arroyo Seco and wood was salvaged from fallen trees and from the 1932 Olympic bicycle track at the Rose Bowl.

The project was sponsored by the city of Pasadena and the Pasadena Garden Club, which diligently maintains the site today, including various well-tended gardens showcasing various types of plants: water-wise and water-spending, butterfly-attracting, natives, and others. The site also offers excellent views of the Colorado Blvd. Bridge.

DIRECTIONS TO THE START

La Casita del Arroyo has a small parking lot, though the gate is closed, unless there is an event taking place there, in which case the lot often fills. I recommend parking at the Lower Arroyo Seco Nature Park and walking up the trail to La Casita.

Arroyo Seco
Lower Arroyo

MONTECITO HEIGHTS | HIGHLAND PARK | SOUTH PASADENA

Walk 23

LOWER ARROYO SECO
Montecito Heights,
Highland Park, South Pasadena

HIGHLIGHTS
3.8 MILES

Although it's a concrete channel through Highland Park and
South Pasadena, the Arroyo Seco features streamside parks
new and old. This walk, directly inside the channel, has historic bridges, tall sycamores and oaks, and interpretive
signs at South Pasadena's Arroyo Seco Woodland and
Wildlife Park.

Access Note: Although many people visit this area every
day, this trip may include places that are not yet officially
open to the public.

STARTING POINT

Montecito Heights Recreation Center, 4545 Homer Street,
Montecito Heights (*Thomas Guide* p. 595, B5).

ALTERNATE STARTING POINT

Arroyo Seco Woodland and Wildlife Park, Pasadena Ave. at
Sycamore Ave., South Pasadena (*Thomas Guide* p. 595, E2).
There is easy access from Metro Bus 176; get off at
Marmion Way (immediately east of the York Blvd. Bridge).
If driving, park on Pasadena Ave.

WALK DIRECTIONS

Walk to the west end of the parking lot and enter the signed
bike path. Share the path with bicyclists. (If you're starting
at the alternative starting point, at the north end of the
walk, enter the Woodland Park, descend to the Arroyo, and
proceed downstream.)

The path turns to the right and parallels the Arroyo Seco.
At approximately 0.3 mile (directly before the pedestrian
bridge), go through the gate on your left. From this point,
you get a good view (up to your left in the hills across the
Arroyo) of the Southwest Museum. It's LA's first museum,
cofounded by Charles Fletcher Lummis in 1906 and opened

Daylighting the North Branch Creek

As you go down the ramp into the Arroyo, look across the channel and spot the medium-size storm drain directly across from you. This is the outlet for the North Branch Creek. Though the creek exists today as an anonymous storm drain that runs underground below Sycamore Grove Park and the 110 Freeway, its topography is still somewhat evident in nearby areas. It exists as a gully perpendicular to Marmion Way just north of the Metro Gold Line Southwest Museum Station.

In other parts of the world, there have been great creek restoration projects known as "daylighting." This process takes the underground water flow and restores it to the surface, enhancing habitat, water quality, and connecting the community with natural water processes.

The nonprofit urban forestry organization North East Trees (NET) and others have advocated daylighting a portion of the North Branch Creek as it runs through Sycamore Grove Park. The restored creek would add a new natural feature to enhance this park. In 2004, the county began working with the city and the community to study how this daylighting could be accomplished.

at the present site in 1914. Also note the outlet of the North Branch Creek (see sidebar).

Take the ramp down into the channel and walk upstream. This takes you under quite a few bridges, but it's not easy to distinguish them from below. In order, you will encounter: Sycamore Park Pedestrian Bridge, Ave. 52 Bridge (1939), Via Marisol Bridge (1939), Arroyo Seco Park Pedestrian Bridge (1951), Ave. 60 Bridge (1926), Ave. 60 Off-Ramp (1940), Metro Gold Line Bridge (1895), Marmion Way Off-Ramp, Marmion Way Bridge (1940), and York Blvd. Bridge (1912).

Many of these bridges were associated with the Arroyo Seco Parkway, which opened in 1940. Today it's called the 110 or Pasadena Freeway. For the most part, the bridges are old, but rather plain in their design elements. Many of the freeway bridges featured decorative designs that were later covered over. The Ave. 52 and Via Marisol bridges have pleasant lighting standards, visible from the walk.

Two of the bridges are exceptional—the York Blvd. Bridge and the Ave. 60 Bridge. The Ave. 60 Bridge has its historic railing and lighting intact. Merrill Butler's team built this gem in 1926. At that time, the bridge was symmetric around the central arch over the Arroyo Seco. With the introduction of the freeway in 1939, however, the bridge was lengthened.

There are great views of the bridge from inside the channel (especially looking downstream), and also from within Arroyo Seco Park. For a closer look, ascend the bike ramp on your right just past the bridge, and then turn right/downstream. The railing is easy to reach. Inside the park, walk downstream (south). Cross under the bridge, and then turn left onto the asphalt path. Turn left and ascend the ramp marked BIKE PATH. Retrace your steps back into the channel.

Continue walking upstream (north) in the channel and look up to the Santa Fe Arroyo Seco Railroad Bridge, designated Los Angeles City Historic-Cultural Monument #339. Completed in 1895, this is the oldest extant bridge over the Arroyo, and the oldest and highest railroad bridge in LA County. Over the years, the bridge has repeatedly been rehabilitated and reworked. Today it carries the Metro Gold Line light rail from downtown LA to Pasadena.

Continuing upstream (north), ascend the ramp at the end of the bike path, which puts you in a parking lot at the north end of Arroyo Seco Park. Veer left to continue upstream. Pass through the gate and walk on the access road between the stables and the Arroyo Seco.

Continue below the 1912 York Blvd. Bridge, an important early connection over the Arroyo. The bridge's historic railing has been replaced, but its massive arches are still impressive from below. It's best viewed from the park upstream.

On the upstream side of the bridge is one of the newest nature parks in the Los Angeles River system. South Pasadena's Arroyo Seco Woodland and Wildlife Park opened in 2004. The 3-acre park incorporates existing heritage oak, sycamore, and walnut trees, as well as new understory

Outlet of the North Branch Creek (see sidebar, page 168)

plantings. It features informative interpretive signage about the plant communities and wildlife of the Arroyo.

Continue walking along the Arroyo channel and turn right on the path just past a large sycamore surrounded by a ring of rocks (just before the golf course). Veer right, then left, and ascend the stairway. At the top of the stairs, turn right onto the bridle trail. As you descend, check out the stepped bio-swale on your left. This feature is designed to concentrate and cleanse storm-water runoff before it enters the Arroyo.

Descend back to the Arroyo access road, turn left, and retrace your steps to the start.

DIRECTIONS TO THE START

BIKE

The walk follows the Arroyo Seco Bike Path in the Arroyo channel, from just above Ave. 43 to just below York Ave. To reach the start from the north, take the bike path to its downstream end at Montecito Heights Recreation Center.

Alternately, from central Los Angeles, use Griffin Ave., a designated bike route and a low-traffic street with plenty of space for bikes. Take Griffin Ave. north, turn left on Ave. 43, and go down the hill. In two blocks, turn left onto Mosher Ave. and look for the trail entry point to your left at the end of Mosher. Alternately, take your bike on the Metro Gold Line and follow the transit directions below.

TRANSIT

Take the Metro Gold Line to the Southwest Museum Station. Walk down the stairs or ramp to North Figueroa Street. Cross Figueroa at Woodside Drive. Enter Sycamore Grove Park (to your left) and proceed to the back (east side) of the park. Walk through the pedestrian tunnel, go up the stairs, and cross the 110 Freeway via the pedestrian bridge. After descending the stairs at the end of the bridge, turn right. At this point, you can begin in mid-walk by proceeding to your right through the gate and down the ramp into the Arroyo, or turn left and walk about a third of a mile to the starting point.

CAR

Exit the 110 Freeway at Ave. 43 in Montecito Heights. At the end of the off-ramp, turn left onto Ave. 43. Turn north onto Mosher Ave. (directly adjacent to the freeway) and park at the lot at the end of Mosher.

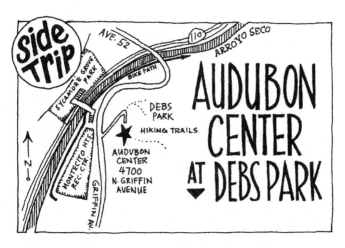

1.4 MILES

LOCATION AND INFORMATION

4700 North Griffin Ave., Montecito Heights (*Thomas Guide* p. 595 B4). For information about the Audubon Center, call 323-221-2255 or see www.audubon-ca.org/debs_park.htm.

DESCRIPTION

This kid-friendly nature center serves as a trailhead for various walks in 282-acre Debs Park, which includes approximately 200 acres of upland wilderness.

The buildings here are nationally recognized for their extensive sustainability features. The center is run entirely on solar power, its wastewater-treatment facility is on site, and it uses storm-water infiltration and recycled building materials.

Young visitors are drawn to the Children's Woodland, which features a small cabin, a stream, a vegetable garden, trees with limbs for climbing (low to the ground), and more.

DIRECTIONS TO THE START

The Audubon Center is within easy walking distance of the Arroyo Seco. To get there from this walk: Begin at the Sycamore Park Pedestrian Bridge by the initial ramp into the channel, and go east to Griffin Ave. Turn right onto Griffin and walk about a hundred yards. The entrance to the center is on your left across the street.

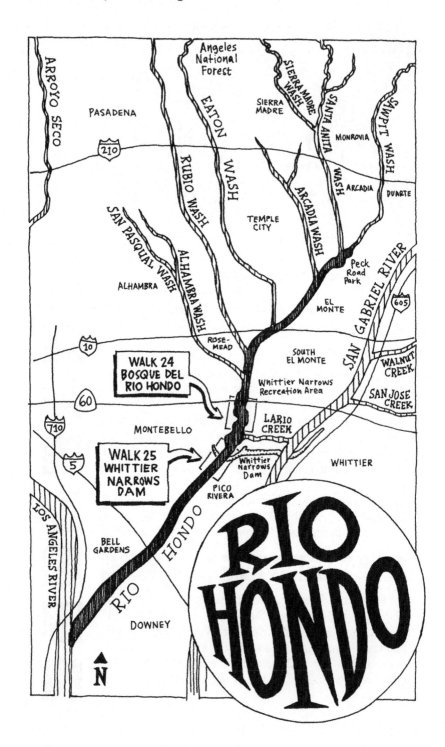

The Rio Hondo, Spanish for "deep river," is the easternmost tributary of the Los Angeles River. The Rio Hondo is most commonly associated with the San Gabriel River, which it parallels through the San Gabriel Valley. Both rivers squeeze together at the Whittier Narrows, with a bypass channel known as the Lario Creek connecting them behind the Whittier Narrows Dam. Both the Rio Hondo and the San Gabriel River bracket a number of communities, including El Monte, Pico Rivera, and Long Beach.

The Rio Hondo originates in the San Gabriel Mountains as a series of waterways, including the Sawpit Wash, Eaton Wash, and Alhambra Wash. The Rio Hondo is generally a large, trapezoidal concrete channel, with a bikeway and several spreading grounds alongside. The one exception to the concrete is the basin behind the Whittier Narrows Dam.

The Rio Hondo wends its way through Monrovia, Irwindale, Arcadia, El Monte, South El Monte, Rosemead, Montebello, Pico Rivera, Commerce, Downey, and Bell Gardens before merging with the LA River in South Gate.

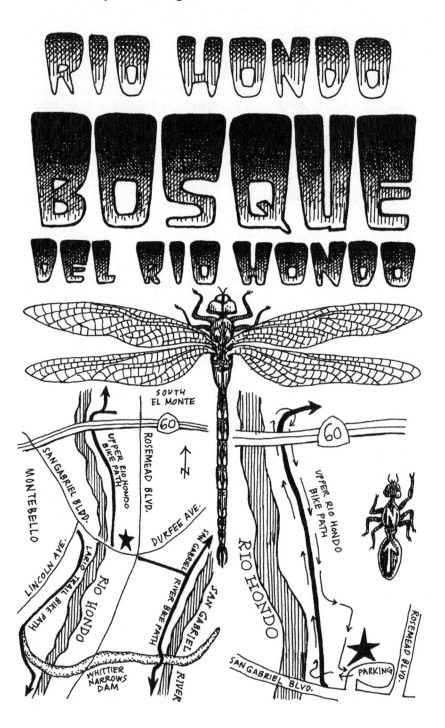

RIO HONDO BOSQUE DEL RIO HONDO

Walk 24

BOSQUE DEL RIO HONDO
South El Monte

HIGHLIGHTS **3.8 MILES**

The Bosque Del Rio Hondo Park (Spanish for "forest of the deep river") is a 5-acre park within the 277-acre Whittier Narrows Recreation Area, a lush and wild natural area with excellent bird-watching in the riparian wetlands. The original San Gabriel Mission was established here in 1771; in 1775, after a flood and fire, the mission was relocated to its present location, above the floodplain, in today's city of San Gabriel. In recent years, the area has been known as Marrano Beach, an unofficial local hangout.

Like other areas behind flood-protection dams, the site features an un-concreted, relatively natural streambed. In addition to the Rio Hondo, which flows year round, the site also features seasonal creeks: Mission Creek and Butterfly Creek. It is plentiful with critters, including herons, coots, ducks, hawks, turkey vultures, rabbits, turtles, frogs, and even (harmless) gopher snakes.

STARTING POINT

Bosque Del Rio Hondo Park, 9300 San Gabriel Blvd., Rosemead (*Thomas Guide* p. 676, F1).

WALK DIRECTIONS

This is a the most natural area described in this book. As such, the site lends itself more to exploration than to the linear walk format used throughout this book. I encourage you to explore and enjoy the nooks and crannies of this park, even though what follows is a relatively linear walk.

There are a few official trails and many easy-to-find unofficial ones. Some years, high waters or downed trees make previous trails un-navigable, and new trails appear. There are many horse trails (suitable for walking) on the west side of the Rio Hondo, accessible by going south on the bike path and walking west across the San Gabriel Blvd. Bridge, then descending the dirt path on your right.

The Army Corps of Engineers

The Whittier Narrows Dam is a project of the U.S. Army Corps of Engineers (USACE), the primary federal agency charged with protecting people and property from floods. You may wonder why the Army has this responsibility. In the early 1800s, the federal government called upon the only engineers they had—those in the Army—to enhance commercial waterways. The Army's civil role for improving waterways stuck and eventually was expanded to include flood control and, later, environmental enhancement and recreation.

Beginning in the 1930s, USACE was charged with fixing the flooding problems on the Los Angeles River. This massive project to encase much of the river in concrete lasted through the 1960s. The armoring has been effective at stopping floods, and, hence, saving lives and preventing property damage. However, these benefits have come at a great cost to wetland habitat, extirpating many species and almost completely disconnecting local communities from the river. Today, the USACE owns and maintains the basins behind local flood-control dams. They lease the Sepulveda Basin land to the city of Los Angeles, generally for a token fee such as $1 per year.

Because of the USACE's primary focus on flood control, FoLAR spent many of its early years in opposition to the agency. In 1996, FoLAR sued to prevent the agency from raising the walls along the lower stretches of the river. This plan, known as the Los Angeles County Drainage Area (LACDA) project, did proceed, with modifications, and is visible on many of the downstream walks.

Today, the relationship between FoLAR and the USACE is becoming one of cooperation. In the last couple of decades, the agency has expanded its mission. Its primary focus is still on flood prevention, but now the mission includes habitat restoration, recreation, and environmental sustainability. In various areas throughout the county, the agency has collaborated with local groups to create multipurpose river revitalization projects. In LA, the agency is working with local partners to study large-scale restoration and recreation in a number of areas along the river.

Flooding problems are complex. Floods are worsened by development throughout a watershed, meaning that a local flood is often a symptom of problems upstream. For example, widespread deforestation can result in increased runoff and flooding. Historically, the solution was to build higher levees and dams. Fortunately, today people worldwide are considering holistic methods such as reforestation, generally in conjunction with some reinforcement of levees. Working with nature can be more expensive in the short run, but it ultimately is more sustainable, while yielding more public and environmental benefits.

For the suggested walk, leave the parking area and head west on the trail that parallels San Gabriel Blvd. Cross Mission Creek on the small wooden footbridge. Cross the paved Lario Bike Trail and look out over the sandy bank of Marrano Beach, a popular area for picnicking and just hanging out.

Backtrack to the bike path. Turn left (north) and walk upstream on the bike path with the Rio Hondo on your left. After walking about 1 mile, cross below the 60 Freeway. The path turns to the right. Turn left (north) at the T-intersection. At nearly 2 miles, the Rio Hondo becomes channelized, and the surroundings are much less green and inviting. Turn back and retrace your steps.

On your return, you can walk along a trail that parallels Mission Creek. Approximately a half mile south of the 60 Freeway, the bike path veers right, with an unpaved trail/access road continuing straight ahead (recognizable because of a line of utility poles on the right). Walk straight onto the trail. Turn left to cross Mission Creek, and then follow the trail/road as it turns right. Keep right, and the trail takes you back to where you started. Turn left to return to the parking lot.

The lush banks of the Rio Hondo upstream of Marrano Beach

DIRECTIONS TO THE START

BIKE

The walk start is easily accessed from the Lario Bike Trail, which runs through the Bosque Del Rio Park. At San Gabriel Blvd., the Lario becomes on-street bike lanes connecting the upstream path on the east bank with the downstream path on the west bank. The entrance to the Bosque Del Rio Park is just east of the upstream bikeway, on the north side of San Gabriel Blvd.

TRANSIT

Take Metro Bus 266 (Rosemead Blvd.) to San Gabriel Blvd. and Durfee Ave. and walk half a block west.

CAR

Exit the 60 Freeway at Rosemead Blvd. in Rosemead/South El Monte and go south on Rosemead Blvd. At the first intersection, turn right on San Gabriel Blvd. The park entrance is on your right. There is a $3 requested fee for parking in the lot.

The Rio Hondo and the New San Gabriel River

In the early days of Los Angeles, the San Gabriel River was a tributary of the Los Angeles River. In the heavy storms of 1868, which caused extensive flooding on the LA River, the San Gabriel River dug itself a new mouth, emptying into the Pacific Ocean at Alamitos Bay, currently the boundary between Los Angeles and Orange counties.

This new course was known simply as the "New River," until it came to be called San Gabriel River. Water continued to flow in the old streambed, which was renamed the Rio Hondo.

Though the Rio Hondo is the largest and most voluminous tributary of the LA River, it's generally associated more with the San Gabriel River. From the base of the foothills of the San Gabriel Mountains in Irwindale, the Rio Hondo nearly parallels the San Gabriel River. Tributaries to its west, such as the Alhambra Wash, feed the Rio Hondo, while tributaries to the east, such as San Jose Creek, feed the San Gabriel.

Some say that the San Gabriel River and the Rio Hondo (hence the LA River) are "joined at the hip," due to what is known as the Lario Creek. The Lario Creek runs east-west in the Whittier Narrows Recreation Area, allowing the San Gabriel to spill into the Rio Hondo and vice versa.

The Lario Bike Trail through the Bosque Del Rio Hondo Park

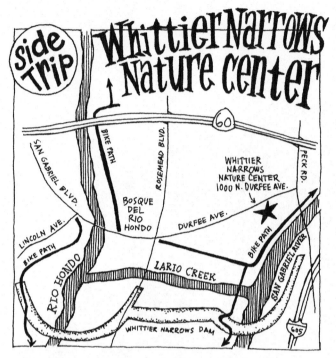

1-4 MILES

LOCATION AND INFORMATION

1000 North Durfee Ave., South El Monte (*Thomas Guide* p. 637, C6). The nature center is open daily from 9:30 a.m. to 5 p.m. For information, call 626-575-5523.

DESCRIPTION

The Whittier Narrows Nature Center features a small but jam-packed nature museum adjacent to more than 200 acres of nature preserve on the San Gabriel River. (Yes, that's that other great river next door. In this book, I've generally stuck to sites within the LA River watershed, but I'm making an exception and including this one because it's so close to the Bosque Del Rio Hondo Park.)

The nature center has interpretive displays on watersheds, local flora and fauna, and even live lizards, spiders, and snakes. The center hosts various events, including school tours, family birding expeditions, and kids' birthday parties.

The preserve features various areas; some are degraded, and some are excellent. The site is good for bird-watching, especially at the wildlife lakes and along the San Gabriel River. Another fun feature is an excellent artistic gate by Brett Goldstone.

Local community advocates are working with the county, the Lower Los Angeles and San Gabriel Rivers and Mountains Conservancy (RMC), local water districts, and others to restore, renovate, and reinvent the site as the San Gabriel River Discovery Center. The project is expected to be completed by 2009. For updates, contact the San Gabriel River Discovery Center at 626-443-1127.

DIRECTIONS TO THE START

From Bosque Del Rio Hondo, go east on San Gabriel Blvd., which becomes Durfee Ave. The nature center is the right. Park in the center's parking lot.

Brett Goldstone's gate at the Whittier Narrows Nature Center

Rio Hondo
WHITTIER NARROWS
DAM

MONTEBELLO, CA

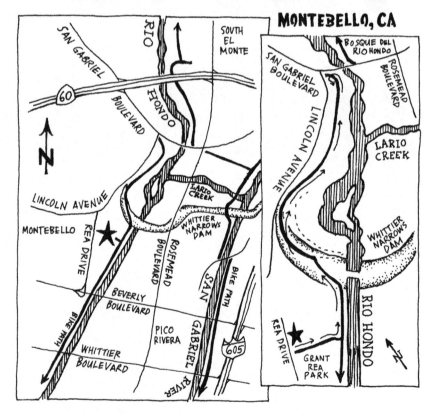

Walk 25

WHITTIER NARROWS DAM
Montebello

HIGHLIGHTS **3.5 MILES**

This walk offers a sharp contrast between the stark concrete channel of the lower Rio Hondo and the lush and wild
natural area behind the Whittier Narrows Dam. The walk
features a panoramic view of the lower flood plains of the
Rio Hondo and San Gabriel River, and a close-up look at the
riparian wetlands of the Whittier Narrows Recreation Area.

STARTING POINT

Grant Rea Memorial Park, Rea Drive between Beverly Blvd.
and Lincoln Ave., Whittier (*Thomas Guide* p. 676, F1).

WALK DIRECTIONS

Enter the park at the trailhead for the Lario Bike Trail (look
for the small sign that identifies this asphalt road as the Rio
Hondo River Bike Trail). As you walk toward the Rio Hondo,
on your right is a sunken baseball field. The field is designed
to be played on most days of the year, but in a large storm,
the field can be flooded. This is the sort of multiple-use flood
protection that FoLAR has championed.

Follow the trail up the ramp across the wooden footbridge
onto the Lario Bike Trail. The stark concrete bed of the
lower Rio Hondo comes into view. Turn left and walk
upstream toward the Whittier Narrows Dam. Share the trail
with bicyclists, who may be moving fast downhill as they
descend the face of the dam. Continue on the bikeway as it
ascends the face of the dam.

At the top of the dam, you encounter a 360° view. Behind
you, there is the dense floodplain development of Pico
Rivera and Montebello and the barren concrete channel of
the Rio Hondo. Ahead, behind the dam, is the relatively wild
reserve of the Whittier Narrows Recreation Area.

If it's rained recently, the basin may be flooded or muddy.
Continue walking west on the bike path, which runs along

the top of the dam. As you pass the small parking lot, check out the US Army Corps of Engineers sign profiling the dam's specifications. Continue upstream on the bikeway as it descends along the west edge of the basin.

At about 1.7 miles, the bikeway ends at Lincoln Ave. This is the suggested turnaround point, but if you want to keep walking, turn to the right (north). Cross San Gabriel Blvd. and turn right (east). Just before Rosemead Blvd., enter the Bosque Del Rio Hondo Park (see Walk 23).

Whittier Narrows Dam

DIRECTIONS TO THE START

BIKE

The walk start is easily accessed from the Lario Bike Trail. Take the Lario to the unmarked exit at Grant Rea Memorial Park, directly below the Whittier Narrows Dam.

TRANSIT

Take Montebello Bus Line 40 or 342 on Beverly Blvd. to the intersection of Beverly and Bradley Ave. Walk one block east to Rea Drive, and then head north into Rea Park.

CAR

Exit the 60 Freeway at San Gabriel Blvd. in Whittier/Rosemead and head southeast on San Gabriel. Turn right on Lincoln Ave. and left on Rea Drive. Look for the small sign denoting the bike path entrance, located near the baseball fields in the north end of the park. Park on Rea Drive or in the park's lot on your left.

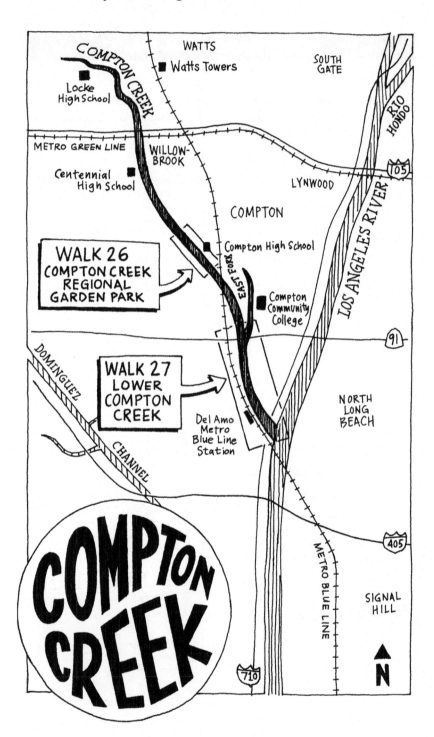

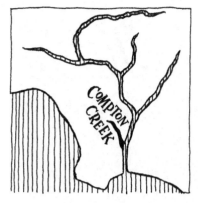

ompton Creek is unique among tributaries to the Los Angeles River in that it drains a watershed that is nearly entirely urbanized. The headwaters of all the other major tributaries are located in relatively pristine mountainous areas. Compton Creek emerges from below the police station at 108th Street and Main Street in South Central Los Angeles. Its headwaters are the street storm drains of Florence, Athens, and the city of LA's Exposition Park area.

The creek flows through the communities of Watts, Willowbrook, Compton, and Rancho Dominguez before its confluence with the LA River near Del Amo Blvd. in North Long Beach.

Much of Compton Creek is relatively anonymous, enclosed in a concrete box channel. The downstream portion, from the 91 Freeway to the river, is fed by underground artesian water upwelling. That area is soft-bottom, and, though much degraded, it's a popular bird-watching area.

There are many efforts underway to restore Compton Creek. Community groups are working with the city of Compton, the LA County Department of Public Works, the Army Corps of Engineers, and others to plan and implement revitalization projects.

COMPTON CREEK

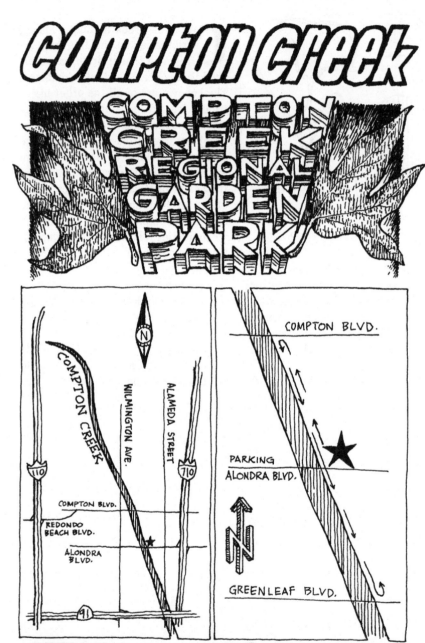

COMPTON CREEK REGIONAL GARDEN PARK

CITY OF COMPTON

Walk 26

COMPTON CREEK REGIONAL GARDEN PARK
Compton

HIGHLIGHTS   **2.5 MILES**

The Compton Creek Regional Garden Park is an ambitious
vision for change that is supported by the community, the
city of Compton, and county and federal elected officials.
The project opened in 2005 with a tree-lined shared bicy-
cle/pedestrian/equestrian path. Future plans include
parks, vegetation, public art, and creekside economic
development.

STARTING POINT
Compton Creek at Alondra Blvd. (*Thomas Guide* p. 734, J5).

WALK DIRECTIONS
At the beginning of the walk is the Alondra Blvd. Bridge,
built in 1938. A second, nearly identical bridge, the
Compton Blvd. Bridge, is nearby upstream. While the
designs are simple, they do feature ornamental concrete
railings and plaques that state: WAR DEPARTMENT—US ENGI-
NEER DEPT.—1938.

Walk upstream on the asphalt path with the row of native
sycamore trees on your right. At Compton Blvd., note the
historic bridge and turn back downstream. When you arrive
at the start at Alondra, cross the street carefully. Cross traffic does not stop.

Below Alondra, the sycamores continue, though somewhat intermittently. In this stretch, there are two somewhat
interesting traces of former bridges at Raymond Street and
Acacia Street. The piers are left in the middle of the channel, and portions of the abutments remain, but the bridge is
no longer around.

At Oleander Ave., carefully cross the street diagonally
and resume walking downstream. The path ends at
Greenleaf Blvd. Turn around and retrace your steps.

DIRECTIONS TO THE START

BIKE

Take the Compton Creek Bike Path (see Bikeway 10). There is easy bike/transit access from Metro Blue Line Compton Station. Ride west on Compton Blvd., then head downstream on the bikeway.

TRANSIT

The start is approximately 1 mile from the Metro Blue Line Compton Station. Walk west on Compton Blvd. and turn left onto Oleander Ave. Turn right onto Alondra Blvd.

CAR

Exit the 710 Freeway at Alondra and go west on Alondra for approximately 2 miles. After crossing Compton Creek, park on Alondra.

Alternately, exit the 91 Freeway at Wilmington Ave. and go north on Wilmington. Turn right on Alondra. Park on Alondra between Center Ave. and Compton Creek.

The sycamore-lined path of Compton Creek Regional Garden Park

compton creek

LOWER COMPTON CREEK

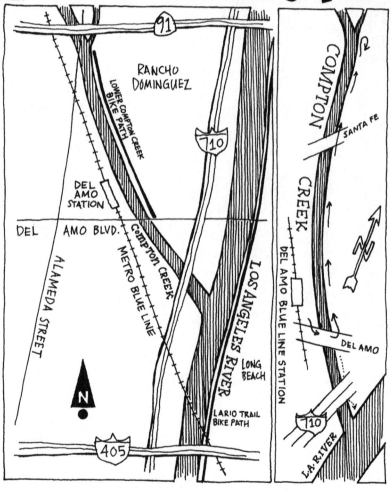

Walk 27

LOWER COMPTON CREEK
Rancho Dominguez

HIGHLIGHTS   2.1 MILES

Compton Creek is the southernmost tributary of the Los
Angeles River. This walk features a soft-bottom area with
wetlands fed by artesian water. Though highly degraded,
this site features significant populations of local and migratory birds.

STARTING POINT

Metro Blue Line Del Amo Station, Del Amo Blvd. at Santa
Fe Ave., Rancho Dominguez (*Thomas Guide* p. 765, B4).

WALK DIRECTIONS

Exit the south end of the Metro parking lot onto Del Amo
Blvd. Go left (east) on Del Amo, across Compton Creek, and
enter the creek via the gate at the far side. Turn left onto the
Lower Compton Creek Bike Path along the top of the levee.

Walk upstream (north) along the creek. This area has
been left soft-bottom, as it is fed from underground artesian
water. The creekbed on your left hosts herons, egrets,
ducks, plovers, and much more. Seasonally, you can spot
various migrating waterfowl. FoLAR's favorite bird expert,
Dan Cooper, has seen rare loggerhead shrikes inhabiting
trees along the east side of the creek.

Continue walking upstream, cross Santa Fe Ave., and
continue upstream on the east side of the creek. The bikeway ends and the terrain becomes inhospitable as you
approach the 91 Freeway, so turn around and retrace your
steps.

For a bit more creek, cross Del Amo Blvd. (carefully, traffic does not stop) and continue downstream on the west side
of the creek. The convenient, flat levee road ends just before
the 710 Freeway, where you can turn around and retrace
your steps back to the Metro station.

DIRECTIONS TO THE START

BIKE

The Lower Compton Creek Bike Path ends at the walk starting point, though the site is generally more easily accessed from the much longer Lario Bike Trail. Exit the bike trail at Del Amo Blvd., the first street exit north of the 405 Freeway and north of the Metro Blue Line. Go west on Del Amo, cross the LA River, go under the 710 Freeway, and the Metro station will be on your right after Compton Creek.

TRANSIT

Take the Metro Blue Line to Del Amo Station.

CAR

Exit the 710 Freeway at Del Amo Blvd. in North Long Beach and go west on Del Amo. The Metro station is on the right after Compton Creek. Park in the south end of the lot along Del Amo. On weekends, there is usually ample free parking in the Metro parking lot. On weekdays, the lot sometimes fills up. If the lot is full, street parking is available on Santa Fe Ave.

Lower Compton Creek

The Arroyo Seco Bike Path in Highland Park

Bikeways

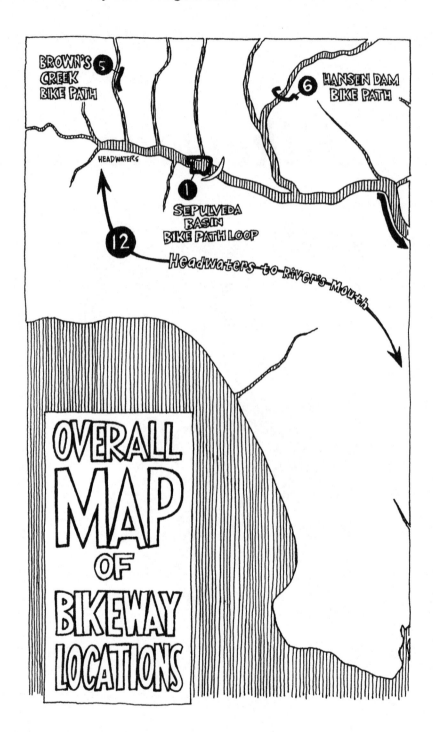

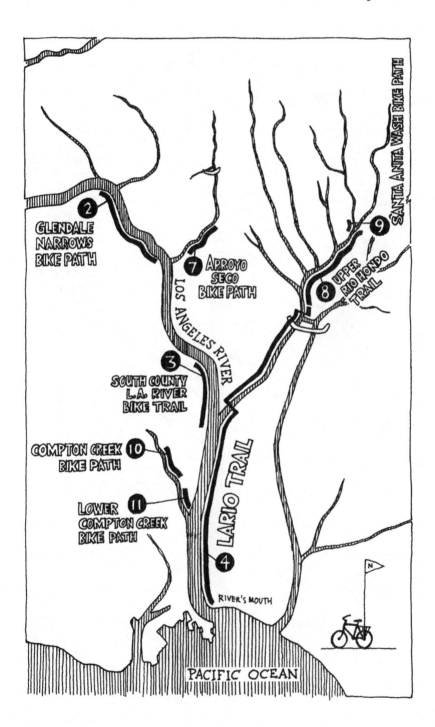

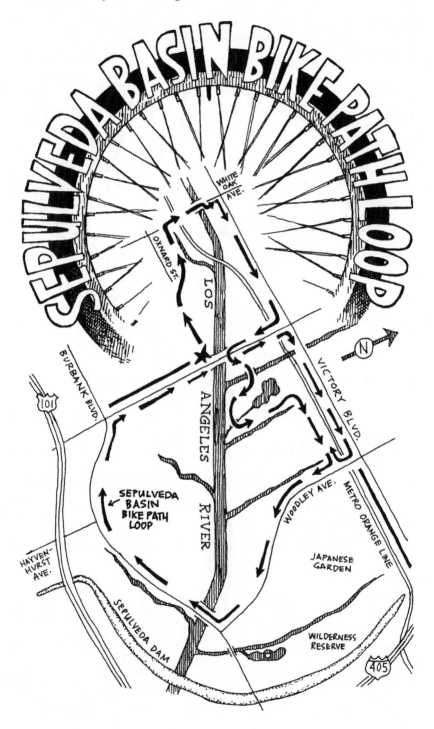

Bikeway 1

SEPULVEDA BASIN BIKE PATH LOOP

9.1 MILES, LOOP

HIGHLIGHTS

The Sepulveda Basin Bike Path is a recreational trail that circulates throughout the 2000-acre Sepulveda Basin Recreation Area, a US Army Corps of Engineers flood-control basin that serves as the Central Park of the San Fernando Valley. The LA River in this area is soft-bottom and full of life. This gently curving loop offers excellent biking for families and those who aren't comfortable riding with traffic. The bike loop crosses the LA River at three places but doesn't really parallel it enough to be considered a true river bike path. Like many of the beach bike paths, on days with nice weather, this popular trail tends to fill up with pedestrians, skaters, and other slower traffic. (For more information about the Sepulveda Basin, see walks 1, 2 and 3.)

STARTING POINT

Parking lot at Balboa Blvd. and the LA River. (*Thomas Guide* p. 561, D1).

ROUTE NOTES

There are essentially three loops (plus a couple of spurs) in this trip. The loop in the northwest area of the park is best done clockwise in order to make easy transitions onto the White Oak Ave. bike lanes, but other than that, the bikeway can be done in any order. The directions below describe one way to loop through nearly all of the bikeway.

The entire Sepulveda Basin is closed and flooded in heavy rains. The trail can be muddy in places shortly after wet weather.

Route Cues

MILE	DIRECTIONS
0.0	From the north end of the parking lot at Balboa Blvd. and the LA River, head left (west) on the bike path.
0.2	Bike path turns right, then left to parallel Oxford Street.
0.5	For fixed-gear fans: The Encino Velodrome is on your right.

Sepulveda Basin Bike Path along Balboa Blvd.

MILE	DIRECTIONS
1.0	Bike path ends at White Oak Ave. Turn right (north) onto the bike lanes.
1.3	Immediately after crossing the LA River, exit the bike lanes, turning right onto the bike path as it goes along the dog park. It's a bit narrow for one block, so be careful of opposing traffic here.
1.4	Bike path turns right and parallels Victory Blvd. At the Encino Office Park, the path becomes an unmarked, wide sidewalk.
2.4	Bike path turns right (unmarked) and parallels Balboa Blvd.
2.8	Bike path crosses beneath Balboa at the LA River. Turns right, then left, then left again to resume traveling along Balboa, this time heading north. If you're pooped out, continue south along Balboa to the starting point directly ahead of you.
3.0	After crossing under the bridge, take the right fork to continue downstream. Keep right and cross Bull Creek. The bikeway turns right, then left around Lake Balboa. The LA River is visible on your right.
3.6	Path bridges over a small concrete creek outlet for the lake, turns left, and parallels Hayvenhurst Creek.
4.1	Bike path descends a hill and turns right.
4.6	At Woodley Ave., turn right.

MILE	DIRECTIONS
5.5	Bike path turns right and parallels Burbank Blvd.
5.6	Bike over the LA River. Be careful: This is a narrow path with two-way bike traffic.
7.2	Keep right as path turns right at Balboa.
7.6	Continue straight ahead as the path crosses the LA River at Balboa. If you're tired, veer left to cross under the bridge and return to the starting point.
8.1	Bike path turns right and parallels Victory Blvd. Enjoy the grove of old oak trees (just east of Hayvenhurst).
9.1	Bike path turns right and parallels Woodley Ave.
9.2	Turn right onto the bike path immediately after the road for the Woodley Lakes Golf Course. If this part looks familiar, it's because you just rode this section, but you were going the other way. Continue around Lake Balboa.
10.6	Just after crossing Bull Creek, take the left fork.
11.1	Keep left, then cross below Balboa Blvd. After crossing under, keep right to return to the start.
11.2	Finish at the Balboa Blvd. parking lot.

Access Points

Note: The Sepulveda Basin bikeway is relatively permeable; it's easily accessed from nearly any point along its path. The following is a list of convenient locations for access.

MILE	DESCRIPTION
0.0	Parking lot at Balboa Blvd. at the LA River.
1.0	Northeast corner of Oxnard Street and White Oak Ave.
1.4	Southeast corner of Victory Blvd. and White Oak Ave.
2.4	Southeast corner of Victory Blvd. and Balboa Blvd.
5.5	Northwest corner of Burbank Blvd. and Woodley Ave.
6.5	North side of Burbank Blvd. at Hayvenhurst Ave.
7.2	Northeast corner of Burbank Blvd. and Balboa Blvd.
9.1	Southwest corner of Victory Blvd. and Woodley Ave.
spur	East side of Haskell Blvd., just south of Victory Blvd.

DIRECTIONS TO THE START

TRANSIT

The bikeway's starting point is located just off the parking lot on Balboa Blvd., on the Sepulveda Basin Bike Path. Getting there is an easy 7-mile ride from the Metro Red Line North Hollywood Station. From the station, bike west on Chandler Blvd., which is located directly across Lankershim Blvd. from the Metro station (Chandler is split into two one-way streets; take North Chandler to go west). Chandler, with intermittent bike lane/route, is a pleasant ride. Continue directly west 4.2 miles until Chandler veers right and puts you on Van Nuys Blvd. Turn left onto Burbank Blvd. Cross over the 405 Freeway and Sepulveda Dam. Enter the Sepulveda Basin Bike Path on your right at the corner of Burbank Blvd. and Woodley Ave. Continue biking west, parallel to Burbank Blvd., and follow the path as it turns right at Balboa Blvd. At the LA River, take the right fork to go left under the Balboa Bridge to the starting location.*

Alternately, take the 236 or 237 Bus on Balboa Blvd. Disembark at the stop just south of the LA River (between Burbank Blvd. and Victory Blvd.).

CAR

Exit the 405 Freeway at Burbank Blvd. in Van Nuys and go west on Burbank. Turn right on Balboa Ave. The starting place for the bikeway is just before the Balboa Blvd. Bridge over the LA River. Parking is available at the parking lot on the west side of the street, just south of the LA River.

Alternately, exit the 101 Freeway in Encino at Balboa Blvd., go north on Balboa, and follow the directions above.

Bike/Transit Note: In the future, the Metro Orange Line will offer enhanced bike and transit access to the basin. At the time of this writing, the line was under construction and expected to open in late 2005. The Orange Line will connect with the North Hollywood Red Line Station, and will have stops at Balboa Blvd. and Woodley Ave. (just below Victory Blvd.). The project transforms an unused rail right-of-way into a bus rapid transitway and includes a bikeway extending from Warner Center to North Hollywood. To reach the start of this bikeway, exit the Orange Line at Balboa and proceed south to the LA River.

Bicyclists may want to visit the nearby Sepulveda Basin Wildlife Reserve (Walk 3)

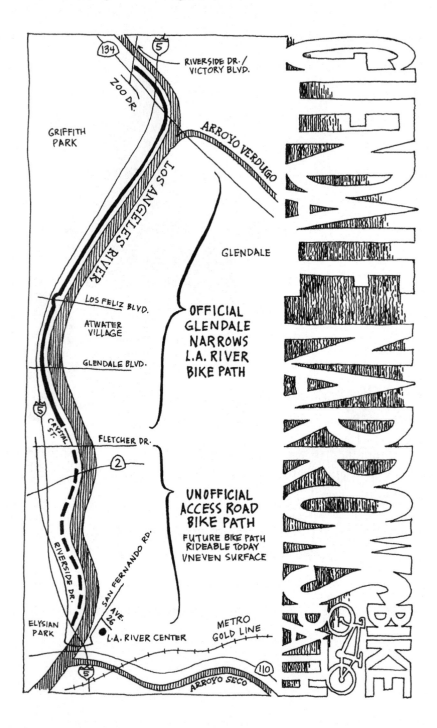

Bikeway 2

GLENDALE NARROWS LA RIVER BIKE PATH

8.3 MILES, ONE-WAY

HIGHLIGHTS

The Glendale Narrows bikeway parallels the unpaved, soft-bottom LA River, making it a great way to see some of the nicest parts of the river. (See more about Glendale Narrows on pages 69 to 105.) This section features various mini-parks, historic bridges, and public art. The bikeway is excellent for families, and also has enough uninterrupted straightaways for experienced rider to cut loose. It is also a full-feature commuter bikeway, with lighting (on until 10 p.m.), call boxes, and convenient entry points at major intersections.

STARTING POINT

Los Angeles River Center and Gardens, 570 West Ave. 26, Cypress Park (*Thomas Guide* p. 594, J6).

ALTERNATIVE STARTING POINTS

The Los Angeles River Bicycle Park, Crystal Street at Fletcher Drive, Los Angeles (*Thomas Guide* p. 594, E3): This is a half block west of the starting place for Walk 11. See full directions on page 90.

Griffith Park Ferrarro Soccer Fields, North Zoo Drive at the 5 Freeway, Los Angeles (*Thomas Guide* p. 564, B4): Exit the 5 Freeway north at Zoo Drive. Turn left and park on North Zoo Drive. There are bike path entries on North Zoo Drive both upstream and downstream of the 134 Freeway bridge. (Note: This parking fills up on weekends.)

ROUTE NOTES

Unlike the other bikeway listings, which go from upstream to downstream, this one directs you to travel upstream from the River Center because it is a convenient starting point and has bathrooms, water, and parking. Note that the final 3 miles of this bikeway (from Fletcher Drive to Barclay Street) may be under construction when you visit. The city of Los Angeles will be building a new bikeway in this area, as well as resurfacing and striping and adding lighting and an undercrossing at Fletcher Drive. Construction is expected to begin in 2006. If you visit when the path is finished, take the path. If you come before it's complete, follow the directions provided here to take the access road.

The gates to this trail are closed and locked when rain is predicted. Approximately 3 miles of this trip are on an access road commonly used as bikeway.

Access Note: Although many people visit this area every day, this trip may include places that are not yet officially open to the public.

Route Cues

MILE	DIRECTIONS
0.0	Begin at the LA River Center and Gardens. Use the bike staging area on the west side of the property (features the only convenient restrooms on the ride). Exit via the west gate. Go left onto San Fernando Road. Be careful of the railroad tracks in the road.
0.3	Turn left under the 5 Freeway to remain on San Fernando.
0.4	Turn right onto Riverside Drive and cross the river on the bridge.
0.7	At the end of your descent from the bridge, just after crossing under the 5 Freeway before you reach the residential area of Elysian Valley, turn right into Egret Park. This is easy to miss, so slow down and look for the first driveway (unmarked). At Egret Park, turn left and bike upstream. You are on an old access road that is commonly used by bicyclists and pedestrians. Caution: The surface is uneven here. Ride over the dips and bumps slowly and carefully.
3.3	At Fletcher Drive, exit the bikeway via the Great Heron Gate. Take the sidewalk to the light at Ripple Street and Crystal Street. Cross Ripple, and then cross Fletcher. Continue upstream on Crystal past the LA River Bike Park to the entrance of the official bikeway.
4.7	Cross Los Feliz Blvd. on the Alex Baum Bicycle Bridge.
6.9	Arrive at the confluence of the LA River and the Arroyo Verdugo, which is somewhat obscured beneath the confluence of the 134 and the 5 freeways.
7.8	Arrive at the end of the bikeway at Riverside Drive.

Access Points

Note: There are many unofficial entry points (generally gaps in fences) at the end of most streets in Elysian Valley (miles 0.7 through 3.3).

MILE	DESCRIPTION	COMMUNITY
0.7	Egret Park on Riverside Drive just downstream of Barclay Street.	Elysian Valley
3.3	Rattlesnake Park, east side of Fletcher Drive at Ripple Street.	Elysian Valley
3.4	Upstream end of Crystal Street (near Fletcher and Ripple).	Elysian Valley
4.0	Upstream (right) side of Glendale Blvd., southbound at Glendale-Hyperion Bridge.	Atwater Village
4.7	Both sides of Los Feliz Blvd.	Atwater Village
6.8	East side of North Zoo Drive, south of the 134 Freeway in Griffith Park.	Griffith Park
7.1	East side of North Zoo Drive, north of the 134 Freeway at Ferraro Soccer Fields.	Griffith Park
7.8	East side of Riverside Drive, between Victory Blvd. and Zoo Drive.	Griffith Park

Leo Limón's stormdrain cat paintings, visible upstream of Los Feliz Blvd.

DIRECTIONS TO THE START

TRANSIT

Take the Metro Gold Line to the Lincoln Heights/Cypress Park (Ave. 26) Station. Exiting the station, turn left (west, toward the 110 Freeway) on Ave. 26. Go under the freeway and, in three blocks, look for the River Center on your left.

CAR

From the 110 Freeway northbound, exit at Figueroa Blvd. (the first exit after the 5 Freeway, on the left side). The exit puts you northbound on Figueroa. Make the first left at Ave. 26 and look for the River Center on your left.

From the 110 southbound, exit at Ave. 26 and turn right on Ave. 26. Cross Figueroa and look for the River Center on your left.

From the 5 Freeway northbound, exit at Figueroa/Ave. 26 (on the off-ramp to the 110 north). Turn left on Ave. 26, cross Figueroa, and look for the River Center on your left.

From the 5 Freeway southbound, exit at Stadium Way and turn right on Stadium. Turn right on Riverside Drive, which crosses the river and becomes Figueroa. Turn left at Ave. 26 and look for the River Center on your left.

There is ample parking at the River Center. Occasionally, for large weddings or other events, the lot can fill, in which case there is street parking on Ave. 26 or San Fernando Road.

Willow tree in river near Griffith Park

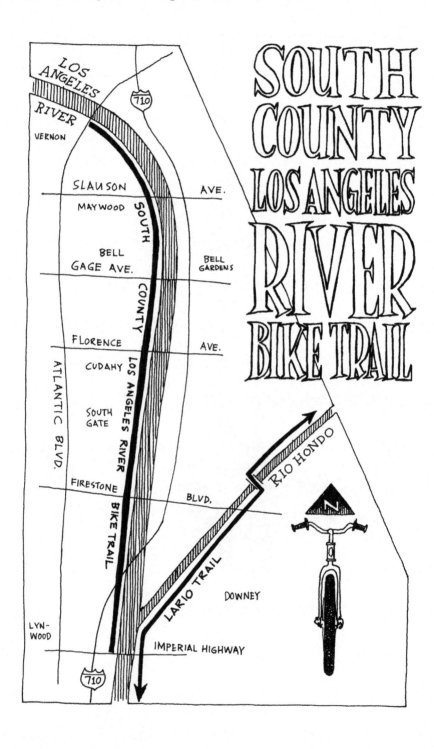

Bikeway 3

SOUTH COUNTY LA RIVER BIKE TRAIL

4.8 MILES, ONE-WAY

HIGHLIGHTS

Riding the South County LA River Bike Trail in combination with the lower end of Lario Bike Trail makes for 17 miles of continuous bikeway on the main stem of the LA River. This trail showcases a stark stretch of river: The channel is all concrete. Some of the path runs alongside working class neighborhoods, but most of it is industrial, with foundries, manufacturing, and railroad uses adjacent.. However, greening projects in Maywood, Cudahy, and South Gate are bringing new life to this long-neglected stretch.

STARTING POINT

Maywood Riverfront Park, Walker Ave. and 59th Place, Maywood (*Thomas Guide* p. 675, F6).

ALTERNATIVE STARTING POINTS

District Blvd. at Atlantic Blvd., Vernon (*Thomas Guide* p. 675, E5): Exit the 5 Freeway or 710 Freeway at Atlantic Blvd. in the city of Commerce and go south on Atlantic. Turn right on District Blvd. The bikeway entrance is on the left 0.1 mile east of Atlantic. Street parking is on District.

Cudahy Neighborhood Park, 5225 Santa Ana Street, Cudahy (*Thomas Guide* p. 705, F2): Exit the 710 Freeway at Florence Ave. and go west on Florence. Turn left onto Wilcox Ave. and left onto Santa Ana Street, and look for the park at the end of Santa Ana. The bikeway entrance is at the back of the park, across River Road.

Southern Ave. Bike Trail and Park, Atlantic Ave. at Southern Ave., South Gate (*Thomas Guide* p. 705, E4): Exit the 710 Freeway at Firestone Blvd. and go west on Firestone. Turn left at Rayo Ave. Rayo ends at a triangular mini-park designed as a parking and staging area for riding the river trail. To reach the bike trail, ride east on Southern Ave. 0.3 mile.

ROUTE NOTES

The gates to this trail are closed and locked when rain is predicted.

Route Cues

MILE	DIRECTIONS
0.0	Enter the bikeway at the gate on east side of Atlantic Ave., just north of District Blvd. in the city of Vernon.
0.8	Maywood Riverfront Park (to be open mid-2006) is visible to the right.
2.7	Cudahy Park is on your right. Note the native sycamore trees planted along the river bike path here. This park has the only bathrooms and water directly adjacent to the bike path.
4.6	Arrive at the confluence of the Los Angeles River and the Rio Hondo.
4.8	Arrive at the end of bike path at Imperial Highway.

Note: To continue downstream, cross the river and proceed downstream on the Lario Bike Trail on the east levee.

Access Points

MILE	DESCRIPTION	COMMUNITY
0.0	East side of Atlantic Blvd., south side of Los Angeles River.	Vernon
0.1	North side of District Ave., just east of Atlantic Blvd. Note that this access point is generally easier to use than the nearby, heavily trafficked Atlantic Blvd.	Vernon
0.8	Slauson Ave. Single access point is upstream of Slauson. Future access planned at Maywood Riverfront Park.	Vernon/Maywood
1.3	Randolph Street.	Bell
1.5	Gage Ave.	Bell
2.1	Florence Ave.	Bell
2.4	Clara Ave. Single access point upstream of Clara. Downstream access at River Road.	Cudahy
2.4	River Road. Access at right-angle turn adjacent to Clara.	Cudahy
2.7	River Road. Access on east side of River Road at Cudahy Park.	Cudahy

MILE	DESCRIPTION	COMMUNITY
3.3	Firestone Blvd.	South Gate
3.7	East end of Southern Ave.	South Gate
4.3	East end of Tweedy Blvd.	South Gate
4.8	Imperial Highway.	South Gate/Lynwood

DIRECTIONS TO THE START

TRANSIT

To reach the starting place, exit the South County bikeway at Slauson Ave., the first bridge downstream of Atlantic Blvd. The unmarked exit is on the upstream side of Slauson. As you exit at Slauson, go left (west) on the frontage road adjacent to Slauson. Turn left onto Alamo Ave., cross Slauson, and then turn left onto 59th Place. The park will be on your right at the end of 59th. The site is also easily accessed from the Metro Blue Line Slauson Station. From there, ride east on Slauson to Alamo Ave. Turn right onto Alamo, and then turn left on 59th.

CAR

Exit the 710 Freeway at Atlantic Blvd. in Vernon/Bell (just south of the intersection of the 5 Freeway). Go south on Atlantic and turn left on Slauson Ave. Turn right on Alamo Ave. and then left on 59th Place. Find street parking on Walker Ave. or 59th. If park construction is complete (expected in 2006), turn left off 59th to enter the parking lot.

Alternately, exit the 710 Freeway at Florence Ave. in Bell/Bell Gardens and go east on Florence. Turn left on Eastern Ave., left on Slauson Ave., and left again on Alamo Ave. Turn left on 59th Place. Find street parking on Walker Ave. or 59th. If park construction is complete (expected in 2006), turn left off 59th to enter the parking lot.

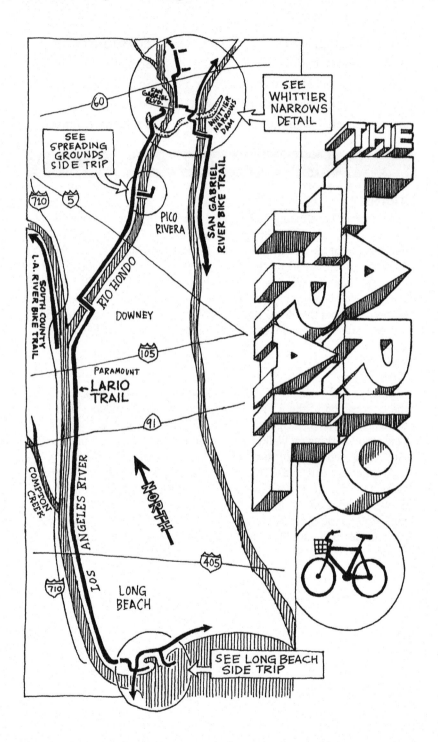

Bikeway 4

LARIO BIKE TRAIL

23.5 MILES, ONE-WAY

HIGHLIGHTS

The Lario Bike Trail is longest river bikeway in the LA River watershed and can be combined with connecting bikeways for even longer rides (but don't worry, there are plenty of parks along the way where you can fill your water bottle). The trail, which gets its name because it runs along the LA River and the Rio Hondo (from Whittier Narrows in South El Monte all the way to the Pacific Ocean in Long Beach), shows many of the faces of the Los Angeles River, from industrial, to residential, to natural, including soft-bottom areas behind the Whittier Narrows Dam and those in the estuary downstream of Willow Street in Long Beach.

STARTING POINT

Bosque Del Rio Hondo Park, 9300 San Gabriel Blvd., Rosemead (*Thomas Guide* p. 676, F1).

ALTERNATIVE STARTING POINTS

Grant Rea Memorial Park, Montebello (*Thomas Guide* p. 676, F1): For full directions, see Walk 25.

John Anson Ford Park, 8000 Park Lane, Bell Gardens (*Thomas Guide* p. 705, H2): Exit the 710 Freeway at Florence Ave. and go east on Florence. Turn right on Scout Ave. and look for the park on your left.

Ralph Dills Park, 6500 San Juan Street, Paramount (*Thomas Guide* p. 735, E4): Exit the 710 Freeway at Rosecrans Ave. and go east on Rosecrans. Turn right on Orange Ave., right on San Luis Street, and go to the end to find the park.

De Forest Park, 6255 De Forest Ave., Long Beach (*Thomas Guide* p. 765, D1): Exit the 710 Freeway at Long Beach Blvd. and go south on Long Beach Blvd. Turn left on 56th Street and left again on Chestnut Ave., which becomes De Forest Ave. The park is on your left. The bikeway entrance is across from Osgood Street.

Willow Street (*Thomas Guide* p. 795, C3): For full directions, see Walk 18.

ROUTE NOTES

There are numerous connections on this trail for longer rides. At its upstream terminus, the Lario becomes the Upper Rio Hondo Bike Trail

(Bikeway 8, 5.2 miles). At San Gabriel Blvd., a spur connects with the San Gabriel River Trail (not covered in this book, 39 miles). Near Washington Blvd. in Pico Rivera, Lario connects with the Rio Hondo Coastal Basin Spreading Grounds Bike Path (side trip, 1.8 miles.) At the river's mouth in Long Beach, cyclists can continue on the Long Beach bike path network (see side trip).

The gates to this trail are closed and locked when rain is predicted. If there is construction just downstream of the 105 Freeway in Paramount (at mile 12.5) ride briefly on the parallel dirt road to pass it.

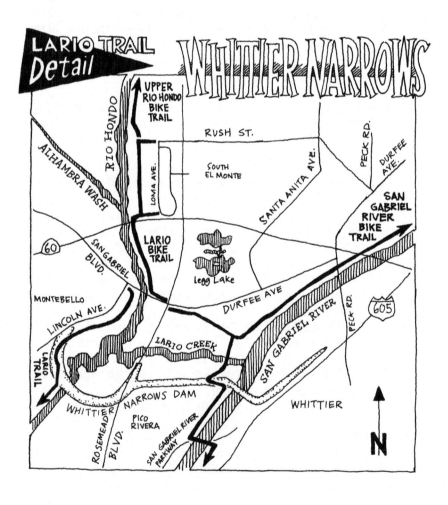

Route Cues

MILE	DIRECTIONS
0.0	Begin at the Whittier Narrows Recreation Area, at the bikeway T-intersection (directly west of Rush Road), where the Upper Rio Hondo Bike Trail becomes the Lario Bike Trail.
0.7	Turn right at the T-intersection and cross below the 60 Freeway.
1.0	The bike path briefly becomes bike lanes. Path turns left on the sidewalk of San Gabriel Blvd. (if you continue on this spur, it takes you to the San Gabriel River Trail). Turn right onto the San Gabriel Blvd. bike lane.
1.1	Turn left at Lincoln Ave. Enter the Lario Bike Trail on the east side of Lincoln Ave., directly south of San Gabriel Blvd.
2.2	Cross the Whittier Narrows Dam. Path ascends and curves left, then descends and curves right. Below the dam are various access roads around the adjacent spreading grounds. Keep left, adjacent to the Rio Hondo main channel.
9.4	Turn left onto the bike/pedestrian bridge just downstream of John Anson Ford Park. At end of bridge, turn right to continue downstream.
11.2	Pass the Rio Hondo and LA River confluence., The Lario Bike Trail continues downstream on the east bank of the Los Angeles River.
11.3	Continue below Imperial Highway. To connect with the South County LA River Trail (Bikeway 3), cross the river at Imperial and ride right (upstream) on the west levee.
13.3	Check out the turtle, shark, and killer whale murals painted on the concrete channel wall.
20.5	When you cross below Willow Street, the concrete ends. The levees are riprap rock and the riverbed is earthen, with plenty of birds.
23.4	Turn left at Golden Shore Marine Reserve Gate.
23.5	Arrive at the end of the Lario Bike Trail. To continue riding on the Long Beach Shoreline Bikeways, see the side trip on page 224.

Access Points

MILE	DESCRIPTION	COMMUNITY
0.0	West side of Loma Ave. at Rush Street.	South El Monte
0.7	West side of Loma Ave. near 60 Freeway.	South El Monte
1.0	North side of San Gabriel Blvd. between Rosemead Blvd. and Rio Hondo.	South El Monte
1.1	East side of Lincoln Ave. immediately south of San Gabriel Blvd.	South El Monte
2.3	Whittier Narrows Dam parking lot on east side of Lincoln Ave.	Montebello
2.9	Grant Rea Park, access point on the east side of Rea Drive, south of Lincoln Ave.	Montebello
3.2	Grant Rea Park, access point on east side of Rea Drive, south of Beverly Blvd.	Montebello
4.3	East side of Bluff Road at Roosevelt Ave.	Montebello
5.1	West side of Paramount Blvd. at Mines Ave. (via the Rio Hondo Coastal Basin Spreading Grounds Bike Path; see side trip).	Pico Rivera
5.9	East side of Bluff Road, north of Sycamore Street.	Montebello
6.4	Slauson Ave. Single access point on east side of Bluff Road, immediately downstream of Slauson Ave.	Montebello
7.2	Treasure Island Park, east end of Allengrove Street.	Downey
7.7	East side of Bluff Road, at Glencliff Drive.	Downey
7.9	East side of Bluff Road, at end of Bluff Road, downstream of Suva Street.	Downey
8.4	Florence Ave.	Bell Gardens
8.8	John Anson Ford Park—two access points at the back of the park.	Bell Gardens
9.4	Crawford Park.	Downey
9.9	Firestone Blvd. Single access point on south side of Firestone Blvd.	South Gate
10.2	Southern Ave.	South Gate
10.5	Garfield Ave.	South Gate
11.3	Imperial Highway.	South Gate

MILE	DESCRIPTION	COMMUNITY
11.9	Hollydale Park—three access points.	South Gate
13.3	Rosecrans Ave.	Paramount
13.5	Ralph Dills Park—two access points.	Paramount
13.8	Compton Blvd. (Somerset Blvd.)	Paramount/Compton
14.4	Alondra Blvd.	Paramount
14.7	East end of 72nd Street.	Paramount/Long Beach
16.2	De Forest Park—access point on east side of De Forest Ave. at Osgood Street.	Long Beach
16.6	Long Beach Blvd.—single access point on west side of Long Beach Blvd. at 56th Street.	Long Beach
17.5	Del Amo Blvd.	Long Beach
19.4	West side of De Forest Ave. at 34th Street (downstream of Wardlow Road).	Long Beach
20.4	West side of De Forest Ave. at 26th Way (immediately upstream of Willow Street).	Long Beach
20.6	West side of De Forest Ave., between 25th Way and 25th Street (downstream of Willow Street).	Long Beach
21.0	Stairway at west end of Hill Street.	Long Beach
21.5	Pacific Coast Highway—single access point at end of bridge on frontage road downstream of highway.	Long Beach
22.2	Anaheim Street—single access point at west side of De Forest Ave. at intersection of bridge on frontage road.	Long Beach
22.6	West side of De Forest at Chester Place.	Long Beach
22.8	Seventh Street tunnel—access via frontage road immediately south of Seventh Street freeway on-ramp.	Long Beach
23.5	West side of Golden Shore Street, south of 710 Freeway.	Long Beach

DIRECTIONS TO THE START

TRANSIT

Take the Metro Bus 266 (Rosemead Blvd.) and get off at San Gabriel Blvd. and Durfee Ave. Ride a half block west.

CAR

Exit the 60 Freeway at Rosemead Blvd. in Rosemead/South El Monte and go south on Rosemead Blvd. At the first intersection, turn right on San Gabriel Blvd. The park entrance is on your right. A fee of $3 is requested for parking in the lot.

1.8 MILES, ONE-WAY

HIGHLIGHTS

This pleasant spur path opened in 2004. It winds along the ponds in the county's spreading grounds. The spreading grounds are important for soaking water into the ground to replenish local groundwater. The bikeway features native understory plantings and a small picnic area only accessible by bike.

Route Cues

MILE	DIRECTIONS
0.0	Enter the Spreading Grounds bikeway from Paramount Blvd. Follow the path as it curves around the spreading ponds.
0.8	Path turns right and parallels Washington Blvd.
1.0	At the Y-Intersection, take the right (north) fork for a half-mile spur loop to a small picnic area, or continue straight ahead (west) to connect to the Lario Bike Trail.
1.1	Turn right, then left onto the bicycle bridge over the Rio Hondo.
1.2	Arrive at the end of the Spreading Grounds bikeway at the Lario trail.

Access Points

MILE	DESCRIPTION
0.0	West side of Paramount Blvd. at Mines Ave.
1.2	East side of the Lario trail just upstream of Washington Blvd. (Lario mile 5.1).

DISTANCE

Shoreline Bike Path: 1 mile, One-way
Long Beach Beach Bike Path: 4.6 miles, One-way
Queensway Bay Bike Path: 0.8 mile, One-way
Long Beach Marina Bike Path: 0.7 mile, One-way

HIGHLIGHTS

At the end of the Lario Bike Trail, you can continue onto a series of spur bikeways that access the Long Beach Aquarium, the Queen Mary, Shoreline Village, the Long Beach Marina, and the beach. Similar to other beach bikeways, these paths are shared with plenty of pedestrians, skaters, and relatively slow-moving bicyclists. The cool ocean breeze and views are great. These paths are not appropriate for high-speed cycling, so just rest, relax, and enjoy.

SHORELINE BIKE PATH

Route Cues

Note: The entire path is shared with pedestrians. Ride slowly. Look out for and yield to pedestrians.

MILE	DIRECTIONS
0.0	The Shoreline Bike Path begins at Golden Shore, across from the downstream terminus of the Lario Bike Trail. Ride south along the parking lot.
0.1	Path curves left and crosses two parking lot entry roads. Then it turns right, then left into the Catalina Cruises terminal. Striping disappears in this area and signage is unclear. Do not turn into parking lot.
0.2	Turn to the right along the waterfront. Path striping resumes. Path turns left and the Queen Mary comes into view.
0.4	Arrive at bikeway T-intersection just after crossing below Queensway Bay Bridge. The Shoreline Bike Path continues straight ahead. The Beach Bike Path is to the left.
0.7	Path curves left and striping again disappears.
0.8	Arrive at bathroom and bicycle parking. Turn left to ascend spiral to lighthouse.
1.0	Path ends at Lighthouse.

LONG BEACH BEACH BIKE PATH

Route Cues

Note: Yield to pedestrians. Path doesn't encounter actual beach for about a mile.

MILE	DIRECTIONS
0.0	Beach Bike Path begins at bikeway T-intersection near Queensway Bay Bridge (Shoreline Bike Path mile 0.4). Ride north and use crosswalk to cross the park road. Turn right (north) onto wide sidewalk bike path.

MILE	DIRECTIONS
0.2	Arrive at bikeway T-intersection. The Beach Bike Path continues straight ahead. The Queensway Bay Bike Path is to the left. Continue straight and cross Aquarium Way.
0.3	Cross Shoreline Drive. Turn right onto bike path paralleling Shoreline Drive.
0.6	Cross Pine Ave. Path goes along edge of lake at Hyatt Hotel.
0.8	Turn right onto far crosswalk to cross Shoreline Drive. Continue straight into Marina Green Park.
0.9	Arrive at bikeway T-intersection. Turn left to continue the Beach Bike Path. The Long Beach Marina Bike Path is to the right.
1.3	Beach Bike Path hits actual beach and continues down the coast.
4.6	Finish at the end of the Beach Bike Path past Belmont Pier.

QUEENSWAY BAY BIKE PATH

Route Cues

Note: This bikeway has almost no pedestrians and one good hill climb. It is recommended for bicyclists trying to get in that last little bit of workout after the Lario Bike Trail.

MILE	DIRECTIONS
0.0	Queensway Path begins at the bikeway T-intersection (mile 0.2 of the Beach Bike Path) just southwest of the aquarium parking lot. Ascend the bikeway on the Queensway Bay Bridge over the mouth of the LA River.
0.5	Bike path ends. Continue straight ahead on bike route on Queensway Drive.
0.8	Bike route ends at unsigned park, with bathrooms and water, right before the Queen Mary.

LONG BEACH MARINA BIKE PATH

Route Cues

Note: This bikeway generally has more pedestrians than bicyclists. Signs posted state 5 mph speed limit. Slow down and enjoy the views.

MILE	DIRECTIONS
0.0	Marina Path begins at the bikeway T-intersection (mile 0.9 of the Beach Bike Path).
0.1	Turn left past the parking lot road. Follow the leftward curve of the jetty.
0.7	Marina Path ends at observation deck, with bathrooms and water.

Access Points

Note: This is not an exhaustive list—it's only a few useful access points. You can get to these paths by heading for the ocean from nearly anywhere in Long Beach.

MILE	DESCRIPTION
0.0	Shoreline Bike Path access on west side of Golden Shore Street, south of 710 Freeway, across from end of Lario Bike Trail.
0.6	Beach Bike Path access point on both sides of Pine Ave., north of Shoreline Drive. This is the most convenient access to/from the Metro Blue Line. Long Beach Transit Mall Station is located about a third of a mile north of the bikeway.
1.5	Beach Bike Path access point from stairway at the southeast corner of Alamitos Ave., Ocean Blvd., and Shoreline Drive.

The Queen Mary in Long Beach, sometimes called "the toothpick in the mouth of the LA River"

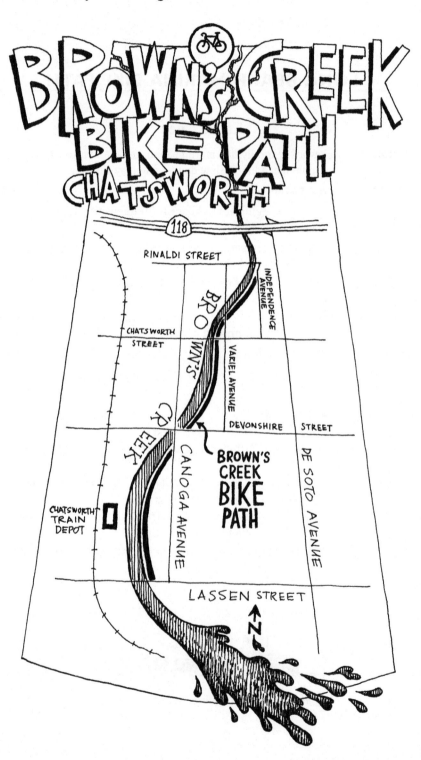

BROWN'S CREEK BIKE PATH CHATSWORTH

118

RINALDI STREET

INDEPENDENCE AVENUE

BROWN'S

CHATSWORTH STREET

VARIEL AVENUE

DEVONSHIRE STREET

CREEK

DE SOTO AVENUE

BROWN'S CREEK BIKE PATH

CANOGA AVENUE

CHATSWORTH TRAIN DEPOT

LASSEN STREET

N

Bikeway 5

BROWN'S CREEK BIKE PATH

1.5 MILES, ONE-WAY

HIGHLIGHTS

Brown's Creek debouches into the Los Angeles River near Mason Ave. in the West San Fernando Valley community of Winnetka. The Brown's Creek Bike Path is a relatively short bikeway that serves mainly as a Chatsworth neighborhood feeder for train commuters. Though the creek is entirely a concrete box channel, the bikeway features landscaping, mini-parks, benches, water, and 1970s-era bridges decorated with river rock at Rinaldi Street, Variel Street, and Chatsworth Street.

The neighborhood retains a somewhat rural character with plenty of equestrian activity. The adjacent train depot features the tiny, folksy Museum of Chatsworth Transportation and Movie History, with historic photography and paraphernalia in the train waiting room. It's open Monday through Friday, 6:15 a.m. to 5:30 p.m.

STARTING POINT

Chatsworth Metrolink/Amtrak Train Station, 10040 Old Depot Plaza Road, Chatsworth (*Thomas Guide* p. 500, A5).

ROUTE NOTES

Unlike the other bikeway listings, which go from upstream to downstream, this one directs you to travel upstream from the Chatsworth Train Station because it is a convenient starting point. The bikeway is not continuous; it requires cyclists to cross streets at grade at all three intersections.

Route Cues

MILE	DIRECTIONS
0.0	Enter the bikeway at Lassen Street, on the east side of Brown's Creek.
0.2	Look for *Welcome to Chatsworth* mural on the right.
0.6	Go left at Devonshire Street to the corner of Canoga Ave. Use crosswalks to cross both Devonshire and Canoga. Continue upstream on the bikeway.
1.1	Cross Chatsworth Street and watch out for traffic.

MILE	DIRECTIONS
1.3	Look for the mini-park with benches and water on the right, before crossing Variel Ave. Be careful: Cross traffic does not stop.
1.5	Bikeway ends at Independence Ave., 0.1 mile south of Rinaldi Street.

Access Points

Note: There are clear, easy access points at all cross streets.

MILE	DESCRIPTION
0.0	North side of Lassen Street, between Canoga Ave. and Old Depot Plaza.
0.5	West side of Canoga Ave., immediately south of Devonshire Street.
0.6	North side of Devonshire Street, immediately east of Canoga Ave.
1.1	Chatsworth Street.
1.3	Variel Ave.
1.5	West side of Independence Ave., 0.1 mile south of Rinaldi Street.

DIRECTIONS TO THE START

TRANSIT
Take Amtrak or Metrolink (Ventura County Line) to the Chatsworth Station. Exit at the south end of the station. Turn left on Lassen Street (easiest to ride briefly on the sidewalk), cross the creek, and turn left onto the bikeway.

CAR
Exit the 118 Freeway at De Soto Ave. in Chatsworth and go south on De Soto. Turn right onto Lassen Street. Turn right on Old Depot Plaza Road and park in lot. Enter the bikeway on Lassen Street.

Brown's Creek Bike Path mini-park at Variel Ave.

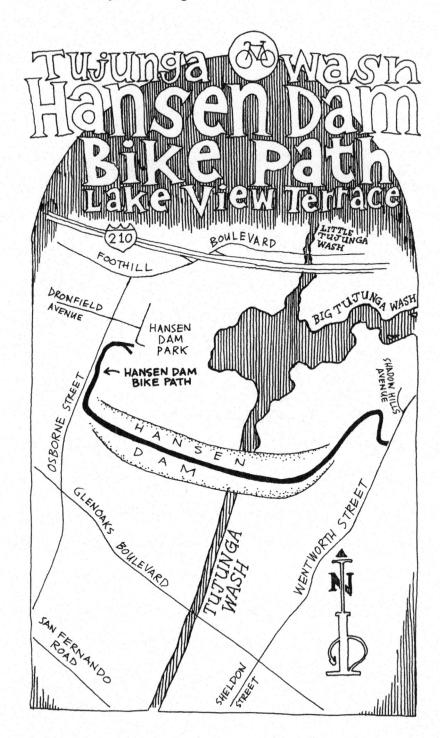

Bikeway 6

HANSEN DAM BIKE PATH

2.5 MILES, ONE-WAY

HIGHLIGHTS

The Hansen Dam Bike Path is popular with pedestrians, runners, and bicyclists. The path, which runs along the top of Hansen Dam on the Tujunga Wash in Lake View Terrace, features expansive views of the San Fernando Valley. The bike path is very wide, so it's easily shared among the various users. For additional information on Hansen Dam, see Walk 20.

STARTING POINT

Hansen Dam Park, Dronfield Ave. at Osborne Street, Lake View Terrace (*Thomas Guide* p. 502, G2).

ROUTE NOTES

The path begins at Hansen Dam Park, just south of the end of Dronfield Ave. The entry point is a bit difficult to find. From the end of Dronfield, turn right (on the unnamed park road). Behind the row of large rocks where the road turns left, there is a small sign stating BIKE PATH BEGIN. In another 100 feet, the bike path begins, curving off to the right (west) toward Osborne Street.

The route cues that follow do not include a short, straight 0.3-mile segment that runs along the park road (perpendicular to Dronfield). At the time of this writing, that segment doesn't connect with anything; in the future, I hope that it will.

Route Cues

MILE	DIRECTIONS
0.0	Begin the Hansen Dam Bike Path at Hansen Dam Park near Dronfield Ave. The bike path curves to the right and ascends parallel to Osborne Street.
0.3	Path curves left, then right at Osborne Street parking lot. Continue left through gate onto top of Hansen Dam.
2.3	Path curves right and descends.
2.5	Path ends at Wentworth Street.

Access Points

MILE	DESCRIPTION
0.0	Hansen Dam Park—southwest side of park road south of Dronfield Ave.
0.3	Parking lot on east side of Osborne between Glenoaks Blvd. and Dronfiled Ave.
2.5	West side of Wentworth Street, a quarter mile south of Shadow Hills Ave.

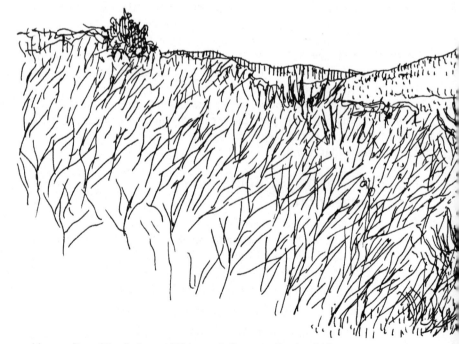

Hansen Dam Bike Path near Wentworth Street in Shadow Hills

DIRECTIONS TO THE START

BIKE

Take the convenient bike lanes on Glenoaks Blvd. Turn northeast (uphill) onto Osborne Street. Turn right onto Dronfield.

TRANSIT

Take the Metro Bus 90/91 on Foothill Blvd., the 92 on Glenoaks, or the 94 on San Fernando Road. Exit at Osborne Street. From Glenoaks or San Fernando Road, go right (uphill) on Osborne Street. From Foothill, go left onto Osborne Street. Enter Hansen Dam Park at Dronfield Ave.

CAR

Take the 210 Freeway and exit at Foothill Blvd. in Lakeview Terrace. Go west on Foothill. Turn left onto Osborne Street and left again onto Dronfield Ave. Turn left at the end of Dronfield onto the unnamed park road. Park in the lot on your left.

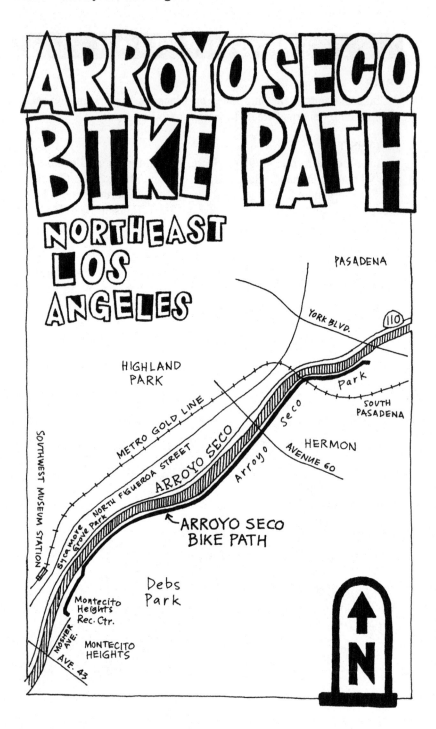

Bikeway 7

ARROYO SECO BIKE PATH

2.I MILES, ONE-WAY

HIGHLIGHTS

The Arroyo Seco Bike Path offers a rare in-channel experience. The bikeway is essentially a slab laid in the bottom of the trapezoidal channel. The stream runs alongside the path. The bikeway is relatively short at this point, but it provides good connectivity to parks along the Arroyo in this area. It's actually a comparatively pleasant and quiet experience, as the sound of the adjacent Pasadena Freeway is muffled when you're below grade. For more details on the area and the bikeway, see Walk 23.

STARTING POINT

Arroyo Seco Park (also called Hermon Park) on Arroyo Drive just south of York Blvd. (*Thomas Guide* p. 595, E2).

ALTERNATIVE STARTING POINT

Montecito Heights Recreation Center (*Thomas Guide* p. 595, B5). For directions, see Walk 23.

ROUTE NOTES

The gates to this trail are closed and locked when rain is predicted.

Route Cues

MILE	DIRECTIONS
0.0	Enter the Arroyo Seco Bike Path at Arroyo Seco (Hermon) Park near the stables downstream of York Blvd.
1.8	The bikeway ramps up to the surface at the Sycamore Grove Park Pedestrian Bridge and exits through gate to continue downstream along top of levee.
2.1	Finish at the end of the bike path at Montecito Heights Recreation Center parking lot.

Access Points

MILE	DESCRIPTION	COMMUNITY
0.0	Arroyo Seco (Hermon) Park, downstream of York Blvd.	Hermon
0.6	Arroyo Seco (Hermon) Park, upstream of Ave. 60. Enter via the upstream end of the parking lot off Via Marisol or via the bike ramp into the park on the downstream side of Ave. 60.	Hermon
1.8	Montecito Heights Recreation Center at Sycamore Grove Pedestrian Bridge, which is accessible from the west side of Griffin Ave., north of Montecito Drive.	Montecito Heights
2.1	Montecito Heights Recreation Center: Enter on the west end of the parking lot at Mosher Ave.	Montecito Heights

DIRECTIONS TO THE START

TRANSIT

There is easy access from Metro Bus 176. Exit at York Blvd., east of the 110 Freeway and go south on Arroyo Drive. The park is on your right.

CAR

Exit the northbound 110 Freeway at Marmion Way and look for the park on the left. Alternately, exit the southbound 110 Freeway at York Blvd. and follow signs to York Blvd. Turn left onto York, cross the Arroyo, and turn right onto Marmion Way. The park is on your right.

FUTURE PROJECT IN THE AREA

Arroyo Seco Bikeway Extension Phase I: The county of LA has funding to extend the Arroyo bikeway downstream 1.7 miles to Ave. 26. Construction is expected to begin in 2006.

Pacific Coast iris at South Pasadena's Arroyo Seco Woodland and Wildlife Park (directly upstream from Arroyo Seco Bike Path; see Walk 23)

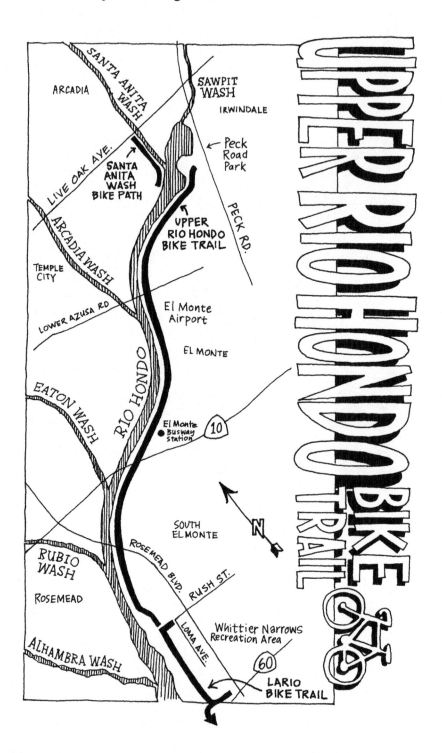

Bikeway 8

UPPER RIO HONDO BIKE TRAIL

5.2 MILES, ONE-WAY

HIGHLIGHTS

The Upper Rio Hondo Trail begins at a tree-lined lake at Peck Road Park in Arcadia and travels along the east side of the stark concrete Rio Hondo. It continues into the verdant Whittier Narrows Recreation Area in South El Monte, where the bikeway ends in name only, continuing as the Lario Bike Trail. Together, these form the longest bike path on the LA River system.

STARTING POINT

Peck Road Park, 5401 North Peck Road, Arcadia (*Thomas Guide* p. 597, F3).

ALTERNATIVE STARTING POINTS

El Monte Busway Station, near the intersection of Santa Anita Ave. and Ramona Blvd. (*Thomas Guide* p. 597, B7): Take one of the many bus lines that stop at this hub: Metro lines 70, 76, 267, 320, 376, 484, 487, and 490, or the Foothill Transit or El Monte trolley service.

Whittier Narrows Recreation Area, Loma Ave. parking lot, south of Rush Street (*Thomas Guide* p. 636, J3): Exit the 60 Freeway at Rosemead Blvd. and go north on Rosemead. Turn left onto Rush Street. At the end of Rush, turn left on Loma Ave. and left into the parking lot. Access the bikeway on the east side of Loma Ave. at Rush Street.

ROUTE NOTES

In the past, a section of Loma Ave. served as an on-road connection between the Upper Rio Hondo Trail and the Lario Bike Trail. Fortunately, the county has since connected these two, blurring the distinction between them. However, some of the old directional signage remains in place, which can be confusing. Also, the gates to this trail are closed and locked when rain is predicted.

Route Cues

MILE	DIRECTIONS
0.0	Begin at the trailhead at Peck Road Park and follow the bikeway downstream (south) along the east side of park.

MILE	DIRECTIONS
1.5	Just past the anonymous confluence with the Arcadia Wash, check out small airplanes taking off and landing at El Monte Airport on your left. The mini-park here could use some greening.
5.1	Concrete channel ends as the bikeway enters the Whittier Narrows Recreation Area. (For more information about this area, see walks 24 and 25.)
5.2	In the Whittier Narrows Recreation Area, at the bikeway T-intersection (directly west of Rush Road), the Upper Rio Hondo Trail becomes the Lario Bike Trail. To continue 23.5 miles to Long Beach on the Lario trail, see Bikeway 4.

Access Points

MILE	DESCRIPTION	COMMUNITY
0.0	Peck Road Park.	Arcadia
1.3	Single access point downstream of Lower Azusa Road.	El Monte
2.6	Single access point downstream of Valley Blvd.	El Monte
2.7	Northwest corner of Pioneer Park.	El Monte
2.9	El Monte Busway Station.	El Monte
3.1	West side of Fletcher Parkway, immediately south of 10 Freeway.	El Monte
3.6	West side of Brockaway Street at Towne Way.	El Monte
4.4	Garvey Ave.	Rosemead/ South El Monte
5.2	West side of Loma Ave. at Rush Street.	South El Monte

DIRECTIONS TO THE START

TRANSIT

Take a bus to the El Monte Busway Station (see bus lines listed on page 241 under alternate starting points). Ride upstream on the bikeway 3 miles to Peck Road Park.

CAR

Exit the 10 Freeway at Peck Road in El Monte and take Peck Road north approximately 3 miles to the park entrance on the left.

Alternately, exit the 605 Freeway at Lower Azusa Road, go west on Lower Azusa, and right on Peck Road.

Entryway to Bosque Del Rio Hondo Park, located on the Lario Bike Trail just downstream of the Upper Rio Hondo Bike Trail

Bikeway 9

SANTA ANITA WASH
BIKE PATH

0.9 MILE, ONE-WAY

HIGHLIGHTS
The Santa Anita Wash Bike Path is a short spur along the west side of the lake at Peck Road Park in Arcadia. This tree-lined bikeway, a pleasant ride near the lake, is frequented by pedestrians walking their dogs.

STARTING POINT
East Live Oak Ave. between Eighth Ave. and Hempstead Ave. in Arcadia East (*Thomas Guide* p. 597, E2).

ROUTE NOTES
This path was originally built as a spur of the Rio Hondo bikeway. Unfortunately, the site is rarely dry enough for bikes not equipped with pontoons to make the connection. The gates to this trail are closed and locked when rain is predicted.

Route Cues

MILE	DIRECTIONS
0.0	Enter the bike path at Live Oak Ave.
0.9	Turn around or end at Peck Road Park spillway.

Access Points

MILE	DESCRIPTION	COMMUNITY
0.0	South side of Live Oak Ave. between Eighth Ave. and Hempstead Ave. Access point is difficult to see: It's immediately east of Arcadia Golf Course.	Arcadia
0.2	Daines Drive Pedestrian Bridge.	Arcadia
0.9	The connection with Upper Rio Hondo Bike Path is closed/submerged.	Arcadia/El Monte

DIRECTIONS TO THE START

TRANSIT

Take Metro line 78 (Huntington/Las Tunas) or Foothill Transit line 492 (downtown LA to Claremont) to the intersection of East Live Oak Ave. and Sixth Ave./Hempstead Ave.

CAR

Exit the 605 Freeway southbound at Arrow Highway in Irwindale. Head west on the Arrow Highway, which becomes Live Oak Ave. Alternately, exit the northbound 605 at Live Oak Ave. in Irwindale and head west on Live Oak. Find street parking on Live Oak near Hempstead Ave.

The Santa Anita Wash Bike Path at Peck Road Park in Arcadia

COMPTON CREEK BIKE PATH

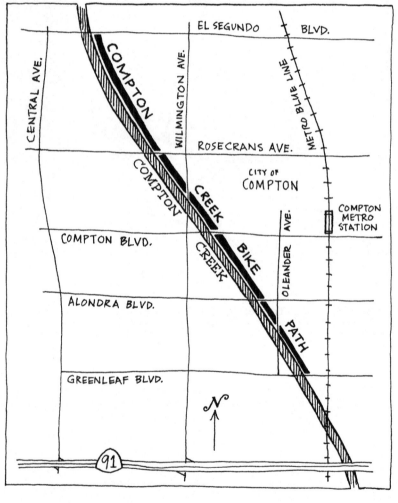

Bikeway 10

COMPTON CREEK BIKE PATH

2.9 MILES, ONE-WAY

HIGHLIGHTS

Two new bikeways opened on Compton Creek in the spring of 2005. The Compton Creek Bike Path is the first phase of a planned greenway trail system that will transform this tributary from a neglected utilitarian culvert into a multiuse community asset for bicyclists, pedestrians, and equestrians. This downstream end of the bikeway is pleasantly shaded by a row of native California sycamore trees. For more information on the envisioned Compton Creek Regional Garden Park, see Walk 26.

STARTING POINT

Compton Creek at Alondra Blvd. (*Thomas Guide* p. 734, J5).

ROUTE NOTES

This bikeway has five at-grade crossings where cross traffic does not stop. Be careful crossing streets.

Route Cues

MILE	DIRECTIONS
0.0	Enter Compton Creek Bike Path at El Segundo Blvd.
1.0	Cross the short, unpaved area, then cross Rosecrans Ave. Be careful at this and other intersections: Traffic does not stop.
1.5	Cross Wilmington Ave.
1.6	Cross Compton Blvd.
2.3	Cross Alondra Blvd.
2.4	Cross Oleander Ave. at an oblique angle, turn right, then left, then right again onto path.
2.9	Arrive at the path's end at Greenleaf Blvd.

Note: To reach the Lower Compton Creek Bike Path, follow the directions below.

2.9	Turn left onto Greenleaf Blvd.
3.4	Turn right onto Santa Fe Ave.

MILE	DIRECTIONS
4.0	Pass below the 91 Freeway. Turn right onto the unpaved access road immediately past the railroad tracks. If you prefer to remain on paved surfaces, continue straight ahead on Santa Fe, which intersects the Lower Compton Creek Bike Path in 0.8 mile.
4.1	Turn left at the upstream end of the Lower Compton Creek Bike Path.

Access Points

MILE	DESCRIPTION
0.0	South side of El Segundo Blvd. between Parmelee Ave. and Compton Ave.
0.1	Parmelee Ave. Pedestrian Bridge.
0.6	West side of Slater Ave. at 136th Street.
0.9	West end of Cressey Street.
1.0	Rosecrans Ave.
1.2	South end of Kemp Ave.
1.2	West end of Elm Street.
1.3	Poplar Street Pedestrian Bridge
1.3	West end of Arbutus Street.
1.4	West end of Palmer Street.
1.5	Wilmington Ave.
1.6	Compton Blvd.
2.3	Alondra Blvd.
2.4	Oleander Ave.
2.5	West end of Claude Street.
2.5	West end of Tichenor Street.
2.6	Caldwell Street Pedestrian Bridge.
2.7	West side of Acacia Ave. at Johnson Street.
2.7	West end of Bennett Street.
2.8	West end of Glencoe Street.
2.9	North side of Greenleaf Blvd. between Oleander Ave. and Willowbrook Ave.

DIRECTIONS TO THE START

TRANSIT

Take the Metro Blue Line to Compton Station and bike west on Compton Blvd. to the Compton Creek Bike Path. Bike downstream to Alondra Blvd.

CAR

Exit the 710 Freeway at Alondra Blvd. and take Alondra west approximately 2 miles. After crossing Compton Creek, park on street. Alternately, exit the 91 Freeway at Wilmington Ave. and go north on Wilmington. Turn right on Alondra. Park on Alondra before you reach Compton Creek.

Compton Creek Bike Path downstream of Alondra Blvd. in Compton

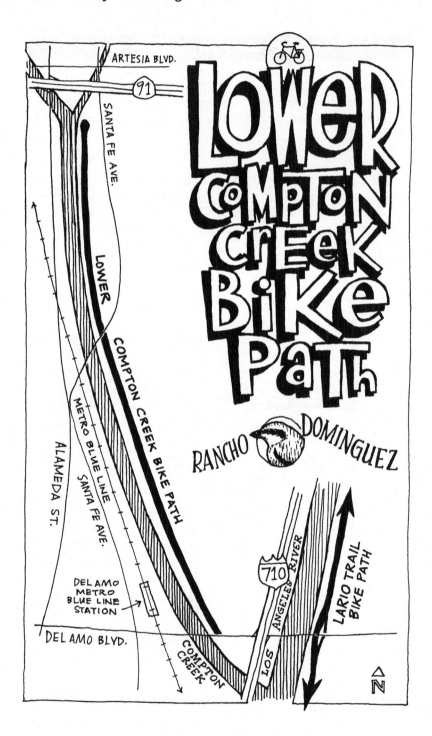

Bikeway 11

LOWER COMPTON CREEK BIKE PATH

1.9 MILES, ONE-WAY

HIGHLIGHTS

The Lower Compton Creek Bike Path is the newest bikeway in the LA River system. It runs nearly 2 miles alongside the soft-bottom area of Compton Creek—a good bird-watching area. The county of Los Angeles opened the Lower Compton Creek Bike Path for its Earth Day 2005 celebration, granting official access to an area that bird-watchers and bicyclists had been using unofficially for some time. River advocates hope that someday this path will be extended to connect the upstream Compton Creek Bike Trail with the Lario Bike Trail downstream (see Walk 27 for additional information).

STARTING POINT

Metro Blue Line Del Amo Station, Del Amo Blvd. at Santa Fe Ave., Rancho Dominguez (*Thomas Guide* p. 765, B4).

Route Cues

MILE	DIRECTIONS
0.0	Begin at the upstream end of Lower Compton Creek Bike Path near the 91 Freeway.
0.8	Carefully cross Santa Fe Ave.; cross traffic does not stop.
1.9	Finish downstream at the end of the bike path at Del Amo Blvd.

Access Points

MILE	DESCRIPTION
0.0	Upstream end of path can be accessed from Santa Fe Ave. Ride west from Santa Fe Ave. on the unpaved path south of the railroad tracks (just south of the 91 Freeway).
0.8	Santa Fe Ave.
1.9	North side of Del Amo Blvd., between the Blue Line station and 710 Freeway.

DIRECTIONS TO THE START

TRANSIT

Take the Metro Blue Line to Del Amo Station.

CAR

Exit the 710 Freeway at Del Amo Blvd. in North Long Beach and go west on Del Amo. The Metro station is on the right after Compton Creek. Park in the south end of the lot along Del Amo. On weekends, there is generally ample free parking in the lot. On weekdays, the lot fills up; if it is full, look for street parking on Santa Fe Ave.

Compton Creek as it meanders through the soft-bottom stretch near Del Amo Blvd.

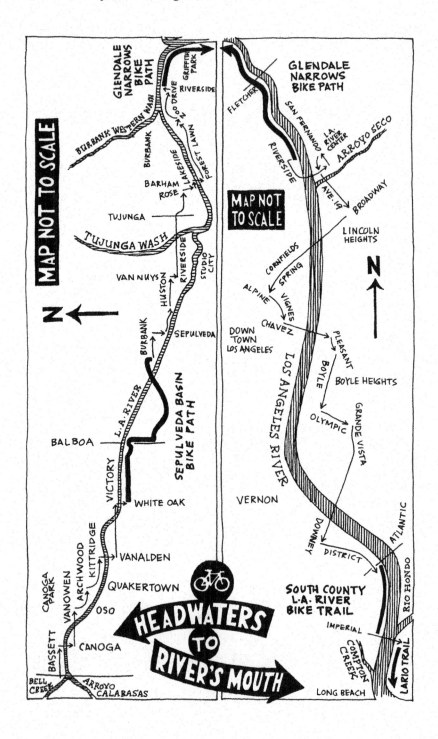

Bikeway 12

HEADWATERS TO RIVER'S MOUTH

55 MILES, ONE-WAY

HIGHLIGHTS

I am frequently asked how to bike the whole river, or how to bike from the Glendale Narrows LA River Bike Path to the beach. While I don't recommend this ride for folks other than the most dedicated creek-freaks (like myself), I've included it here because it's a way to experience the trajectory of the entire river. If you're looking for a long bike ride that's all on bike path, see the Lario Bike Trail, described in Bikeway 4.

Stretching from the start of the LA River in Canoga Park to its mouth in Long Beach, this trip is quite an undertaking. The ride crosses the San Fernando Valley mostly on streets, takes the Glendale Narrows LA River Bike Path, and then follows streets through downtown LA before resuming the bike path in Vernon and continuing 17 miles to Long Beach.

STARTING POINT

The confluence of Bell Creek and Arroyo Calabasas, Canoga Park, (intersection of Owensmouth Ave. and Bassett Street (*Thomas Guide* p. 530, A6).

Bikeway 12: Streets vs. Bike Paths

This "whole enchilada" ride is approximately half on street and half on bikeways. It breaks down as follows:

West SF Valley	on street	6 miles
Sepulveda Basin	bike path	3 miles
East SF Valley	on street	13 miles
Glendale Narrows	bike path	7 miles
Downtown	on street	9 miles
S. County LAR	bike path	5 miles
Lario	bike path	12 miles

ROUTE NOTES

The headwaters of the Los Angeles River are at the confluence of Bell Creek and Arroyo Calabasas, adjacent to Canoga Park High School. This is where the LA River proper begins, though its headwaters are much farther upstream, in the creeks and arroyos that run into the canyons of the Santa Susana, Santa Monica, and San Gabriel mountains. When you're at the headwaters, note the native plantings on the north bank of the river and Bell Creek. Unfortunately, these are inaccessible to the public, but they will be part of a planned headwaters commemoration park.

In late 2005, Metro is expected to open a 14-mile Metro Orange Line bikeway that will cross the San Fernando Valley. That may well be a better way to get through the Valley portion of this ride. For now, I've specified a route following fast and direct existing streets that works well for the experienced vehicular/touring cyclist. If you are a casual cyclist merely wishing to explore the Valley, a more river-adjacent meandering neighborhood route might be desirable. For this sort of ride, it's possible to follow Valleyheart Drive for much of the east Valley. This is an enjoyable ride, but its many stops and lack of signals at crossings make it somewhat impractical for riding the entire length of the river.

In the downtown area, the route features relatively direct streets that avoid most of the railroad tracks. I worked with others to come up with this routing for the Los Angeles County Bicycle Coalition's annual LA River Ride, which includes roughly a metric century ride from Griffith Park to Long Beach and back. It's been tested and refined over the five years of this ride, and it seems to work pretty well. As it passes through industrial areas, however, you will encounter a fair amount of truck traffic at weekday commute times. On the weekends, these streets are nearly deserted. There are still a few railroad tracks to cross, so be careful. Cross with your wheels perpendicular to the tracks.

This bikeway is different than the others. It combines multiple bikeway facilities previously covered: Sepulveda Basin (Bikeway 1), Glendale Narrows (Bikeway 2), South County (Bikeway 3), and Lario (Bikeway 4). This can be ridden as a long ride, or it can be used to bike from one bike path to another. Access points are not listed here; please see the individual bikeway sections for those. The gates to these trails are closed and locked when rain is predicted.

Access Note: Although many people visit this area every day, this trip may include places that are not yet officially open to the public.

Route Cues

MILE	DIRECTIONS	COMMUNITY
0.0	Start on the Owensmouth Ave. Bridge. The headwaters of the Los Angeles River are immediately west of the bridge at the confluence of Arroyo Calabasas and Bell Creek. Ride east on Bassett Street	Canoga Park
0.2	Turn right onto Canoga Ave.	Canoga Park
0.3	Turn left onto Vanowen Street.	Canoga Park
1.6	Turn right onto Oso Ave., which turns left onto Archwood Street.	Winnetka
2.0	Turn right onto Quakertown Ave., which turns left onto Kittridge Street.	Winnetka
3.2	Turn right onto Vanalden Ave.	Reseda
3.4	Cross the river on the Vanalden Footbridge (no curb cut).	Reseda
3.5	Turn left onto Victory Blvd.	Reseda
5.3	Turn right onto White Oak Ave. (bike lanes).	Reseda
5.7	At Oxford Street, turn left onto the Sepulveda Basin Bike Path. The unmarked entry to the bike path is located past the Metro Orange Line Busway and immediately before Oxnard Street. I suggest making a sharp left turn (nearly a U-turn) at Oxnard. Inexperienced bicyclists may prefer turning left from the bike lane onto the nearby crosswalk.	Reseda
6.5	Path enters the Sepulveda Basin Recreation Area and veers right.	Sepulveda Basin
6.5	Turn left at the T-intersection and remain on the concrete path.	Sepulveda Basin

MILE	DIRECTIONS	COMMUNITY
6.7	Turn left. Path curves left, then U-turns back around to the right and crosses below the Balboa Ave. Bridge. Path again U-turns to the right. Turn left to proceed south on the path along Balboa Ave. adjacent to the golf course.	Sepulveda Basin
7.4	Path curves left and proceeds east along Burbank Blvd.	Sepulveda Basin
9.1	Just after crossing the river, at Woodley Ave., turn right to exit the bike path. Cross Burbank Blvd. and turn left. There is a short, narrow, paved side path to your right. It's often muddy or filled with other debris, so I suggest riding east with traffic on Burbank Blvd.	Sepulveda Basin
9.7	At the bottom of the hill, turn right onto Sepulveda Blvd.	Sherman Oaks
10.4	Just past the fire station on your right (and just before the LA River), turn left onto North Valleyheart Drive.	Sherman Oaks
11.0	Cross Kester Ave., continue straight as Valleyheart becomes Huston Street.	Sherman Oaks
11.5	Turn right on Van Nuys Blvd.	Sherman Oaks
11.6	Turn left onto Riverside Drive.	Sherman Oaks
15.6	At Tujunga Ave., veer right to remain on Riverside Drive.	North Hollywood
17.7	Turn right onto Rose Street.	Burbank
18.2	Rose Street ends. Turn left onto Lakeside Drive.	Burbank
18.3	Turn right onto Barham Blvd.	Burbank
18.5	Turn left onto Forest Lawn Drive.	Griffith Park
20.5	Turn right onto Zoo Drive and enter Griffith Park.	Griffith Park
20.6	Turn left (at Griffith Park Drive) to remain on Zoo Drive.	Griffith Park

MILE	DIRECTIONS	COMMUNITY
21.6	Turn left onto Riverside Drive.	Griffith Park
21.7	Turn right onto the Glendale Narrows LA River Bike Path.	Griffith Park
24.8	Veer left to ascend the Alex Baum Bridge over Los Feliz Blvd.	Los Feliz
26.2	Official bike path ends. Continue straight on Crystal Street.	Elysian Valley
26.3	Cross Fletcher Drive and go through the Great Heron Gate. Continue downstream on the access road, which has uneven surface at points.	Elysian Valley
28.8	Access road ends at Egret Park, where the natural area ends and the concrete channel begins (careful, this is easy to overshoot). Turn right, then left onto Riverside Drive.	Elysian Valley
29.1	Turn left onto San Fernando Road.	Cypress Park
29.2	Turn left onto Ave. 19.	Cypress Park
29.9	Turn right onto Broadway.	Lincoln Heights
30.0	Get in the middle lane and continue straight onto Spring Street.	Lincoln Heights
31.2	Turn left onto Alpine Street (becomes Vignes Street).	Chinatown
31.7	Turn left onto Cesar Chavez Ave.	Union Station
32.3	Turn right onto Pleasant Ave.	Boyle Heights
32.7	Veer right onto Boyle Ave. (at Mariachi Plaza).	Boyle Heights
34.3	Boyle ends. Turn left onto Olympic Blvd.	Boyle Heights
35.0	Turn right onto Grande Vista Ave. (becomes Downey Road). Warning: The worst train tracks are here; be careful.	Boyle Heights
36.5	Turn left onto District Blvd. There are a few more train tracks here.	Vernon

MILE	DIRECTIONS	COMMUNITY
38.0	Just past Atlantic Blvd., turn left onto the South County LA River Bike Trail.	Vernon
42.8	The bikeway ends at Imperial Highway. Continue below Imperial Highway, then make a right U-turn and turn right onto Imperial. Cross the river and turn right onto the Lario Bike Trail.	South Gate / Lynwood
55.0	Lario Trail Bike path ends at Golden Shore Wetlands.	Long Beach

The LA River's headwaters at the confluence of Arroyo Calabasas and Bell Creek in Canoga Park

The 1938 Riverside Drive Bridge at Bette Davis Picnic Area in Griffin Park

HISTORIC BRIDGES

From 1910 to 1932, the city of Los Angeles constructed a dozen magnificent bridges over the Los Angeles River in the downtown area. The bridges were the city's attempt to resolve the problem of congestion among automobiles, trains, streetcars, and pedestrians, but the solution was not an entirely utilitarian one—it was also an opportunity to create lasting civic monuments.

The monumental bridges are most concentrated in the downtown area and the Arroyo Seco, but many additional great bridges are found throughout the city, from San Pedro to Brentwood to Lake View Terrace, and in many adjacent cities, including Pasadena, Glendale, Burbank, and Long Beach.

Although these bridges aren't natural features of the river, they do serve many river-restoration purposes. They evoke the history of the city, create a sense of place, and represent important public investment.

In the late 1990s, as I was preparing river walking and bicycling tours, I began to familiarize myself with the downtown bridges. Because they are generally omitted from architectural and other guides to the region, local bridges are somewhat difficult to research. Every time I think I've seen them all, I look around and discover another bridge. As I explored tributaries, I encountered other historic bridges. In 2000, the reconstruction and rededication of the North Broadway Bridge and the designation of 15 local bridges into the Historic American Engineering Record spurred local interest in this region's historic bridges.

Sadly, a lot of the bridges designed by Merrill Butler, the guiding hand behind the city's bridge program, no longer exist. (For more information on Butler, see the sidebar in Walk 15, page 123.) This is especially true for the smaller bridges he built in the San Fernando Valley, but it also includes a few central Los Angeles River bridges such as the Allesandro Street Viaduct and the Aliso Street Viaduct (these gave way to the 2 and 101 freeways, respectively).

To help promote LA's historic bridges, I have created this listing. It is not exhaustive; it includes bridges, 50 years and older, that I have found charming or aesthetic. These bridges have not necessarily been officially acknowledged as cultural, historic, or engineering landmarks.

Nonetheless, I see the "lesser" bridges among these as contributing structures to a larger cluster of great historic bridges in Southern California.

The bridges here are listed in upstream to downstream order, beginning with those on the river and followed by those on the tributaries. Following the waterway bridges, I've including a listing of other historic bridges, such as street grade separations, listed east to west.

I've also included a subjective rating of each bridge, from one to three stars:

> ★　Good and/or interesting, but probably not worth bicycling across town for.
>
> ★★　Has interesting features, but not quite spectacular. This includes many bridges where the arch below remains, but the railing has been replaced.
>
> ★★★　Highly recommended.

Listings begin with the most common name of the bridge. This is followed by the formal name of the bridge (if different than the common name). Most of the downtown bridges are technically viaducts, a type of bridge that spans more than one thing—in this case, the downtown bridges span river and railroads.

Each listing includes the date, designer (if known), a brief description, and location. In a few cases, I'm unsure of the actual date of the bridge. Often, historic bridges have plaques documenting the date and other aspects of the bridge, but many of these plaques are removed when deteriorating railings are replaced. Bridges that are also featured in walks include the walk number for further details.

Generally, the bridges listed here are within the Los Angeles River watershed and greater downtown Los Angeles, but I have included some notable exceptions outside these areas. I've generally omitted the railroad bridges; although they're historic, most are lean on aesthetics.

Following are the abbreviations used here, including websites referencing historic structures:

GRHP:　Glendale Register of Historic Places, www.planning.ci.glendale.ca.us/list.asp

HAER:　Historic American Engineering Record, www.cr.nps.gov/habshaer/haer/

LACFCD:　Los Angeles County Flood Control District

LAHCM:　Los Angeles City Historic-Cultural Monument, cityplanning.lacity.org/

NRHP: National Register of Historic Places,
www.cr.nps.gov/nr/

PL: Pasadena Landmark,
www.ci.pasadena.ca.us/landmarks/historicreg.asp

SPCL: South Pasadena Cultural Landmark,
www.ci.south-pasadena.ca.us/about/tour.htm

USACE: US Army Corps of Engineers

WPA: Works Progress Administration

The 1927 Seventh Street Bridge over the LA River in downtown. To save costs, the upper deck was built atop a 1910 at-grade bridge (see Walk 15).

The 1938 Riverside Drive Bridge at Bette Davis Park

LOS ANGELES RIVER BRIDGES

★★ **Lankershim Blvd. Bridge/Universal City Bridge** (1940, Merrill Butler, WPA, Universal City): This bridge was completed in 1926 but was washed out in the 1938 floods. The current bridge at this location, a WPA bridge apparently based on the previous one, was completed in 1940. The intersection has since been widened. The downstream side of the bridge dates to 1940, while the upstream side is a historically accurate replica. The railing is similar to the nearby Barham Bridge over the 101 Freeway. The railing is somewhat marred by attached contemporary lighting and signals. (*Thomas Guide* p. 563, B5)

★★ **Riverside Drive Bridge** (1938, Butler, at Zoo Drive, Griffith Park): This bridge is a later streamlined example of Merrill Butler's work. For more details, see Walk 7.

★ **Los Feliz Blvd. Bridge/Tropico Bridge** (1925, John C. Shaw with Butler, Atwater Village): This bridge is rather anonymous today, as the ornamental concrete railing was replaced with nondescript metal railing. For more details, see walks 8 and 9.

★★★**Glendale Blvd. Hyperion Ave. Bridge/Victory Memorial Viaduct** (1927, John C. Shaw with Butler, Atwater Village, HAER, LAHCM #164): This monumental architectural jewel commemorates the US victory in World War I. For more details, see walks 9 and 10.

★★★**Fletcher Drive Bridge** (1927, Butler, Atwater Village, HAER, LAHCM #322): This noble bridge features distinctive ornamental pylons with large ornate lanterns. For more details, see walks 10 and 11.

★★ **Riverside Drive Bridge/Riverside Drive-Dayton Ave. Viaduct** (1929, Butler, at Figueroa Street, Elysian Valley): This bridge features ornamental concrete railing and lampposts. For more details, see Walk 13.

★ **Pasadena Freeway Bridge/Figueroa Street Viaduct** (1936, Lincoln Heights): This art deco bridge featured the largest girder span in the nation when it was built. For more details, see Walk 13.

★★★**North Broadway Bridge/Buena Vista Viaduct** (1911, Homer Hamlin and Alfred F. Rosenheim, Lincoln Heights, HAER): This excellent bridge is the oldest of the historic bridges on the river, setting a high standard for all that followed. For more details, see Walk 14.

★★★**North Spring Street Bridge** (1927, John C. Shaw with Butler, Lincoln Heights, HAER):This bridge features ornate concrete railing, decorative lighting, and two graceful arches. For more details, see Walk 14.

★★ **Main Street Bridge** (1910, Henry G. Parker, Lincoln Heights HAER): This is the only at-grade bridge remaining downtown, presenting some conflicts between road users and railroads. Note that the deck details have been removed and replaced with nondescript barriers, but the arches below remain. It is best viewed from the southeast river bank (near Gibbons Street) or from the North Spring Street Bridge. (*Thomas Guide* p. 634, J1)

★★★**Cesar Chavez Ave. Bridge/Macy Street Viaduct** (1926, Butler, downtown, HAER): In my opinion, this monumental bridge is the most beautiful bridge in Los Angeles. It was the longest span in the city in its day. Dedicated to Junipero Serra and located on the historic El Camino Real, it features Spanish colonial revival design commemorating the city's Spanish beginnings. There is easy transit access from Union Station/Patsaouras Plaza. There are excellent ground-level views from Keller Street off Ramirez Street (behind Piper Technical Center). (*Thomas Guide* p. 634, H3)

★★★**First Street Bridge/First Street Viaduct** (1929, Butler, downtown, HAER): This 1300-foot-long bridge features elaborate pylons, lighting, railing, and two graceful arches. For more details, see Walk 15.

★★★**Fourth Street Bridge/Fourth Street Viaduct** (1931, Butler, downtown, HAER): This great bridge features gothic-revival-style railing, pylons, and lighting. For more details, see Walk 15.

★★★**Sixth Street Bridge/Sixth Street Viaduct** (1932, Butler, downtown, HAER): At nearly 1 mile, this bridge was the longest concrete bridge in the world in its day. For more details, see Walk 15.

★★★**Seventh Street Bridge/Seventh Street Viaduct** (1927, Butler, downtown, HAER): As a money-saving measure, this beautiful bridge was built on top of an earlier, 1910 at-grade bridge. For more details, see Walk 15.

The unusual Del Mar Ave. Bridge over Alhambra Wash (see details on page 292)

★★★ **Olympic Blvd. Bridge/Ninth Street Viaduct** (1925, Butler, downtown, HAER): This elaborate gem features gorgeous ornamental pylons and an S-shaped acanthus leaf railing motif. It was painstakingly restored in 1995. It is best viewed from the southeast, near Rio Vista Ave. (*Thomas Guide* p. 634, J7)

★★★ **Washington Blvd. Bridge** (1930, Butler, downtown, HAER): This great at-grade bridge features beautiful friezes depicting the process of designing and constructing bridges. (*Thomas Guide* p. 674, J1)

★★ **26th Street Bridge** (date unknown, Vernon): This is an odd, smaller bridge that was built perhaps in the '20s or '30s. Its construction preceded channelization, as it overshoots the current channel by about 15 feet on its west end. It appears that the deck was subsequently widened. The railing is unremarkable, but the arches below are excellent. It is best viewed from the Soto Street. (*Thomas Guide* p. 674, J2)

★★ **Soto Street Bridge** (1928, Vernon): The deck is contemporary and unremarkable. The six beautiful arches below are best viewed from Bandini Street Bridge. (*Thomas Guide* p. 674, J2)

★★ **Atlantic Blvd. Bridge** (1931, Vernon): This very pleasant county bridge features ornamental concrete railing, elaborate supports, and multiple shallow arches. For more details, see Walk 16.

★ **Clara Street Bridge** (1939, Cudahy): This is a modest neighborhood bridge. (*Thomas Guide* p. 705, F2)

Historic Bridges of Long Beach

To me, the six historic bridges of Long Beach tell the story of the gradual end of City Beautiful and the onset of the freeway era. Bridges at Atlantic Blvd., Artesia Blvd., Long Beach Blvd., Wardlow Road, Willow Street, and Anaheim Street were constructed from 1937 to 1951. They're not showy, but they have flourishes, especially in the lighting. As time progresses, the arches below the bridges flatten out, and the lighting goes from stylized to anonymous.

** **Atlantic Blvd. Bridge** (1937, Long Beach): The Atlantic Blvd. Bridge has a graceful curve and pleasant concrete railing. From below, the spans have slight arches. However, it is in need of restoration, as the railing is damaged in a few areas. Good views are available from the deck or from the bikeway downstream. (*Thomas Guide* p. 735, D6)

* **Artesia Blvd. Bridge** (1949, Long Beach): This is very similar to the Long Beach Blvd. Bridge (see below), but shorter and without plaques. (*Thomas Guide* p. 735, D7)

* **Long Beach Blvd. Bridge** (1946, G.E. Kearns, Long Beach): This long bridge features unremarkable metal railings with stylized, early cobra lighting. It includes a pair of plaques commemorating Long Beach's elected officials of the day, as well as the bridge's builder and designer, G.E. Kearns and Donald R. Warren Co., respectively. It is best viewed from the bikeway downstream. (*Thomas Guide* p. 765, C2)

* **Wardlow Road Bridge** (1951, Long Beach): This long bridge has 13 arched spans and vintage cobra lighting. It is best viewed from the bikeway downstream. Enter at the end of West 34th Street. (*Thomas Guide* p. 765, C7)

* **Willow Street Bridge** (1946, Long Beach): This is a rather plain bridge with commemorative plaques and antique lighting standards. For more details, see Walk 18.

* **Anaheim Street Bridge** (1952, Long Beach): This bridge shows the last vestiges of ornamentation at the onset of the freeway era. It has no arches and unremarkable metal railing, but it does feature somewhat interesting older braced cobra lighting and large commemorative plaques at each end. (*Thomas Guide* p. 795, C6)

Gothic-styled lighting standard on the 1931 Fourth Street Viaduct in downtown LA (see details on page 270 and in Walk 15)

TRIBUTARIES' BRIDGES

PACOIMA WASH BRIDGES

★ **Foothill Blvd. Bridge** (1923, San Fernando): The bland railings appear to be of a more recent vintage, but there are two pleasant arches below. It's difficult to get a good long view. (*Thomas Guide* p. 482, D5)

★ **San Fernando Road Bridge** (1925, Pacoima): This is a fine bridge with concrete railing, decorative approach walls, and twin arches below. It's also difficult to get a good long view. (*Thomas Guide* p. 502, B1)

TUJUNGA WASH BRIDGES

★★★ **Foothill Blvd. Bridge** (1937, Lake View Terrace): This wonderful, long, gently curving bridge was featured in the movie *Chinatown*. It features handsome concrete railing, elegant concrete lighting standards, and multiple arched spans below, but it is somewhat marred by some sort of boxes recently attached below the deck (possibly cell phone transmitters). It is best viewed from downstream along the access road east of the bridge. (*Thomas Guide* p. 503, D1)

★★ **San Fernando Road Bridge** (1935, Sun Valley): This is a long bridge, featuring concrete railing and six arched spans below. The length of the bridge indicates the width of the Tujunga Wash prior to channelization: The bridge is more than six times wider than the current concrete channel below. It is best viewed from upstream. (*Thomas Guide* p. 502, F5)

BURBANK WESTERN WASH BRIDGES

★ **Magnolia Blvd. Frontage Road Bridge** (1949, Burbank): The five bridges from Magnolia to Alameda Ave. are nearly identical, featuring decorative concrete railing and quarter-circle rounded approach walls. They're unassuming, friendly, neighborhood-scale bridges. Magnolia Blvd. and Olive Ave. Frontage Road bridges, with larger recent bridges spanning the wash, rail, and highway, each have only one historic railing intact. (*Thomas Guide* p. 533, G7)

★ **Olive Ave. Frontage Road Bridge** (1949, Burbank): See description for Magnolia, above. (*Thomas Guide* p. 533, G7)

★ **Verdugo Ave. Bridge** (1949, Burbank): See description for Magnolia. (*Thomas Guide* p. 563, H1)

★★ **Lake Street and Providencia Ave. Bridge** (1949, Burbank): This bridge, an all-curved, back-to-back pair of parentheses, wins my praise for the best local bridging of a four-way intersection. While you're there, check out the adjacent mini-park commemorating the historic compass point sycamores planted in 1817 to mark the midpoint between Los Angeles and San Fernando. (*Thomas Guide* p. 563, H1)

★ **Alameda Ave. Bridge** (1949, Burbank): See description for Magnolia. (*Thomas Guide* p. 563, H2)

★ **Victory Blvd. Bridge** (1940, Burbank): The bridges at Victory and Riverside are nearly identical. Each features concrete posts with decorative metal railing, and an arch below. (*Thomas Guide* p. 563, H2)

★ **Riverside Drive Bridge** (1940, Glendale): See description for Victory, above. (*Thomas Guide* p. 563, H3)

ARROYO VERDUGO (VERDUGO WASH) BRIDGES

★ **Cañada Blvd. Bridge—Upstream** (1933, USACE, Glendale): This bridge features a concrete railing with a harlequin pattern, with diamonds. (*Thomas Guide* p. 534, H5)

★ **Glorietta Ave. Bridge** (1941, LACFCD, Glendale): This bridge appears to be based on the basic pattern of the Opechee Way Bridge (see below), but it is slightly altered and actually improved, including vertical elements extending below deck. It is best viewed from upstream in Glorietta Park, east of the bridge. (*Thomas Guide* p. 534, H6)

★ **Opechee Way Bridge** (1940, USACE, Glendale): The Opechee, Wabasso Way, and Mountain Street bridges are identical. They are similar to the Cañada Blvd. Bridges, but without the diamonds. (*Thomas Guide* p. 534, H7)

★ **Wabasso Way Bridge** (1938, USACE, Glendale): See description for Opechee, above. (*Thomas Guide* p. 534, H7)

★ **Cañada Blvd. Bridge—Downstream** (1938, USACE, Glendale): This bridge was originally built in 1933, but in 1938, it was washed out and rebuilt. It has the same pattern as Cañada upstream and is best viewed from Verdugo Park. (*Thomas Guide* p. 564, H1)

★ **Mountain Street Bridge** (1936, USACE, Glendale): See description for Opechee. (*Thomas Guide* p. 564, H1)

★ **Glenoaks Blvd. Bridge** (1937, USACE, Glendale, GRHP #36): Glenoaks, Geneva Street, and Kenilworth Ave. bridges are nearly identical. These very muscular bridges are constructed of riveted girders forming an arch with vertical supports. The system is called the Vierendeel Truss, invented by Arthur Vierendeel in Belgium in 1896. The truss is described on a plaque on the Brand Blvd. Bridge: The plaque states that the first Vierendeel Truss bridge in the US was built in 1937 at Glendale's Central Ave., where it stood until 1985. (*Thomas Guide* p. 564, G3)

★ **Geneva Street Bridge** (1937, USACE, Glendale, GRHP #34): See description for Glenoaks, above. (*Thomas Guide* p. 564, F3)

★ **Kenilworth Ave. Bridge** (1937, USACE, Glendale, GRHP #35): See description for Glenoaks, above. (*Thomas Guide* p. 564, D3)

★ **Concord Street Bridge** (1936, USACE and WPA, Glendale, GRHP #37): This oddity looks to me like a railroad bridge that has been adapted for street use. It is very different from the Vierendeel design but similarly overly muscular. (*Thomas Guide* p. 564, D3)

★ **San Fernando Road Bridge** (1939, USACE, Glendale): This modest bridge features ornamental concrete railing, identical to Compton Creek bridges. (*Thomas Guide* p. 564 C4)

ARROYO SECO BRIDGES

★★ **Devil's Gate Dam** (1920, Pasadena): This isn't a bridge, but it shares some of the same design features—ornamental lighting, concrete form railing, and arches below. There are good views from Oak Grove Drive between Berkshire Place and Windsor Ave. Access the top of the dam from La Cañada Verdugo Road, east of Windsor Ave. in Altadena. (*Thomas Guide* p. 535, E6)

★ **Washington Blvd. Bridge** (1939, WPA, Pasadena): There are five very similar bridges in this stretch: Washington, Seco Street, and three footbridges. Their arches all feature an art deco sun motif below the

The Berkshire Place Bridge over Flint Canyon Creek in La Cañada Flintridge (see details on page 280)

railing. Washington and Seco have WPA plaques. Seco is the easiest bridge to view (from the adjacent parking lot); golf cart bridges obscure Washington. (*Thomas Guide* p. 565, F1)

★ **Seco Street Bridge** (1939, WPA, Pasadena): See description for Washington. (*Thomas Guide* p. 565, F3)

★★★**Holly Street Bridge/Linda Vista Bridge** (1925, Pasadena): This elegant bridge features ornate concrete railing, antique lighting, and a large central arch. For more details, see Walk 21.

★ **Arroyo Blvd. Bridge** (1927, Pasadena): This modest concrete bridge does not actually go over the Arroyo but a side canyon. For more details, see Walk 21.

★★★**Colorado Blvd. Bridge** (1913, John Drake Mercereau, Pasadena, NRHP, PL): This graceful masterpiece is the only Los Angeles County bridge listed in the national register of historic places. For more details, see Walk 21.

★★★**Loma Road Bridge** (1914, Pasadena): Though the nondescript railing is new, the tall arches below are excellent, albeit slightly deteriorating. The city of Pasadena is planning to restore this bridge. There are good views from Arroyo Blvd. near Bradford Street, but it is best viewed from underneath. Enter the Lower Arroyo Nature Park via the (unmarked) walkway at the intersection of California and Arroyo boulevards. (*Thomas Guide* p. 565, F6)

★★★**San Rafael Ave. Bridge** (1922, Pasadena): This pleasant, tall bridge has its railing and lighting intact. The impressive arches below have been restored and look somewhat contemporary. There are good views from Arroyo Blvd.; it is best viewed from underneath. Enter the Lower Arroyo Nature Park via the (unmarked) gap in the fence at the bottom of Busch Garden Court. (*Thomas Guide* p. 565, F7)

★ **San Pascual Ave. Bridge** (1939, Garvanza): This modest, low bridge features ornamental concrete railing. (*Thomas Guide* p. 595, F1)

★★ **York Blvd. Bridge** (1912, Highland Park): This important early bridge features massive solid arches. For more details, see Walk 22.

★ **Marmion Way Bridge** (1940, WPA, Highland Park): This plain bridge features a plaque crediting the Federal Works Agency and former President Franklin D. Roosevelt For more details, see Walk 22.

★ **Metro Gold Line Bridge/Santa Fe Railroad Bridge** (1895, Highland Park, LAHCM #339): This is the oldest and tallest railroad bridge in LA County. For more details, see Walk 22.

★★★**Ave. 60 Bridge** (1926, Butler, Hermon): This wonderful bridge features ornate concrete railing and a large central arch over the Arroyo. For more details, see Walk 22.

★ **Arroyo Seco Park Pedestrian Bridge** (1951, Hermon): This small span features concrete railing. For more details, see Walk 22.

★ **Via Marisol Bridge** (1939, Hermon): This pleasant bridge features antique lampposts. For more details, see Walk 22.

★ **Ave. 52 Bridge** (1939, Highland Park): This bridge is similar to Via Marisol, above. For more details, see Walk 22.

★★ **Ave. 43 Bridge** (1939, Butler, Montecito Heights): The earlier bridge at this site washed out in the 1938 floods. The current bridge's railing is intact, but it has been marred by an added chain-link fence. It includes pleasant lighting standards, walls, and angles. There are good views from Carlota Blvd. (across from the Lummis Home). (*Thomas Guide* p. 595, B5)

★ **Pasadena Ave. Bridge** (1940, WPA, Heritage Square): The lighting and railing are contemporary and unremarkable on this bridge, but it does have a plaque crediting the Federal Works Agency and former President Franklin D. Roosevelt. (*Thomas Guide* p. 595, A6)

★★★**Ave. 26 Bridge** (1925, Butler, Cypress Park/Lincoln Heights): The original modern Ave. 26 Bridge opened in 1925. It was extended in 1939 in conjunction with the construction of the 110 Freeway. The widening matches the earlier bridge, though there are slight differences. The eastern span of the bridge features slightly different lighting than the western span. The ornate arch over the Arroyo is a great deal more appealing than the adjacent nearly flat span over the freeway. It is best viewed from below. Today, see it from the McDonald's parking lot on the downstream west side. There should be good views from the planned Arroyo Seco Bike Path on the upstream east side, expected to be completed in 2006. (*Thomas Guide* p. 594, J6)

** **San Fernando Road Bridge** (1913, Cypress Park/Lincoln Heights): According to historic photos prior to channelization of the Arroyo, this bridge had two arch spans. Only one span remains today. The historic railing has been replaced with utilitarian contemporary metal railing. It is best viewed from the Ave. 19 Bridge. (*Thomas Guide* p. 594, J7)

FLINT CANYON CREEK BRIDGE
** **Berkshire Place Bridge** (1924, La Cañada Flintridge): This is a perfect little arched bridge in a lush, green setting. It is best viewed from below. If driving, park in the turnout east of the bridge. Walk across the bridge, turn right, and enter the (unmarked) hiking/equestrian path located at the end of the hedge across from Dover Road. (*Thomas Guide* p. 535, D6)

RIO HONDO BRIDGE
** **Firestone Blvd. Bridge** (1932, South Gate): This pleasant, historic bridge is in very good condition, with intact railing (though small sections have been cut to add incongruous contemporary lighting). It features decorative terra-cotta tiling (the same tiles are on the Valley Blvd. Bridge over the Alhambra Wash and on the Sierra Madre Blvd. Bridge over the Sierra Madre Wash). It is interesting to note that the bridge span is nearly 50% longer than the present-day Rio Hondo, indicating that the channel was significantly narrowed during channelization. It is best viewed from the bikeway downstream. (*Thomas Guide* p. 705, G4)

The 1926 Ave. 60 Bridge over the Arroyo Seco (see page 279 and Walk 22 for details)

SAWPIT WASH BRIDGE

★ **Huntington Drive Bridge** (1928 and 1952, Monrovia): This bridge features concrete railing and a gutter impression date of 1952. (*Thomas Guide* p. 567, J5)

SANTA ANITA WASH BRIDGE

★★ **Foothill Blvd. Bridge** (1928, Arcadia): This is another bridge that is much longer than the current concrete channel below it. It features ornamental concrete railing and is dated on the outside of the deck. (*Thomas Guide* p. 567, D3)

SIERRA MADRE WASH BRIDGES

★ **Sturtevant Drive Bridge** (1934, Sierra Madre): This pleasant, short bridge has decorative concrete railing. (*Thomas Guide* p. 567, B1)

★ **Grandview Ave. Bridge** (1939, WPA, Sierra Madre—Arcadia): This bridge is unremarkable, but it features WPA plaques. (*Thomas Guide* p. 567, C1)

★ **Sierra Madre Blvd. Bridge** (1953, Arcadia): This bridge features concrete railing with terra-cotta tiles. (*Thomas Guide* p. 567, C2)

EATON WASH BRIDGES

★★ **Colorado Blvd. Bridge** (1925, Pasadena): In situation similar to Valley Blvd. over the Alhambra Wash, this bridge is nearly invisible, due to decking upstream and downstream. Only the downstream decorative concrete railing remains, featuring posts similar to Las Tunas Drive Bridge. (*Thomas Guide* p. 566, F4)

★ **Las Tunas Drive Bridge** (1927, Temple City): This two-span bridge features ornate concrete posts somewhat similar to the North Broadway Bridge over the LA River. Identical posts appear on Hermosa Drive and San Gabriel Blvd. bridges over the Rubio Wash and the Valley Blvd. Drive Bridge over the Alhambra Wash. This bridge's posts are somewhat obscured by added chain-link fence. (*Thomas Guide* p. 596, H3)

RUBIO WASH BRIDGES

★ **Hermosa Drive Bridge** (1927, San Gabriel): This short, low bridge has ornate concrete post railing. (*Thomas Guide* p. 596, F3)

★ **San Gabriel Blvd. Bridge** (1914, San Gabriel): This two-span bridge features ornate concrete post railing. (*Thomas Guide* p. 596, F4)

ALHAMBRA WASH BRIDGES

*   **Valley Blvd. Bridge** (1931, San Gabriel): This is an example of the unfortunate disrespect afforded our waterways and historic infrastructure. When I first noticed this bridge, around 2001, the railing was intact, although a parking area for the adjacent shopping mall had covered up the downstream side of the bridge. More recently, the area upstream was redeveloped, covering all but the railing of the bridge. Now a sort of mysterious urban oddity, the ornamental concrete railing features terra-cotta tiles, some of which are damaged. I fear that, instead of restoring the railing, it may be demolished. Perhaps the wash and the bridge can be daylighted. (*Thomas Guide* p. 596, E7)

*   **Garvey Ave. Bridge** (1935, Rosemead): This bridge features a concrete railing and a date impression on the low approach wall. (*Thomas Guide* p. 636, F2)

COMPTON CREEK BRIDGES

*   **Compton Blvd. Bridge** (1938, USACE, Compton): The Compton Blvd. and Alondra Blvd. bridges feature ornamental concrete railing, identical to the San Fernando Road Bridge over the Arroyo Verdugo. For more details, see Walk 26.

*   **Alondra Blvd. Bridge** (1938, USACE, Compton): See description for Washington. For more details, also see Walk 26.

*   **Alameda Street Bridge** (1937, USACE, Compton): This bridge is similar to Compton Blvd. and Alondra Blvd. bridges, but longer. (*Thomas Guide* p. 735, A7)

ADDITIONAL
HISTORIC BRIDGES

★ **Columbia Street Bridge over Metro Gold Line** (1910, South Pasadena): This bridge features concrete railing and arches. It is best viewed from Fair Oaks Ave. (*Thomas Guide* p. 595, H1)

★★ **Oaklawn Bridge and Waiting Station** (1906, Greene & Greene, South Pasadena, SPCL #3): This is the only bridge designed by the famed architects who would later design Pasadena's Gamble House. One of the first concrete bridges in the county, it now serves as a pedestrian bridge. It features five arches, a quaint craftsman-style bus stop shelter, and a decorative obelisk. (*Thomas Guide* p. 595, H1)

★★ **Monterey Road Pass** (1930, Butler, Monterey Hills): Locals call this the "upside down bridge." It features elegantly styled retaining walls and antique lighting standards. (*Thomas Guide* p. 595, D4)

★ **Soto Street Bridge/Soto Street Grade Separation over Mission Road** (1936, Butler, El Sereno): This bulky, arched structure has contemporary lighting and railing. (*Thomas Guide* p. 595, C7)

★★ **Soto Street Bridge over Valley Blvd.** (1936, Butler, Boyle Heights): This bridge features tall, sharp lighting standards and a railing similar to the Sunset Bridge over Silver Lake Blvd. It is best viewed from Valley Blvd east of Soto Street. (*Thomas Guide* p. 635, C2)

★★★ **Fourth Street Bridge over Lorena Street** (1928, Butler, Boyle Heights, HAER, LAHCM #265): Another great Merrill Butler masterpiece, this bridge features angular geometric details above and graceful curving arches below. (*Thomas Guide* p. 635, C3)

★ **State Street Bridge over 10 Freeway** (1925, Boyle Heights): This bridge, originally over railroad tracks, has been greatly extended and reworked. There is only a very short section of the original acanthus flower railing (identical to the Olympic Blvd. Bridge), but much of the underside remains. It is best viewed from Pomeroy Ave. (*Thomas Guide* p. 635, B3)

** **Cesar Chavez Ave. Bridge over 10 Freeway** (circa 1920s, Boyle Heights): Originally a grade separation for Macy Street above the railroad tracks, this bridge features an ornamental concrete railing and unique lighting. From the south side of the bridge, you can view another old grade separation remnant at the intersection of the 10 and 101 freeways. (*Thomas Guide* p. 634, J3)

** **Vignes Street Undercrossing/Vignes Street Grade Separation** (1938, Butler, near Union Station): This is similar to the Cesar Chavez Ave. Undercrossing. (*Thomas Guide* p. 634, H3)

** **Cesar Chavez Ave. Undercrossing/Macy Street Grade Separation** (1937, Butler, along Union Station): According to a June 23, 1936, *Los Angeles Times* article, there was an interesting controversy around the construction of this beautiful bridge. The project had been approved, but no progress could be made until streetcar companies took action to reroute their trains. The impasse was broken when city staff, overseen by Butler himself, actually used jackhammers and acetylene torches to cut the railroad tracks, stranding commuters. Streetcar officials rushed to the scene and hastily negotiated with city engineer Lloyd Aldrich and Butler. There are good views on both ends. This undercrossing is included in the grounds of Union Station, officially the Los Angeles Union Passenger Terminal, which are listed in the NRHP and designated LAHCM #101. (*Thomas Guide* p. 634, H3)

* **Park Row Drive Bridge** (1941, Elysian Park): This tall bridge features an ornate arch below. For more details, see Walk 14's side trip.

** **110 Freeway Tunnels /Figueroa Street Tunnels** (four tunnels built between 1931 and 1936, Elysian Park): These four tunnels feature ornate concrete detailing. (*Thomas Guide* p. 594, H7)

** **Temple Street Bridge/Temple Street Grade Separation over Figueroa** (1939, Butler, WPA, downtown): Constructed by the WPA, this bridge features elaborate ornamental concrete walls and rails. It is best viewed from Dewap Road.(*Thomas Guide* p. 634, F3)

** **First Street Bridge/First Street Grade Separation over Second Street** (1942, Butler, Temple Beaudry): This bridge, sometimes called the Beverly-Glendale Bridge, was intended to streamline an intersection made difficult by the crossing of multiple streetcar lines. Note the naming confusion at this intersection where Beverly Blvd. becomes

First Street and Glendale Blvd. becomes Second Street. It is best viewed from Lucas Street. (*Thomas Guide* p. 634, E2)

* **Sunset Blvd. Bridge over Glendale Blvd.** (1934, Butler, Echo Park): This bridge features ornate concrete railing. (*Thomas Guide* p. 594, E7)

* **Sunset Blvd. Bridge over Silver Lake Blvd.** (1934, Butler, Silver Lake, HAER, LAHCM #236): This historic bridge features attractive metal railing on deck and groin vault arches and large city seals below. (*Thomas Guide* p. 594, C6)

*****Franklin Ave. Bridge** (1926, John A. Griffin with Butler, over Monon Street in Los Feliz, HAER, LAHCM #126): Referred to in the plaque as a "picturesque" and "useful span," this bridge is commonly called the "Shakespeare Bridge" because of its gothic ornamental towers. Note that the view from below is impressive. The space below is open and airy, and the pointed arches echo the design of the railing. To get there from the bridge, go east on Franklin Ave., left on Saint George Street, left on Lyric Ave., and left on Monon Street. The bridge is at the end of the street. (*Thomas Guide* p. 594, B3)

** **Sunset Blvd. Bridge over Myra Ave.** (1929, Butler, East Hollywood): This bridge features ornate concrete railing and a large central arch below. (*Thomas Guide* p. 594, B5)

* **Temple Street Bridge over Silver Lake Blvd.** (1934, Butler, Silver Lake): This bridge features ornate metal railing with concrete posts. The Temple Street and Sunset Blvd. bridges were designed to work in tandem to relieve 1930s congestion on Silver Lake Blvd. (*Thomas Guide* p. 594, B7)

*****Elberon Ave. Bridge** (1936, Butler, San Pedro): The detailing on this bridge is the same as the Gaffey Street Bridge but slightly more modest, and it is arched below. It's best viewed from Gaffey Street north of Elberon. (*Thomas Guide* p. 824, B4)

*****Gaffey Street Bridge** (1935, Butler, San Pedro): This beautiful bridge features exquisite lighting atop adorned pedestals with benches. Most of it is in good shape, but the railing is broken and worn in places. There are many good views, including from atop the adjacent pedestrian bridge. Also view it from below by going east on Summerland Ave. Descend the stairs to the left on Summerland Place (or bike/drive left on Cabrillo Ave.). Proceed left (downhill) on Oliver Street to the bridge. The underside is not arched, but the side view shows plenty of ornamental detailing. From the north end of the Gaffey Street Bridge, look east for a good view of the 1963 Vincent Thomas Bridge. (*Thomas Guide* p. 824, B4)

** **West Blvd. Bridge over Venice Blvd.** (1933, Butler, Mid-City): This is a long, graceful bridge featuring ornamental railing and lighting. (*Thomas Guide* p. 633, E5)

** **Fern Dell Drive Bridge** (1923, Griffith Park): This modest, arched bridge has decorative concrete railing. (*Thomas Guide* p. 593, H2)

** **Pilgrimage Bridge over 101 Freeway** (1940, Butler, WPA, near Hollywood Bowl): This bridge features ornamental concrete railing, unique concrete early cobra lighting, a WPA plaque, and arches below. (*Thomas Guide* p. 593, E2)

** **Mulholland Drive Bridge over 101 Freeway** (1940, Butler, near Hollywood Bowl): This bridge features art deco-style concrete railing and unique early cobra lighting. (*Thomas Guide* p. 593, E2)

** **Barham Blvd. Bridge over 101 Freeway** (1940, Butler, WPA, Universal City): This bridge features extensive retaining walls carved into the Cahuenga Pass. The ramps originally served as off-ramps. There is a WPA plaque located at the middle of the north railing. (*Thomas Guide* p. 563, D7)

* **101 Freeway Bridge over Lankershim/Hewitt Station Underpass** (1938, Butler, Universal City): This pleasant ornamental concrete bridge is easily accessed from the Metro Red Line Universal City Station. (*Thomas Guide* p. 563, B6)

* **Bel Air Road Bridge** (1923, Bel Air): This sweet little bridge has a bell motif on the outside of each span. (*Thomas Guide* p. 592, C7)

***Westridge Road Bridge** (1928, Butler, between 1740 and 1750 Westridge Road, Brentwood): This is a great bridge over an arroyo along Mandeville Canyon. It's a bit far from the LA River watershed, but it is stylistically similar to the downtown bridges, albeit smaller. Its unique feature is that it incorporates a mix of rusticated rock surface with concrete. The view from below is good but somewhat obscured by vegetation. Access the bridge from the end of the unnamed short spur road at 1712-1714 Westridge. (*Thomas Guide* p. 631, E2)

Bridges with Official
Historic-Cultural Monument Status

The only Los Angeles River watershed bridge to be listed in the National Register of Historic Places is Pasadena's Colorado Blvd. Bridge over the Arroyo Seco.

Since its founding, FoLAR has advocated for official recognition of the historic river bridges. Much progress was made toward this goal in the summer of 2000 when the federal Historic American Engineering Record (HAER) documented 15 Los Angeles bridges (12 over the LA River) as historically significant engineering landmarks. HAER acknowledged the importance of the original bridges as well as the contemporary rehabilitation and restoration. HAER produced a beautiful collection of drawings and photos documenting the bridges, and this wonderful pamphlet is available at local libraries and online at the city's Bureau of Engineering website: eng.lacity.org/projects/bridge/historical_gallery/index.htm.

Cities in this area have been slower to acknowledge officially the historic nature of the bridges they've constructed. The cities of Glendale, Los Angeles, Pasadena, and South Pasadena have designated some bridges, but many more worthy structures are unacknowledged. For example, in Los Angeles, only two out of more than a dozen great LA River bridges have been designated, and none are downtown.

Official historic designations are noted in the bridges listed here. Many of the agencies that provided the historic designations have additional information, including photographs, available on their websites (see list on pages 266 and 267).

The 1927 Fletcher Drive Bridge over the LA River, designated Los Angeles City Historic-Cultural Monument #322 (see walks 10 and 11)

Cruising Merrill Butler's Los Angeles

This bicycling or driving tour features 14 City Beautiful landmarks. It's 17 miles, with a few hills, and begins at the Los Angeles River Center: 570 West Ave. 26. (For directions to the start, see Walk 13.)

Route Cues

MILE	DIRECTIONS
0.0	Exit the Los Angeles River Center from the front (north) entrance, and turn right (east) onto Ave. 26.
0.2	Cross the 1925/1939 **Ave. 26 Bridge** over the Arroyo Seco.
0.8	Turn right onto Daly Street, which becomes Marengo Street.
2.2	Turn right onto State Street.
2.4	Cross the 1925 **State Street Bridge** over the 10 Freeway. Note the section of intact railing on your left.
2.7	Turn right onto Bridge Street. Note the Michael Amescua Gate at Proyecto Jardín on your left.
3.2	Turn right onto Cesar Chavez Ave.
3.3	Cross the 1920s **Cesar Chavez Ave. Bridge over the 10 Freeway**.
3.5	Cross the 1926 **Cesar Chavez Ave. Bridge** over the LA River.
3.9	Go through the 1937 **Cesar Chavez Ave. Undercrossing** at Union Station.
4.8	Turn left onto Figueroa Street.
5.0	Go under the 1939 **Temple Street Grade Separation** over Figueroa.
5.4	Turn right onto Second Street, which becomes Glendale Blvd.
5.9	Cross below the 1942 **First Street Grade Separation** over Second Street.
7.1	Cross below the 1934 **Sunset Blvd. Bridge** over Glendale Blvd.
7.1	Keep right and veer right onto Lake Shore Ave.
7.2	Take the first right onto Montana Street.
7.2	Take the first right onto Lemoyne Street.
7.4	Take the first right onto Sunset Blvd.
7.4	Cross the 1934 **Sunset Blvd. Bridge** over Glendale Blvd.
8.2	Cross the 1934 **Sunset Blvd. Bridge** over Silver Lake Blvd.

MILE	DIRECTIONS
8.3	Turn right onto Parkman Ave., then immediately turn right on Silver Lake Blvd.
8.3	Cross below the **Sunset Blvd. Bridge** over Silver Lake Blvd.
8.4	Take the first right onto Parkman Ave.
8.5	Take the first left onto Sunset Blvd.
9.4	Immediately past Santa Monica Blvd./Sanborn Ave., turn left onto Manzanita Street.
9.5	Take the first right onto Gateway Ave.
9.5	Take the first right onto Myra Ave.
9.6	Cross below the 1929 **Sunset Blvd. Bridge** over Myra Ave.
9.7	Turn left onto Fountain Ave.
9.9	Turn right onto Talmadge Street.
10.5	Turn right onto Franklin Ave.
10.7	Cross the 1926 **Franklin Ave. "Shakespeare" Bridge**.
10.8	At the end of the bridge, turn left onto Saint George Street.
10.9	Take the first left onto Lyric Ave.
11.0	Take the first left onto Monon Street.
11.2	View the 1926 **Franklin Ave. "Shakespeare" Bridge** from below. Go back north on Monon Street.
11.3	Turn right onto Lyric Ave.
11.4	Turn left onto Saint George Street.
11.8	Turn right on Rowena Street.
11.9	Take the first left on Hyperion Ave.
12.1	Cross the 1927 **Glendale Hyperion Viaduct**.

Note: At this point, the driving and bicycling routes diverge:

Bicycle Directions

12.6	Keep left and make a U-turn at Glenfeliz Blvd. After turning, keep right to remain on Glendale Blvd.
12.9	Turn right onto the LA River bikeway on-ramp.
12.9	Turn right onto the bikeway heading downstream.
13.0	Cross below the 1927 **Glendale Hyperion Bridge**. Continue downstream with good views of the 1927 **Fletcher Drive Bridge** before and past it.

MILE	DIRECTIONS
13.7	Continue straight onto Crystal Street at end of the bikeway.
13.8	Turn left at Fletcher Drive, then immediately turn right through the Great Heron Gates onto the access road. Caution: There is an uneven surface for the next 3 miles.
16.4	Turn right at Egret Park.
16.4	Turn left onto Riverside Drive.
16.5	Cross the 1929 **Riverside Drive Bridge**.
16.7	Turn left onto San Fernando Road.
16.8	Take the first right to remain on San Fernando Road.
17.0	Turn right into the River Center (west entrance).

Car Directions

12.9	Turn right onto Larga Ave.
13.6	Turn right onto Fletcher Drive.
13.7	Cross the 1927 **Fletcher Drive Bridge**.
14.0	Turn left onto Riverside Drive.
16.4	Cross the 1927 **Riverside Drive Bridge**.
16.6	Turn left onto San Fernando Road.
16.7	Take the first right to remain on San Fernando Road.
16.9	Turn right into the River Center (west entrance).

Odds and Ends

There are a few bridges that aren't all that good-looking, but they tell stories. I have included these oddities because I found them interesting. These are only for the discerning palette.

LOS ANGELES RIVER BRIDGES

Barham Blvd. Bridge (originally built in 1935, with a 1975 addition, Toluca Lake—Burbank): This bridge is completely unremarkable from above. From below, it's possible to see the older bridge upstream (which appears to have been rather unadorned to begin with) and the later addition downstream. It is easiest to view from the parking lot at 6735 Forest Lawn. (*Thomas Guide* p. 563, D5)

Firestone Blvd. Bridge (originally built in 1950, with later addition, South Gate): The downstream portion of this bridge is similar to others nearby built in the late 1940s—not flashy, but exhibiting a bit of character. The original downstream metal railing and small concrete wall features are intact, but the bridge was later expanded asymmetrically, approximately doubling the deck to the upstream side. The upstream portion is a featureless fence. The view from the bike path below also shows the contrast. (*Thomas Guide* p. 704, F4)

EATON WASH BRIDGES

Del Mar Blvd. Bridge (originally built in 1926, with later addition, East Pasadena): Completely contemporary and unremarkable on the surface, this bridge has a hidden ornate arch below. It is best viewed from Eaton Blanche Park. (*Thomas Guide* p. 566, F5)

Garibaldi Ave. Bridge (1953, Temple City): This unusual arched bridge is the only one of its kind I've encountered. After 1940, there aren't a lot of arched bridges; most are flat. This 1953 bridge is very plain, kind of institutional, but arched at a time when bridge builders weren't doing arches. (*Thomas Guide* p. 596, G2)

ALHAMBRA WASH BRIDGE

Del Mar Ave. Bridge (1935, San Gabriel): This is an interesting bridge, probably not unique in its day, but the only one of its kind that I encountered in the Los Angeles River watershed. The bottom layer of the bridge is a steel girder arch; atop that arch, the concrete sidewalk has a series of small arches. (See illustration on page 271.)(*Thomas Guide* p. 596, E7)

AFTERWORD

A Clear Future for the LA River

by Ed P. Reyes

G rowing up in Cypress Park, my boyhood friends and I would gather along the Los Angeles River in the hot summer days of the late '60s and early '70s. Peewee, John, Pio, Mike, and my big brother, Richard, would glide along the edge of the river on our Stingray bikes. We stopped in our favorite spot, where we would sit on sun-scorched rocks and drop fishing lines into "the hole," a deep remainder of sewage flow where tar-colored catfish managed to survive. We were Tom Sawyers on a concrete river, and we competed to see who could catch the biggest catfish or find the oddest-looking tadpoles.

The river took us away from the violence that was a common experience in the neighborhood. Areas where the soft river bottom broke through its cement straitjacket were natural settings much lacking from our neighborhoods. Our private oasis created a sanctuary from the noise of the cars and the hustle of the streets. The river gently rolled past and gurgled in the pools that emerged. Ducks and other wildlife would fly by and swim around us.

Today, I serve as the Los Angeles city councilmember representing the neighborhoods where I grew up. I have endeavored to reinvest in my community, to bring people together, and to bring opportunities and outlets for our youth. The revitalization of the Los Angeles River is a tremendous opportunity to meet these goals and much more.

For many years, Los Angeles has treated its river as a backyard—a place to hide the unattractive parts of the city. Freeways and rail tracks suffocate the river, utility lines surround it, and industrial lots encase it. The challenge before us now is to turn our neglected backyard into our front yard, to showcase the natural resource that gave birth to this great city. I believe that the Los Angeles River can be restored to a place that we can all celebrate: a welcoming greenway for our region.

Soon after my election to the Los Angeles City Council, I invited my colleagues to form the City's Ad Hoc Committee on the Los Angeles River. The River Committee, which I chair, brings together five councilmembers to focus on the future of our river. The committee has raised the visibility of river issues within the city and laid the foundations for long-term river revitalization. I am grateful to all the city staff members who have contributed and continue to contribute to this important effort.

I have worked with many community groups, including FoLAR, to turn the tide of disinvestment in our river communities. These efforts are bearing fruit. Former railroad yards at the Cornfields and Taylor Yard, instead of remaining industrial brownfields, will soon be large, new, urban state parks serving the youth and families of park-poor communities. The planned parks incorporate multiple uses that allow the diversity of Los Angeles peoples to come together and redefine their relationship with the river and each other.

And that's just the start! From the San Fernando Valley to Boyle Heights, the city of Los Angeles is embarking on an ambitious revitalization plan for the 31 miles of river within its jurisdiction. These efforts will address environmental issues—by enhancing water and air quality and restoring habitat—and they will set the stage for neighborhood revitalization. I encourage all Angelenos, especially those living in the neighborhoods along the river, to participate in the city's revitalization planning process.

This will be a long-term project. It's not about the next election cycle, but about the quality of life for my sons and daughter, and for their children. Revitalizing the Los Angeles River is a legacy that we can leave for future generations. I have seen firsthand the tremendous change that has taken place in other cities that have dared to dream, to put forth a vision for river revitalization and to make it happen.

The river's soothing ability is a gift we take for granted. This book is one step toward building this sense of place, where communities gather in the newly staged front yard of our region. As we create the priorities defined by the communities along the river, we can accelerate the healing process for our river, its tributaries, and our beaches. It begins by taking the first steps down by the Los Angeles River.

—*Ed P. Reyes is a Los Angeles city councilmember representing the First District, which includes portions of the LA River and Arroyo Seco. He chairs the city council's Planning and Land Use Management and Ad Hoc River committees.*

Ten Not-Always-Simple Things You Can Do to Save the LA River

Explore

Familiarize yourself with the river. Get a sense for how it changes through the seasons. Use this book, but also go and visit the section of the river that is closest to where you live. It may be a small tributary or a huge concrete channel. The tributaries are just as important to work on because the entire system is interconnected. As you go down to the river and familiarize yourself with it, you will get ideas on what can be done to care for it. Listen to what the river tells you.

Bring friends on these walks. Many Angelenos have no idea where their river is, even though many of us drive over it every day.

When you visit another city, check out the river there. Since the dawn of civilization, all around the world, cities have grown up on rivers. Cities from Seoul (South Korea) to Zurich (Switzerland) are reclaiming and restoring their rivers. In the US, there are many excellent river projects. Some in similar climates to LA are: Guadalupe River (San Jose, California), San Antonio River (San Antonio, Texas), the Platte River (Denver, Colorado), and various East Bay California creeks, including Cordonices Creek and Blackberry Creek (both in Berkeley). When you travel, take some time to check out other rivers and projects going on to get ideas for what might be possible in LA.

Educate Yourself

There are many excellent books on the history of the LA River and there are also ample resources on the internet. Use the list beginning on page 303 to get started.

Find out about the watershed you live in, and which sub-watershed you're in. When water runs off the building where you live, where does it go? Get involved as locally as possible. Find old maps of your neighborhood and see where the creeks and rivers ran and where they are now.

Join Cleanup Events

When it rains, all the trash in our streets washes down into our creeks, rivers and our beaches. So any cleanup you participate in helps the river. Each May, FoLAR hosts our annual La Gran Limpieza—the Great LA River Cleanup. This event brings together thousands of volunteers at more than a dozen sites from Long Beach to Tujunga. Check the FoLAR website for information.

Ultimately, it's more difficult to get the trash out of the river than it is to prevent the trash from getting there in the first place. Of course, one way to help this is to always put your trash in the trash can, to recycle when you can, and to generate less trash in the first place by bringing reusable canvas bags to the store or bringing reusable containers for take-out at restaurants.

Volunteer

Groups that work on LA River issues need your help. Sometimes it's fun stuff, like leading walks, planting trees, or taking samples for water-quality monitoring. More often, it's pretty mundane things, like licking envelopes and making phone calls. Contact FoLAR or any of the other groups (listed on page 303) and ask how you can volunteer.

Get Political

Find out who represents you on your local city council or county board of supervisors; get the names of your state and federal representatives. Write and tell them that your local river is important to you, and ask them to let you know what they're doing to help. When it's election time, vote for politicians who are taking leadership on river issues.

State and local park and water bonds have been critical for funding projects on the LA River. California's Proposition 12, Proposition 13, and Proposition 40 provided the funds for Taylor Yard, the Cornfields, and much more. State Proposition 50 and Los Angeles Proposition O will be very important in funding efforts to restore natural processes that clean up our waters. Volunteer for and vote yes on future ballot measures that support river restoration.

If you're not sure about a specific ballot proposition, call or email FoLAR. Due to its nonprofit status, FoLAR doesn't endorse politicians, but staff members can provide you with background information to help you make an informed decision.

Conserve Water

The LA River has become degraded in part because of Southern California's insatiable demand for water. Most of the water we use now is imported from far away. Our use of this water means less water for a healthy environment where we're getting it from.

Using less water can take a lot of forms. There are small personal steps, like fixing leaks, taking shorter showers, and turning off the water while we brush our teeth. Various water-saving devices are available, including low-flow toilets and shower heads. For the most serious, it can mean using graywater systems to capture and reuse water.

Watersheds and Watershed Management

Watershed is a fancy word that a lot of people don't understand. It refers to the whole area that drains into one river (or creek). It's kind of like a bathtub—no matter where you put water in it, the water will all drain down to that one little hole. No matter where rain falls in a watershed, that rain will drain down to that watershed's river. Generally, the border between two watersheds is a ridgeline at the top of a mountain range.

The example I like to give when I explain the concept is a leaf. A watershed is like the whole leaf, the veins of the leaf are the creeks, and the stem is the river.

The Los Angeles River watershed covers about 850 square miles, including the entire San Fernando Valley and the western portion of the San Gabriel Valley. It also includes a lot of Los Angeles—downtown LA, east LA, and northeast LA—but west LA and much of central LA are in the Ballona Creek watershed. The LA River watershed includes more than three dozen cities, from Pasadena to Long Beach to Calabasas to Monrovia to Montebello. Maps of various LA County watersheds are available on a few different websites, including that of the LA County Department of Public Works: ladpw.org/wmd/watershed/LA/.

Watersheds have sub-watersheds for each tributary. You may live in the LA River watershed and the Tujunga Wash sub-watershed, so water that runs off your yard enters the Tujunga Wash before entering the LA River.

Locally, there are a number of good examples of watershed management. We still need plenty more, of course. Some of these include:

Los Angeles Media Tech Center (2706 Media Center Drive, Los Angeles): This industrial park (unfortunately developed at a corner of Taylor Yard) included parking lots that drain into landscaped medians. Instead of untreated storm water draining to the LA River nearby, the runoff collects and waters on-site landscaping. This breaks down pollutants and contributes to reduced flooding and increased overall sustainability in water usage.

TREES Project Hull House (1828 West 50th Street, Los Angeles): This single-family home was retrofitted with cisterns, retention grading, and drywells. The home is able to retain all the site's storm water from very large rainstorms. The cisterns store 3600 gallons for later use during dry weather. Berms and landscaping capture additional storm water to infiltrate it on-site. Tours are available from TreePeople: 818-753-4600 or www.treepeople.org.   *continued on the next page*

Watersheds, continued

Los Angeles Zoo parking lot (5333 Zoo Drive, Los Angeles):
There is a long swale with native plants that circles the zoo parking lot, cleansing runoff. This is the first phase of a larger project.

Bimini Slough Ecology Park (184 Bimini Place, Los Angeles):
This small park (which I had a hand in establishing) was created by the Bresee Foundation, with the help of the nonprofit group North East Trees (NET). A 500-foot section of Second Street was closed, asphalt was removed, and a park was created. Running the length of the park is a "bio-swale," essentially, a creekbed. It's nearly dry most of the year, but it takes runoff from the street and cleans it through natural filtration and infiltration. Small parks like this can be placed at various points throughout the watershed to manage runoff, restore nature, and provide recreation.

Plant Natives

On of the most important places to conserve water is outside. A lot of the plants in our landscape won't grow here unless we water them a whole lot. Foremost among these are our grass lawns. I certainly enjoy playing Frisbee on a nice grass lawn at the park, but there are a few too many lawns in LA—and they consume a lot of water. They also can require pesticides and fertilizers, and the runoff from this degrades water quality in our creeks and rivers.

If we're not going to have lawns, what should we have? A sustainable yard features California native plants. These species are perfectly adapted to living on the rainfall they get (though you generally need to water them some to get them established). Many native plants are beautiful, and they provide habitat for our local birds and insects. Perhaps most importantly, they reconnect us with the important natural heritage of our bioregion.

Watershed Management

The health of our rivers is tightly connected with the health of the watersheds that drain into those rivers. When we restore natural processes wherever our rain falls, we naturally break down pollutants and prevent them from entering our waterways. If we detain and infiltrate or store this water, we can recharge our aquifers and even prevent some flooding.

There are various techniques, some easy, some difficult, that help us manage our watershed. Relatively easy things include planting trees, turning rain gutters so they drain into our yards, removing concrete wherever possible, and including strategic swales and berms to slow and retain water in our landscaping. Larger efforts include installing cisterns, French drains, soakaway pits, and restoring creeks (see Watersheds sidebar, page 297).

Don't Drive—or, Drive Less

Well, maybe I shouldn't expect too much, this is LA, after all. But driving less, or walking, biking, and taking public transit more, are some of the most important things you can do for the health of our river. Our car usage has a variety of negative effects on our local waterways. Cars generally require impermeable surfaces—roadways, parking lots, driveways, and more, which we have in abundance here. Car operation also results in chemical contaminants leaking onto our roadways. Rain carries these into our creeks and rivers.

To the extent possible, walk or use a bicycle for short and medium trips. Bicyclists and pedestrians become more intimately familiar with the contour of their land and watershed. As a cyclist, I know which way the water flows, because that's where I can coast downhill. As I ride around town, I notice gentle valleys in the landscape—these were once creeks and might be creeks again someday.

Daylight the Creek in Your Neighborhood

For a challenging task, how about bringing that creek (the one that used to run through your neighborhood) back to life? This will probably take a while, not to mention some serious engineering, a few permits from your local municipality, and a lot of your friends' and neighbors' support.

To start, figure out where that creek was in your neighborhood. There are a few ways to do this. You may be able to talk to your elderly neighbor and find out. You can also track down historical maps of the area, get storm drain maps from your local government (though a lot of these drains run in straight lines that water would never choose to do), or walk or bike and notice where your streets dip down.

The next step is choosing a site. Successful daylighting projects in other areas frequently take place on public property. Parks and schools are probably easiest, but this is also possible in parking lots, vacant areas, and even streets (though you may have to close or shrink these).

Work with local community groups, watershed groups, and municipal leaders to come up with a plan for how the creek will work, and how the project will be funded.

Once you've got all that done, dig up the creek. Bring that water to the surface. Nature is pretty good about taking over at that point. Just add water.

Resources

Books

Bakalinsky, Adah, and Gordon, Larry. *Stairway Walks in Los Angeles.* Berkeley, CA: Wilderness Press, 1990.

Brundige, Don and Sharron. *Bicycle Rides: Los Angeles County,* 4th ed. San Pedro, CA: B-D Enterprises, 2000.

Carle, David. *Introduction to Water in California.* Berkeley, CA: University of California Press, 2004.

Carle, David. *Water and the California Dream: Choices for the New Millennium.* San Francisco: Sierra Club Books, 2000.

Caughey, John and LaRee. *Los Angeles: Biography of a City.* Berkeley, CA: University of California Press, 1977.

Clarke, Herbert. *An Introduction to Southern California Birds.* Missoula, MT: Mountain Press Publishing Company, 1989.

Cooper, Daniel S. *Important Bird Areas of California.* Pasadena, CA: Audubon California, 2004.

Crocker, Donald W. *Within the Vale of Annandale: A Picture History of South Western Pasadena and Vicinity,* 3rd ed. Pasadena, CA: San Rafael Scouts, 1975.

Cronin, John, and Kennedy Jr., Robert F. *The Riverkeepers.* New York: Touchstone, 1999.

Davis, Mike. *Ecology of Fear: Los Angeles and the Imagination of Disaster.* New York: Metropolitan Books, 1998.

Eberts, Mike. *Griffith Park: A Centennial History.* Los Angeles: The Historical Society of Southern California, 1996.

Fitch, Janet. *White Oleander.* Boston: Little, Brown and Company, 1999.

Gebhard, David and Winter, Robert. *Los Angeles: An Architectural Guide.* Salt Lake City, UT: Gibbs Smith, 1994.

Gumprecht, Blake. *The Los Angeles River: Its Life, Death, and Possible Rebirth.* Baltimore, MD: The John Hopkins University Press, 1999.

Hargreaves, George, ed. *LA River Studio Book.* Cambridge, MA: Harvard University Graduate School of Design, 2002.

Hise, Greg, and Deverell, William. *Eden by Design: The 1930 Olmsted-Bartholomew Plan for the Los Angeles Region.* Berkeley, CA: University of California Press, 2000.

Johnston, Bernice Eastman. *California's Gabrielino Indians.* Los Angeles: Southwest Museum, 1962.

MacAdams, Lewis. *The River: Books One & Two.* Santa Cruz, CA: Blue Press, 1998.

MacAdams, Lewis. *The River: Books One, Two & Three.* Santa Cruz, CA: Blue Press, 2005.

Majot, Juliette, ed. *Beyond Big Dams: A New Approach to Energy Sector and Watershed Planning.* Berkeley, CA: International Rivers Network, 1997.

McCully, Patrick. *Silenced Rivers: The Ecology and Politics of Large Dams.* London: Zed Books, 2001.

Moore, Charles, et al. *The City Observed: Los Angeles.* Santa Monica, CA: Hennessey & Ingalls, 1998.

Morrison, Patt. *Río LA: Tales from the Los Angeles River.* Los Angeles: Angel City Press, 2001.

Mount, Jeffrey F. *California Rivers and Streams: The Conflict between Fluvial Process and Land Use.* Berkeley, CA: University of California Press, 1995.

Orsi, Jared. *Hazardous Metropolis.* Berkeley, CA: University of California Press, 2004.

Piotrowski, Scott R. *Finding the End of the Mother Road: Route 66 in Los Angeles County.* Pasadena, CA: 66 Productions, 2003.

Pomeroy, Elizabeth. *Lost and Found: Historic and Natural Landmarks of the San Gabriel Valley.* Pasadena, CA: Many Moons Press, 2000.

Riley, Ann L. *Restoring Streams in Cities: A Guide for Planners, Policy Makers, and Citizens.* Washington, DC: Island Press, 1998.

Robbins, Chandler S., et al. *Birds of North America.* Racine, WI: Golden Press, 1983.

Robinson, W. W. *Panorama: A Picture History of Southern California.* Los Angeles: Title Insurance and Trust Company, 1953.

Roy, Arundhati. *The Cost of Living.* New York: Modern Library, 1999.

Samudio, Jeffrey, and Lee, Portia. *Los Angeles California* (Images of America Series). Chicago: Arcadia Publishing, 2001.

Schad, Jerry. *Afoot and Afield in Los Angeles County,* 2nd ed. Berkeley, CA: Wilderness Press, 2000.

Smith, Elizabeth A. T. *Urban Revisions: Current Projects for the Public Realm.* Cambridge, MA: MIT Press 1994.

Somer, Richard, and Jones, Mary Margaret, eds. *Supernatural Urbanism: Los Angeles River Studio.* Cambridge, MA: Harvard University Graduate School of Design, 2003.

Turhollow, Anthony F. *A History of the Los Angeles District, U.S. Army Corps of Engineers 1898-1965.* Los Angeles: US Army Engineer District, Los Angeles, 1975.

Weltman, Gershon, and Dubin, Elisha. *Bicycle Touring in Los Angeles.* Los Angeles: Ward Ritchie Press, 1972.

Brochures, Studies, Pamphlets, Articles

California Coast & Ocean, Vol. 9, No. 3. Oakland, CA: Coastal Conservancy, Summer 1993.

Chinatown, Self-Guided Historic Trails. Los Angeles: Angels Walk LA, 2003.

Common Ground from the Mountains to the Sea: San Gabriel and Los Angeles Rivers Watershed and Open Space Plan. Sacramento, CA: California Resources Agency, San Gabriel and Lower Los Angeles Rivers and Mountains Conservancy, Santa Monica Mountains Conservancy, 2001.

Condon, Patrick, and Moriarty, Stacy, eds. *Second Nature: Adapting LA's Landscape for Sustainable Living.* Los Angeles: TreePeople, Metropolitan Water District of Southern California, et al., 1999.

Dallman, Suzanne, and Piechota, Tom. *Storm Water: Asset Not Liability.* Los Angeles: Los Angeles & San Gabriel Rivers Watershed Council, 1999.

Escher, Frank, and GuneWardena, Ravi. *Cruising Industrial Los Angeles.* Los Angeles: Los Angeles Conservancy, 1997.

Gustaitis, Rasa. "Los Angeles River Revival," *California Coast & Ocean,* Vol. 17, No. 2. Oakland, CA: Coastal Conservancy, Autumn 2001.

Hall, Jessica, et al. *Seeking Streams: A Landscape Framework for Urban and Ecological Revitalization in the Upper Ballona Creek Watershed.* Pomona, CA: California State Polytechnic University Pomona Department of Landscape Architecture, 2001.

Historic-Cultural Monuments. Los Angeles: City of Los Angeles Cultural Affairs Department Cultural Heritage Commission.

Juan Bautista de Anza: Official Map and Guide. San Francisco: National Park Service, US Department of the Interior, 1996.

Living Lightly in Our Watersheds: A Guide for Residents of the Arroyo Seco Watershed and Surrounding Communities. Los Angeles: North East Trees, 2004.

Local Birds of Los Angeles County. Woodside, CA: Local Birds Inc., 1996.

Los Angeles River Bikeway and Greenway Planning Study. Los Angeles: North East Trees, 2002.

Los Angeles River Bridges. Washington, DC: Historic American Engineering Record, National Parks Service, US Department of the Interior, 2000.

Mikesell, Stephen D. "The Los Angeles River Bridges: A Study in the Bridge as a Civic Monument," *Southern California Quarterly,* 68: 365-386, Winter 1986.

Price, Jennifer. "A Field Guide to the LA River," *LA Weekly,* Vol. 23, No. 38, August 10-16, 2001.

The River Through Downtown. Los Angeles, CA: Friends of the Los Angeles River, 1998.

Trim, Heather. *Beneficial Uses of the Los Angeles and San Gabriel Rivers.* Los Angeles: Los Angeles & San Gabriel Rivers Watershed Council, 2001.

Woods, Sean. *Wetlands of the Los Angeles River Watershed: Profiles and Restoration Opportunities.* Oakland, CA: Coastal Conservancy, 2000.

Maps

Thomas Guide: Los Angeles County Street Guide. Chicago: Rand McNally, 2005.

Topo!: Los Angeles, Santa Barbara and Surrounding Recreational Areas. San Francisco: Wildflower Productions, 1999.

River Organizations

SELECTED NONPROFIT GROUPS

Friends of the Los Angeles River
FoLAR protects and restores the Los Angeles River.
323-223-0585
570 West Ave. 26, Suite 250
Los Angeles, CA 90065
www.folar.org

Arroyo Seco Foundation
The ASF preserves the Arroyo Seco and promotes awareness of natural resources.
626-584-9902
PO Box 91622
Pasadena, CA 91109
www.arroyoseco.org

Audubon California
Audubon conserves and restores natural ecosystems and operates nature centers (see Walk 23's side trip).
916-649-7600
711 University Ave.
Sacramento, CA 95825
www.audubon-ca.org

Bresee Foundation
Bresee operates the Bimini Slough Ecology Park.
213-387-2822
184 Bimini Place
Los Angeles, CA 90004
www.bresee.org

California Native Plant Society, Los Angeles Chapter
CNPS fosters understanding of and preserves California's native flora.
818-881-3706
3908 Mandeville Canyon Road
Los Angeles, CA 90049
www.lacnps.org

Friends of Atwater Village
FoAV volunteers improve the Atwater neighborhood through projects including river cleanups, murals, and the Red Car River Park (see Walk 10).
323-913-2999
3371 Glendale Blvd., Unit 110
Los Angeles, CA 90039
www.friendsofatwatervillage.org

Heal the Bay
HTB makes Southern California coastal waters safe and healthy for people and marine life.
310-453-0395
3220 Nebraska Ave.
Santa Monica, CA 90404
www.healthebay.org

International Rivers Network
IRN supports local communities working to protect their rivers and watersheds.
1847 Berkeley Way
Berkeley, CA 94703
510-848-1155
www.irn.org

Los Angeles and San Gabriel Rivers Watershed Council
The Watershed Council preserves, restores, and enhances the Los Angeles River and San Gabriel River watersheds.
213-229-9952
700 North Alameda Street
Los Angeles, CA 90012
www.lasgrwc.org

Los Angeles Conservancy
The LA Conservancy preserves the architectural and cultural heritage of greater LA.
213-623-2489
523 West Sixth Street
Los Angeles, CA 90014
www.laconservancy.org

Los Angeles County Bicycle Coalition
The LACBC improves the bicycling environment and quality of life in LA County.
213-629-2142
634 S. Spring, Suite 821
Los Angeles, CA 90014
www.labikecoalition.org

North East Trees
NET has built more than a dozen mini-parks along the LA River.
323-441-8634
570 West Ave. 26, Suite 200
Los Angeles, CA 90065
www.northeasttrees.org

The River Project
The River Project conserves and enhances LA County's natural resources and watersheds.
818-980-9660
11950 Ventura Blvd., Suite 9
Studio City, CA 91604
www.theriverproject.org

Santa Monica Baykeeper
Santa Monica Baykeeper protects and restores the Santa Monica Bay, San Pedro Bay, and adjacent waters.
310-305-9645
PO Box 10096
Marina del Rey, CA 90295
www.smbaykeeper.org

Sierra Club, Angeles Chapter
The Sierra Club protects and restores the natural and human environment.
213-387-4287
3435 Wilshire Blvd. #320
Los Angeles, CA 90010
www.angeles.sierraclub.org

Surfrider Foundation
Surfrider preserves our oceans, waves, and beaches.
949-492-8170
PO Box 6010
San Clemente, CA 92674
www.surfrider.org

Theodore Payne Foundation for Wildflowers and Native Plants
Theodore Payne Foundation promotes the preservation of California native flora.
818-768-1802
10459 Tuxford Street
Sun Valley, CA 91352-2116
www.theodorepayne.org

TreePeople
TreePeople plant trees, raise environmental awareness, and restore watersheds.
818-753-4600
12601 Mulholland Drive
Beverly Hills, CA 90210
www.treepeople.org

The Trust for Public Land
TPL conserves land and protects our natural and historic resources.
213-380-4233
3250 Wilshire Blvd., Suite 2003
Los Angeles, CA 90010
www.tpl.org

Urban Creeks Council
The Urban Creeks Council preserves and restores urban creeks and their riparian habitat.
510-540-6669
1250 Addison Street, #107C
Berkeley, CA 94702
www.urbancreeks.org

The Village Gardeners of the Los Angeles River
The Village Gardeners create and maintain the Village Gardens of Sherman Oaks (see Walk 5).
818-981-1606
PO Box 6061-589
Sherman Oaks, CA 91413

SELECTED GOVERNMENT AGENCIES

California Coastal Conservancy
The Coastal Conservancy protects and restores the California Coast.
510-286-1015
1330 Broadway, 11th Floor
Oakland, CA 94612
www.coastalconservancy.ca.gov

California State Parks
State Parks protects California's natural and cultural resources and creates recreation opportunities.
818-880-0350
1925 Las Virgenes Road
Calabasas, CA 91302
www.parks.ca.gov

Los Angeles City
Various city departments, including Sanitation, Engineering, Recreation and Parks, and Transportation are responsible for creating and maintaining parks, bikeways, bridges, and other LA River features.
213-473-8230
www.lariver.org

Los Angeles County
Various county departments help manage the LA River and administer the ongoing Los Angeles River Master Plan process. County river activities are coordinated by the Los Angeles County Public Works Watershed Management Division.
800-675-4357
900 S. Fremont Ave.
Alhambra, CA 91803
www.ladpw.org/WMD/watershed

Lower Los Angeles and San Gabriel Rivers and Mountains Conservancy
The RMC preserves open space and habitat to provide recreation, education, wildlife habitat restoration and protection, and watershed improvements. Their LA River jurisdiction includes stretches from the city of Vernon downstream, as well as the Rio Hondo and Compton Creek.
626-458-4315
900 South Fremont Ave.
Annex Building Second Floor
PO Box 1460
Alhambra, CA 91802
www.rmc.ca.gov

Santa Monica Mountains Conservancy/Mountains Recreation and Conservation Authority
SMMC/MRCA preserves and enhances Southern California places to form a system of urban, rural, and river parks; open space; trails; and wildlife habitats accessible to the general public.
323-221-8900
570 West Ave. 26, Suite 100
Los Angeles, CA 90065
www.lamountains.com

Southern California Regional Water Quality Control Board
The SCRWCB preserves and enhances California's water resources.
213-576-6600
320 West Fourth Street, Suite 200
Los Angeles, CA 90013-2343
www.waterboards.ca.gov/losangeles

United States Army Corps of Engineers, Los Angeles District
The USACE provides engineering services to the nation, including planning and operating water resources projects that reduce flood danger and enhance environmental protection.
213-452-3908
PO Box 532711
Los Angeles, CA 90053-2325
www.spl.usace.army.mil

INTERNET RESOURCES

Los Angeles Bike Paths has descriptions and maps of bike paths in LA County: www.labikepaths.com.

Los Angeles Unified School District River Connection features a virtual tour of the Los Angeles River: www.lalc.k12.ca.us/target/units/river/riverweb.html.

Occidental College Los Angeles River Project documents the series "Re-Envisioning the Los Angeles River," co-sponsored by Occidental College's Urban and Environmental Policy Institute and FoLAR: www.lariver.oxy.edu.

Web de Anza has extensive documentation of early Spanish exploration of the west, including the Anza and Portola expeditions. It features maps, chronologies, glossaries, and original Spanish texts with English translations: anza.uoregon.edu.

Index

Photo by Angel Orozco

ABOUT THE AUTHOR AND ILLUSTRATIONS

Joe Linton is an artist and activist who works as a fine artist, graphic artist, and illustrator. To see additional artwork by Joe, visit his website at www.handmaderansomnotes.com. Joe is involved with various local progressive urban environmental causes, including Friends of the Los Angeles River, the Los Angeles County Bicycle Coalition, the Bus Riders Union, and Los Angeles Eco-Village.

All the illustrations were done using a Koh-i-nor Rapidograph pen (mostly the gray 0/.35) on smooth Bristol paper. Illustrations were done in the field, without using photographs or other references (with the exception of a photograph of Ernie La Mere and a few birds). While a few scenes have been simplified somewhat, nothing was invented, so the birds or people that appear in the drawings were present when the drawings were done. Generally, very little pencil pre-drawing was done; most were drawn directly with pen on paper. Very little manipulation of images was done after scanning for publication.

About Friends of the Los Angeles River

Friends of the Los Angeles River (FoLAR) is the oldest LA River advocacy organization, and, in my opinion, has the most steadfast and uncompromising vision for the river. FoLAR has consistently worked toward a vision of the river as a greenway from the mountains to the sea. The group's insistence on the importance of this vision sometimes means taking unpopular positions, including initiating legal challenges to projects that would further degrade the river.

FoLAR pursues many projects at any given time, and these range from bikeway advocacy to creating a river school to water-quality monitoring to tracking government agencies. Projects vary from year to year, so check out www.folar.org for what is going on now.

If you've enjoyed this book, and you're walking and biking the LA River, loving it for what it is and wanting to see it become healthier, greener, and friendlier, you'll want to become a Friend of the Los Angeles River. For information on joining FoLAR, see page 316.

FoLAR's Monthly Walks

Each month, FoLAR hosts a "Down by the River" walk. These guided tours take place the third Sunday of each month, except December. The starting time is 4:30 p.m. most months, or 3:30 p.m., October through February. The casual, non-strenuous walks are open to all ages and usually last approximately 90 minutes.

Many walks highlight newly completed or upcoming projects on the river, sometimes featuring a speaker who discusses natural, cultural, or historic topics. Walks are canceled if it's raining.

The walk schedule is posted at FoLAR's website (www.folar.org), and announcements are sent out the week of the walk via an email list. The walks are free to FoLAR members; a $5 donation is requested from nonmembers.

CPSIA information can be obtained
at www.ICGtesting.com
Printed in the USA
LVOW03s1230150317
527289LV00001B/1/P